Rediscovering the West

SUNY SERIES IN WESTERN TRADITIONS
David Appelbaum, Editor

Rediscovering the West

An Inquiry into Nothingness and Relatedness

Stephen C. Rowe

STATE UNIVERSITY OF NEW YORK PRESS

Published by
State University of New York Press, Albany

© 1994   State University of New York

For information, address State University of New York Press,
State University Plaza, Albany, N.Y., 12246

Production by Christina Tartaglia
Marketing by Dana E. Yanulavich

Library of Congress Cataloging-in-Publication Data

Rowe, Stephen C., 1945–
     Rediscovering the West : an inquiry into nothingness and
relatedness / Stephen C. Rowe.
          p.   cm.
     Includes bibliographical references and index.
     ISBN 0–7914–1991–6 (hc : alk. paper). — ISBN 0–7914–1992–4 (pb :
alk. paper)
     1. East and West. 2. Nothing (Philosophy) 3. Relation
(Philosophy) 4. Philosophy. 5. Religion. 6. Spiritual life.
7. Education, Humanistic. 8. Rowe, Stephen C., 1945– .
I. Title.
BF1999.R716   1994
190—dc20   93–37857
                                                                              CIP

10 9 8 7 6 5 4 3 2 1

Contents

Part III Relatedness as Practice

Acknowledgments

I AM GRATEFUL to Grand Valley State University for sabbatical leaves at the beginning and end of this inquiry, and for a challenging and vital learning community throughout. Without the primary practice of teaching and learning—its joys and sorrows, its serendipity and vexation—this book never would have been.

In the larger world of conversation about challenge and vitality, there are some senior mentors who have provided objectivity and encouragement: Masao Abe, Teresa Bernardez, John B. Cobb, Jr., Martin E. Marty, and Jacob Needleman. Their willingness to be present for me and for us all constitutes worldliness in a way that surpasses the grandeur of any sand dune or mountain with which I have ever communed.

Closer to home, I am blessed with friends and colleagues who ripple out into that larger world in circles of conversation, companionship, and support. Here I can only thank a few: Forrest H. Armstrong, Richelle Bono, Barry Castro, Michael DeWilde, J. Ronald Engel, Ursula Franklin, Mark Henderson, Jon Jellema, Jacqueline Johnson, Cheryl Jones, Lana Hartman Landon, Nick Leighton, Lauren Lepow, Robert W. Mayberry, Rosalind Srb Mayberry, Peimin Ni, Daniel Noel, Barbara M. Roos, Kristin S. Rowe, Marybeth Atwell Rowe, and Judy Whipps.

PROLOGUE

I

W HAT YOU HAVE before you is an inquiry, a practice in the Western tradition of liberal education. Revitalization of ourselves and our culture is what this inquiry is about. The beginning point is our actual situation: an unsteadiness in our relations with each other, a certain dullness within ourselves, and an underlying absence of vision or deep orientation, as though we have forgotten how to live a human life. We need revitalization before we forget that revitalization is what we need.

The guiding aim of this inquiry is a response to the imperative of human growth that is essential to our situation, our need to develop toward full maturity. I seek to address the most basic though rarely stated fact of life in our time: that human beings must mature into beings who are more alert, more compassionate, and more intelligent, who know the proper function of the intellect within human life, or cease to exist. The related fact that this maturation must be entered into and directed largely as a voluntary act serves to focus the aim of this work as a practice, as a matter of what we do and how we are, a matter of what we are becoming, not just of what we think.

This inquiry actually began as an attempt to draw on the tradition of Zen, to say how Zen can be a valuable resource for revitalization in the turbulent world of today. But an unexpected thing occurred in the adventure of exploring the possibilities of Zen. The more I delved into Zen and how it relates to our experience in the post-traditional present, the more I began to rediscover what is great in the Western tradition. Perhaps the classical Zen masters would approve of what happened: the result of contact with Zen was contact with myself. Zen was indeed nothing other than my own real self.

What I found was revitalization as a Westerner, but not in a way that closes off the East and the rest of the world. In fact, I found that the revitalized Western orientation actually makes it possible for me to draw on the insights of the East more honestly and more deeply than before. This, in turn, showed me how much of our previous response to contact with Eastern sources has been an expression of Western irrationalism, an escapist reaction to the prevailing technological rationalism that is unsatisfactory to the human spirit.

Through encounter with both Zen and my own tradition, I found a way of becoming a world citizen from the West, and I found access to a vitality described by some in the East-West dialogue today as the energy of moving toward a new, worldwide universality. My essential experience in this process was one of becoming more truly myself at the very same time I was becoming more fully open to the other.

Here, then, is the central thread through the inquiry that follows: that encounter with the otherness of the East provides the ground upon which it becomes possible to reclaim our own Western integrity, while at the same time we are enabled to open to the realities of such otherness as Zen. The awareness of this process can be extended to encounter with otherness in many forms—with my fellow citizen, my student, my family members and coworkers, as well as with the more general realities of other cultures and the feminine aspect of our very humanity—because of the nature of the Western tradition. For its genius lies not in a particular doctrine or intellectual formulation, not in a given set of beliefs; it turns out to exist in nothing "out there" or separate from our most profound experience of being fully present. The genius of the Western tradition lies in a way of being, one that locates the vitality of life and even the divine in the dynamics of encounter itself, in dialogue, in the full human relationship, in that paradoxical relationship of compassionate openness to the other in which we find ourselves being who we really are.

The purpose of this book is to make this genius more widely accessible, to develop interpretation that is faithful to it, and so to contribute to the support it needs in order to remain and be more fully present on the earth. This purpose is focused through the very strenuous voluntary and personal act of revitalization as it is being undertaken in this very moment by the author and by the reader—by us. What I seek to share is a way of being and developing through which revitalization is possible, and the marvelous complementarity between Western and Eastern perspectives as a source of interpretation, discipline, and inspiration.

II

But none of this can be accomplished from the outside. Therefore this book must be an exercise in the very way of being it seeks to elucidate; it must be a practice rather than a merely theoretical discourse.

The proper use of the intellect is fundamental to the practice of my own lifelong discipline of liberal education in teaching philosophy and religion. Without awareness of what lies beyond the intellect, education becomes endless intellectualization, piling one book of conceptualization upon another, misplacing our education in mere *in-formation* and endless *re-search*, rather than understanding education as pursuit of *trans-formation*. For education in the full sense entails the transformative movement through and beyond the intellect, the simultaneous movement to our own real self and to the actuality of the world, to the point of vital coincidence between self and world out of which arises our full presence.

Following the practice of liberal education, this book is concerned with the immediate, personal, experiential act of revitalization through transformation, and the cultural and political consequences that can issue from this act. Accordingly, its medium is not the traditional theory making of speculative reason, but rather, in the company of such contemporary interpreters as Hans-Georg Gadamer, self-formation or development.[1] Along these lines this work can also be regarded as an attempt to reinvigorate the ecstatic reason of the pre-Aristotelian Greeks, which is shared by some of the later Western mystics and liberals. Through the very old and nearly forgotten Western art of inquiry, I seek to present my own process of rediscovering the West in a way that allows the reader to participate fully—not in the rehearsal of conceptual conclusions, but in the actual event of revitalization. Indeed, I am convinced that the only possible value of this work, or others like it, is in what it offers to the reader's own process of inquiry and development.

This inquiry moves through three parts. Part I, Seeing the World with Zen, is an exploration of the current world situation. In particular, I investigate the claim of the Japanese Kyoto school of philosophy which has emerged in postwar Japan as an attempt to bring together East and West, specifically the spirit of Eastern meditation and the methods of Western thought. Its claim is to possess the world synthesis that is needed for the future of humankind in the emerging global period. Upon the ground of the present meeting of Eastern and Western traditions, I also inquire about the status of Western culture and the matter of its revitalization. This includes the sense that we must integrate those dimensions of human experience that had been culturally defined as "other" during the traditional period. Part I centers on the search for post-traditional wisdom, and the Kyoto school's claim that a new world synthesis can arise out of the embracing of the experience of "homelessness" and nihilism which they understand to be integral to life in the present.[2]

Part II, Rediscovering the West, on that same ground of our present world situation, inquires into Western culture and tradition focusing on the question of what the West has to offer in the global period. The vitality of the West, which becomes available to us in the midst of the coming together of traditions in our era, is associated in our time with the image of "the survivor," with genuine liberalism, and with the radiant lives of Socrates and Jesus. This specifically Western vitality, we discover, is relational, focusing on the achievement of full human presence through encounter with each other.

Part III, Relatedness and Practice, moves to the immediate question of practice and transformation, the concrete question of what we are to do and to be on the post-traditional landscape. This question is taken up in terms of both the Western vision of relatedness as the holy place or locus of the ultimate and the integration of essential insights from the otherness of the East, especially its emphasis on spiritual development through the experience of Nothingness. Through the issue of practice, a postliberal liberalism becomes accessible as a live option for us today, as a way of revitalization.

III

What do I mean when I speak of revitalization?

Western culture is presently in disarray and paralysis. This becomes evident in the midst of emerging world civilization, with the meeting of parts of the world that up to now have been kept apart and organized primarily by Western assumptions and technologies of superiority. It is profoundly ironic that in the upheaval of the present meeting the West does not fare well, even though the coming together of world civilization was induced largely by Western activities. The reasons for this are several, and will be taken up in the inquiry that follows. For now, however, what is crucial to our discussion is the urgent need of the West to achieve revitalization if it is to persist as a viable culture. And this becomes a matter of great concern for the whole world, since the West still wields enormous physical power, even if its spiritual vitality is in eclipse.

The signs of the Western trouble are all around and are rather obvious, perhaps so pervasive that they become difficult to see. In cultural terms the trouble can be described as a function of the dominance of two opposing orientations to thought and action in the post-traditional twentieth century in the West. I discuss them here because they represent, in distilled form, basic moods that are afoot in the culture.

One orientation is relativism, the reduction of all values to personal preference and hence of civilization itself to "the war of all against all." The crucial factor of generosity is lost, the ability to move beyond immediate self-interest and contribute to the common good, the ability to relate rather than merely exchange. The second orientation is absolutism, the authoritarian imposition of one set of values in such a way that individual freedom, choice, and integrity are denied. Generosity is lost here also, perhaps even more obviously, since individuals within absolutism are not even permitted exchange in relation to self-interest, but must submit strictly to the categories of race, gender, and class they represent. Together these orientations of relativism and absolutism describe the dilemma or "Catch-22" of the West at this late point in its history: there are two choices, neither of which is viable, but we are forced to choose between them as the only available options.

Near the end of the twentieth century the dilemma is manifest in the opposition between deconstructionism and neoconservatism. Critic Jacques Derrida and the deconstructionists wish to tear down what they take to be the pretenses and illusions of Western culture, particularly the imperialism of its logocentric foundationalism, which is to say its consensus about transcendent truth and objectivity known exclusively through a certain sort of reason. The tearing down is presumably for the sake of some later reconstruction, but this never quite happens; and the deconstructionist mood, while hypercritical of anything Western, is associated with a tendency to accept uncritically anything that is "other." The problem is that there is no vision of something valuable or sustaining in Western culture that lies beneath those problematic aspects that developed in the traditional period. Hence the deconstructionists become like those most dangerous characters in Plato's *Republic* who are *almost* at the highest stage of realization: "delighting like puppies in tugging and tearing at anyone who comes near them."[3] They relativize, contributing to what David Bromwich calls "a culture of suspicion," a culture in which everything is seen as a projection of someone's self-interest.[4]

On the other side, political philosopher Allan Bloom and the neoconservatives react against the frustrating relativism of contemporary society, its lack of coherence, discipline, and authority, the trivialization of culture and the reduction of greatness to the lowest common denominator of consumerism. Against all this they assert some version of what they take to be "tradition." The chief problem with the neoconservative stance, beyond evasiveness about just what is the wisdom of this "tradition," and a confusion of tradition with merely external authority, is its inability to identify anything positive in the present to which the supposed wisdom of tradition might have any relation whatsoever. In fact, the neoconservatives tend toward disdain for anything present, and do not engage it in any real dialogue.

Meanwhile, these schools of Western thought and action—and the popular cultural moods which they both reflect and generate—necessarily exist within a larger world context. By "necessarily" I mean that we can no longer ignore global interdependence, the legitimacy of culture and lifeways other than our own, and the tenuous emergence of world community. Photography of Planet Earth from outer space comes to be seen as the most vivid symbol of our era.

From this standpoint, viewing the ground of emerging world civilization, the two chief schools to which I refer can only be seen as symptoms of the Western trouble. Relativistic deconstructionism leads to the oblivion of outer space, and to the uncritical embracing of whatever is insistently "other." Absolutistic neoconservatism rigidly refuses the realities of our global circumstance, practicing constriction and denial—as though refusing the fact that the world is round, or that it reposes, as the photos so clearly show, in the midst of the great void. Both schools are defensive, reactive. Neither orientation contains the zest of vigorous relation, or the energizing vision that is associated with a civilization that is thriving.

IV

My experience, and this inquiry, affirms that there is a way out of this dilemma; a third alternative, a way of revitalization, is available. This way, through which we can become world citizens from the West, centers on a certain mode of relationship that is implicit in "dialogue" and "liberal education." This way of relationship entails paradox: we can only discover and have access to that which is great and sustaining in the West when we enter into genuine dialogue with the rest of the world. And dialogue that is genuine involves more than either uncritical acceptance and capitulation to the other or holding to the superiority of one's own position. Real dialogue involves the paradox of being open and being definite at the same time.

This is challenging. It requires that we enter into relationship with a way of presence that is larger than just the intellect, especially the intellect as it has come to be understood throughout the traditional period in Western culture. For Western culture, as early as the influence of Aristotle, fell into an idolatry of the intellect, a worshiping of intellectual formulation rather than God. This idolatry arose from the assumption that theory must always be prior to practice, such that practice and action and presence are seen only as the implementing of that which has been essentially settled elsewhere and expressed in purely intellectual construction. William James refers to this assumption as "vicious intellectualism," and states that it is the reason "philosophy has been on a false scent since the days of Socrates and Plato,"[5] because intellectualism reflects and generates insensitivity and even violence to the actuality of lived experience. Alfred North Whitehead points to the same assumption with his phrase "the fallacy of misplaced concreteness":[6] the actuality of life is missed and denied in the name of conceptual order. In the present, Madeleine L'Engle speaks in a voice that clearly reflects the same awareness: "My intellect is a stumbling block to much that makes life worth living: laughter, love, a willing acceptance of being created. The rational intellect doesn't have a great deal to do with love, and it doesn't have a great deal to do with art."[7] Revitalization requires that we move beyond intellectualism to reclaim love and art.

From the standpoint of this realization, the deconstructionists are right: we must get beyond what has become the logocentrism of the West. But they are wrong in their implication that we should throw out the intellect altogether, and that it is possible to enter into relationship with either complete openness or complete subjectivity. We cannot dismiss the intellect, but must achieve the maturity from which we are able to let it serve its proper function within a human life. And we cannot exempt ourselves from the necessity of declaring our own location, our position, what it is that we stand for. Here the neoconservatives are correct in their stipulation that we must know ourselves, know our own tradition and wisdom as a condition of entering into authentic relationship with others. But they are wrong in suggesting that we can know ourselves in isolation, and know ourselves apart from the openness of real encounter.

Once again, dialogue requires the simultaneity of openness and definiteness, the relative and the absolute, the subjective and the objective; dialogue entails a third reality that is no mere mixture of the other two, a reality that can only be apprehended and lived from within our occasional experiences of human maturity. The reality of it lies beyond Catch-22 or dilemma, beyond the polarization and paralysis that is so typical of our time. It is in this vein, for example, that the Americans Charles Sanders Peirce and Josiah Royce have spoken of the necessity of "thirdness,"[8] and more recently Stanley Rosen has said that we need to become "trinitarians,"[9] pointing to the essential growth and maturity our era requires. It is also in this vein that Socrates, referring now to the ancient sources of this third way, once declared that "there is no greater evil one can suffer than to hate reasonable discourse."[10]

But given the more immediate cultural inheritance as described by James, Whitehead and L'Engle, it is very difficult to practice dialogue or have access to the ancient wisdom. "Dialogue" is reduced to either relativistic chitchat or surreptitious forms of absolutism. And "democracy," the Western vision of a whole society of dialogue, is reduced to either mere polling of personal preferences or a lie that hides the inevitability of dominance by the wealthy. We lack models, ways of support, discipline, and development for the crucial third option to become available. But my suggestion is that there is a Western subtradition that does offer just these things, that provides not only a way of *conceiving* dialogue, a way of envisioning or seeing it in its full magnificence, but also a way to *engage* dialogue as a transformative practice. This subtradition is embodied in the historic practice of liberal education in ways that can be helpful to us in the present.

Liberal education is grounded in the "examined life" of Socrates: "I tell you that to let no day pass without discussing goodness and all the other subjects about which you hear me talking and examining both myself and others is really the very best thing that a man can do, and that life without this sort of examination is not worth living."[11] It is in the spirit of this examination of life, then, that I use the term "inquiry," and through this book propose liberal education as a genre of revitalization.[12]

V

Some readers of this project in manuscript warned me about my use of the term "post-liberal liberalism" to describe the way of being that emerges at the end of this inquiry. They were concerned about the potentially alienating effect of the word "liberalism," which has clearly become a term of spite for almost everyone, though for widely divergent reasons. Friendly readers suggested that I call the Western vision that emerges through the practice of inquiry something else.

I have really had to struggle with this: Do I have some secret reason for wishing to alienate my reader—or to turn him or her away before he or she even begins the first page? Does the inquiry itself fail to escape the cultural contradictions and antagonisms it seeks to address and move beyond?

I am not sure I can answer these questions. But I do know that the issue of what to call that treasure I rediscover in my searching serves to identify the necessity out of which this work arises, and its real audience as well. The necessity is born of poignant experience with people who have forgotten, sometimes unwittingly rejected, or never received their own tradition. So many of us in this culture are well-intending and active people who would have been liberals in the past, who now are anxious to be anything but—so discredited has "the L-word" become in a culture at war with itself. With such a stance, we show a dangerous nonrecognition of what is great in our heritage and thus of who we are and who we might become.

The danger becomes visible in several ways: as a gullibility in the willingness of such post-liberals to embrace anything that is "other" or "politically correct," as a subtle cynicism in the unconscious resignation to a worldview founded on the simple and nasty clashings of interest and power, and as an instability resulting from intense desire to participate in something "new" that is vital. The danger for us in such a situation is that we have no coherent nurture or discipline for our best inclinations, nothing like a tradition to house and stabilize our growth or even to provide a point of departure. In this state such sincere people can easily become something other than what they intended or imagined. Their good intentions are so very fragile and protean.

My daughter, who is a college senior, an avid citizen, and herself a post-liberal, read parts of this book in manuscript form. She called one night to share her sudden realization that after some years of study, she really had no idea of what liberalism is. In the vigorous conversation that followed I found myself suggesting several things genuine liberalism is *not*: isolated individualism, rationalization of middle-class interest, political indecisiveness, the welfare state, or naive optimism about "doing good" and the possibility of progress. In fact, these late modern meanings inevitably become confused and frustrating, since they are social and political expressions of liberalism (at one time or another and for better or worse) that float around on the surface of our era, disconnected from their deeper cultural moorings.

In the conversation I found myself going further: In its deeper moorings, I found myself saying, liberalism is a little like Zen, a subtradition that inherently refuses containment in any specific doctrine, an energizing vision of becoming fully human that can be found within a variety of social, political, and economic arrangements, any of which need to be regarded as incomplete and revisable. And in both liberalism and Zen there is potentially confusing talk of death and rebirth and human maturity. Unlike Zen, liberalism centers not on "sitting" or meditation, but rather on relationship and community as the place in which we are able to achieve our full humanity. Liberalism is an ideal of mutuality as the locus of full participation in the deepest force of creativity and compassion, an ideal that applies as much to the self and its interpersonal relationships as it does to the body politic, and even to our relationship with God or the ultimate conditions of existence. But as a most ambitious ideal and as a delicate possibility within the Western heritage (one that has been easy neither to speak nor to live), "liberalism" is a term that has been greatly misused. This has been especially the case in the modern period, beginning in the seventeenth century, in which the term increasingly fell captive to the values of competition, controlling reason, materialism, and privacy, a set of values that together constitute what we have come to know and criticize as the modern worldview.

The comparison with Zen seemed to hit home, since my daughter, like many others today, in some ways understands Eastern culture better—or at least more sympathetically—than she does the Western tradition. And yet what I said was not about to help much in her meetings the next day with activist groups or her class on political economics. Something more needs to be said in order to make available the depth and full implication of real liberalism in the world of forgetting and dreaming we share today.

She and I agree that there is some very hard and very basic work that needs to be undertaken. And we, along with many of our friends and mentors, know that this work has to do with the birthing of something new, something that requires our own ethical and spiritual growth as well as new forms of political action that would save the planet. And what I want to say in this inquiry is that an essential component of this work is reappropriation of the old, coming into full possession and appreciation of what is great in our own Western past.

What we need is new, a human development and world citizenship that go beyond the limitations of our history and mythology. But though this movement to the new entails a leap and the inclusion of that which has been other in the past, it requires continuity also. Here is the necessity of this inquiry: in it I seek to engage the work of reappropriation, the work of bringing the old to the new, the work in which each becomes more vital as it comes into dialogical relation with the other.

This brings me back to liberal education as a genre of revitalization, and to the significance of the reader's own inquiry. This book is written in such a way that its effectiveness is dependent upon the reader; it is neither intellectualist treatise nor entertaining revelation of personal detail. What is written here assumes the integrity of the reader's own inquiry, even while it also seeks to awaken and nurture the developmental process of dialogue. The effectiveness of this work, then, hinges on the way in which liberal education requires that we examine ourselves through entering the "thirdness" of dialogue, pursuing questions with others (including our own children, and other surprising sources of wisdom) about such matters as "goodness"—or revitalization. From my own perspective, whether this is a "good" book or not depends on this simple point: does it contribute to the transformative practice of the reader or not?

VI

What you have before you, then, is an exploration, a search—a practice. From the standpoint of completion, I see that this work is a presentation of a developmental process through which we as Western people can appropriate what is great and sustaining in our own tradition. The movement is from a certain spitefulness toward liberalism and our past to a position beyond and apart from the Western tradition altogether, and finally to a new point of access to what is noble and sustaining in the Western heritage—a movement perhaps parallel to the one indicated in the well-known Zen saying: "First a mountain, then no mountain, then a mountain." The access one achieves through this movement is not just to ideas, or identification of "classics" to be admired on the shelf in disappointed remove from what is actually going on in our time. It is access to a real energy, a source, something that is as intimately personal as it is generally cultural. This access is possible neither by relativistic standing still and tearing down the Western tradition nor by absolutistic drawing back into defensive assertion of it. It becomes possible only by moving through the paralysis of the present and forward, into encounter with the multicultural realities of the world—in this particular inquiry through encounter with Zen.

This is an extremely delicate and strenuous process because death and rebirth are essential to revitalization. Out of the death of both the transcendent religiosity of the modern period and the secular consumerism of the twentieth century there emerges a spirituality of simultaneous immanence and transcendence, a spirituality of embodiment and presence. Out of the death of the individualistic liberalism of the modern period there arises a relational liberalism in the emerging global period. We experience the death of ourselves as beings who compete with one another, who relate only at the level of negotiating and trading material and emotional "goods" and even the spiritual goods of a heaven of radically limited occupancy in a place far removed from where we are. Out of this death there arises a rebirth of ourselves as "survivors," as persons who are in contact with the aspect of ourselves and others that is associated with the greatness of such beings as Socrates and Jesus. And this vital contact comprises the kind of experience through which the fully human being emerges, and with it the vocation of nourishing and expanding the divinity of the person, the culture, and the globe.

Finally, and crucially for inquiry as a mode of transformation, revitalization involves the death of intellectualism and a rebirth of the intellect as essential tool in human transformation. Socratic dialogue and liberal education move through and beyond the intellect into the domain of human action, transformation, and creativity to which the intellect can only point. William James is especially helpful on this crucial achievement of the proper function of the intellect—neither clinging to it rigidly so that it usurps human presence and the immediacy of actual experience, nor throwing it out altogether:

> The return to life can't come about by talking. It is an *act*; to make you return to life, I must set an example for your imitation. I must deafen you to talk, to the importance of talk, by showing you, as Bergson does, that the concepts we talk with are made for purposes of *practice* and not for purposes of insight. . . . An *intellectual* answer to the intellectualist's difficulties will never come.[13]

The intellect must serve a way of being and relating that is ultimately beyond its grasp. And yet there is no way around the intellect. In the fullness of its vision, liberal education enables us to bring the intellect into the service of transformation in the direction of the human.

However, it must be said as emphatically as possible that this movement beyond intellectualism is *not* anti-intellectualism, irrationalism, emotionalism, or nihilism. The mere antithesis of intellectualism is a most dangerous stance, which sometimes presents itself as an initial stage in the process of transformation. As with all preliminary stages, there is the danger of arrest and of the confusion of a particular stage along a journey with its final destination. The movement beyond intellectualism is rigorous, subtle; it requires both persistence and patience, and compassion for others and oneself. Hence the temptation of the merely antithetical orientation of irrationalism is understandable, as is also the temptation of drawing back altogether from life in the strenuous present into dogmatic assertion of intellectualist "answers."

The underlying reason for the strenuousness and the accompanying temptations is that the transformative movement necessitates encounter with Nothingness—or death. Major diagnosticians of Western culture have identified this encounter as necessary to the revitalization of this culture. Karl Jaspers, for example, has said that "if man is not to be allowed to founder in the mere persistence of life, it may seem essential that in his consciousness he shall be confronted with Nothingness; he must recall his origin."[14] Stanley Rosen, speaking of the Western tradition in philosophy, has said that "if philosophy is to be preserved . . . it must come to terms with the *NIHIL ABSOLUTUM*" that was articulated and ironically even popularized by Nietzsche.[15] In positive terms, Robert Pirsig, in his popular *Zen and the Art of Motorcycle Maintenance*, tells a story of how we can move beyond Nothingness as oblivion to draw on "the silence that allows you to do each thing just right."[16] Likewise, much of the feminist upheaval of our era can be seen as the work of the positive recovery of Nothingness or silence. Consider, for example, the following statement from Adrienne Rich:

> We begin out of the void, out of darkness and emptiness. It is part of the cycle understood by the old pagan religions, that materialism denies. Out of death, rebirth; out of nothing, something.
>
> The void is the creatrix, the matrix. It is not mere hollowness and anarchy. But in women it has been identified with lovelessness, barrenness, sterility. We have been urged to fill our "emptiness" with children. We are not supposed to go down into the darkness of the core.
>
> Yet, if we can risk it, the something born of that nothing is the beginning of our truth.[17]

The common element in these several voices is the movement from Nothingness as terror, oblivion, or annihilation to Nothingness as our most profound companion and source, as synonymous with the true self we so desperately seek in the various identity crises of our era.

But in our culture most of us never reach the positive sense of Nothingness. We become arrested in the preliminary and negative forms of this fundamental experience: in cynical relativism, "psychic numbing,"[18] or simply in shallow and less than fully human lives of incessant busy-ness and consumerism.

As a way to the positive sense of Nothingness, the Eastern co-participants in the global dialogue of our era offer the paradoxical suggestion that revitalization requires radicalizing that experience of Nothingness, entering it, embracing it, fully experiencing it as Absolute Nothingness—*sunyata*. The suggestion is that through this radicalizing rebirth occurs, birth of our own genuine self.

The apparent preposterousness of this suggestion, and its complete affront to the control-oriented intellect and ego-self, begins to wane as the dialogue with the East enables us to rediscover our own Western wisdom.

Our Western inheritance begins to radiate in a new way. We learn to draw on the "human wisdom" of Socrates' "not-knowing," the kind of awareness that enables us to be in touch with our "prophetic" inner voice[19] and to fully employ the intellect in the service of this awareness. We experience firsthand the reality of Paul's confession in the New Testament: "I have been crucified with Christ; it is no longer I who live, but Christ who lives in me . . . " (Galatians 2:20). In terms of the Hebrew Bible, we find within ourselves— and as our very self—that Nothingness out of which Yahweh created everything. We find within ourselves the Nothingness that is paradoxically the source of everything, including human beings who are created, in our full presence, "in God's image"—as creators.

PART ONE

SEEING THE WORLD WITH ZEN

Mankind owes its existence not to the dreams of humanists nor to the reasoning of the philosophers and not even, at least not primarily, to political events, but almost exclusively to the technological development of the Western world. When Europe in all earnest began to prescribe its laws to all other continents, it so happened that she herself had already lost her belief in them.

Hannah Arendt

From what position is it possible to grasp mankind as a single, living, self-aware entity? I believe that the foundation of this position is for *each of us* to awaken to his or her true Self, that is, each individual must break through his or her ego structure, thereby realizing original Self. At the same time that this is a thoroughly individual 'Subjective' matter, it is also a thoroughly universal, objective one. Why is this so? . . . If we turn our backs on the world, there can be no investigation of the self; if we avoid our conflicts with history, which often progresses beyond human control, there can be no awakening to the true Self. The true investigation of the self is always the investigation of the world and of history.

Masao Abe

Emptiness is something we are aware of as an absolute near side. It opens up more to the near side than we, in our ordinary consciousness, take our own self to be. It opens up, so to speak, still closer to us than what we ordinarily think of as ourselves. In other words, by turning from what we ordinarily call 'self' to the field of *sunyata* [Emptiness, Nothingness], we become truly ourselves. . . . We take leave of the essential self-attachment that lurks in the essence of self-consciousness and by virtue of which we get caught in our own grasp in trying to grasp ourselves.

Keiji Nishitani

ONE

Western Teetering and the Japanese Claim

*T*HE MODERN PERIOD of exuberant Western and American expansion is over. A new, multicultural period of globalism and Asian entitlement has begun. In the midst of the vast uncertainties of this transitional time, some Japanese claim to have what America needs, to have, in fact, what is needed by all developed societies in the post-traditional, late twentieth century. The core of what they offer is mysticism, spiritual development as the necessary complement to the rational development that came out of the West.

In the social commentary in their own popular media, the Japanese address what they take to be the root of the many problems besetting our society now. They address not just the education problem or the family problem, not only the problems with leadership, work, and authority, or the several problems of a society based on materialism and consumption, but a deeper problem of which these are only expressions. They speak of our problem as a culture: our not really knowing how to live in the world community that has arisen from our own technologies and adventures. They speak of the problem of our moral disarray, political confusion, and religious unsteadiness, and the fact that in all three of these crucial subdivisions of culture we teeter between lethargy and fanaticism. It is at this root level that some in Japan perceive their superiority, and claim to have an orientation to life in general, a worldview, that other cultures can adopt and inevitably will have to adopt as they learn the hard lessons of this turbulent era.

It is important to understand this claim—what it is, why it is made, and what its benefits and dangers are. This importance is evident in immediately practical terms, as Japanese products and investors flood American markets. There is an undeniable vitality to the Far East, as though the energy of history itself were now focused through that region. And there is the simple fact that the Japanese are our neighbors now, if not just "down the road" then surely as fellow citizens in the new reality of humankind that is emerging in our time. We and they, as those who are among the first generations of world citizens, must learn to address and understand one another for the sake of peace and the future of our children.

The Japanese themselves have developed popular ways of engaging the question of their advantage in the new world situation: *nihonjin ron*, a theory of Japaneseness, appears as the topic of television series, books, and various forms of public discussion. A recent bestseller, for example, *The Japanese Brain: Its Singularity and Universality*, by Tadanobu Tsunoda, is an explicit attempt to demonstrate cultural superiority based upon racial superiority.[1] Clearly the Japanese claim is not without dangers.

One very effective forum in which to engage this claim in dialogue and benefit from what it has to offer, as well as to submit it to critical scrutiny, is the Kyoto school of philosophy. Very briefly put, the Kyoto school makes two basic points, each of which indicates the uniqueness of the Japanese position in a different way. First, because of the peculiar combination of Western and Eastern values that have intermingled there for some time, Japan is said to be "a kind of laboratory for an experiment in a future world culture."[2] Hence the Kyoto school has thought itself able to synthesize Eastern and Western perspectives, and thereby "to lay the foundations of thought for a world in the making, for a new world united beyond differences of East and West."[3] Perhaps the Kyoto school is in an especially advantageous position to pursue this ambitious work, since Japanese discursive philosophy is barely a century old, and since it was organized from the outset around the attempt to articulate Asian insights in Western philosophical categories.

If the first point about the Kyoto school has to do with the advantages of the location and previous experience of Japan as a laboratory for the future, the second has to do with content. Here the sense of superiority becomes explicit. Japan claims to have an answer that is appropriate to the conditions of all modernized societies, East and West, characterized as they are by technological rationalism, materialism, and implicit if not explicit atheism. What is this picture of a modernized society, and what is the Japanese answer?

The introduction of modern values to any society drives that society away from its traditional base. At first this movement away from tradition is unconscious and may even seem pleasant, as real or apparent gains in standards of living and public health develop, and as people orient themselves to modern values of consumption and production. It is only later that the problems are revealed: meaninglessness, alienation, "homelessness," diffuse anxiety—the well-documented horrors of post-traditional, secular, industrial-technological, consumer society. The Kyoto school understands these horrors in terms of encounter with Nothingness, and it holds that the experience of this encounter is unfamiliar to all traditional cultures *except* that of Japan.

The encounter with Nothingness that is induced by modernization disorients most societies, as is expressed in "anything goes" relativism, or in reactionary reassertions of what is supposed to have been lost, or in fascist attempts at delivering something new. But for Japanese culture the encounter with Nothingness is *not* new. In fact, it is at the very basis of traditional Japanese culture. For this reason it has been possible for Japan to modernize so successfully and without loss of its tradition. Here is the root of the feeling of superiority, and what Japan has to offer the world: a way of moving beyond the negativity of nihilism as an initial response to the encounter with Nothingness, into a positive understanding of Nothingness and thereby a "new world."

Eskimos have many different words for snow; so familiar and various is that stuff to them that distinction of its several types is required. Something similar is true in Japan—in Buddhism *per se*—with Nothingness, *sunyata*. Only a few of its many meanings, most of them preliminary at that, are negative. The other meanings are positive, so that the encounter with Nothingness can be the occasion for moving beyond the uncomfortable transitional quality of our period into an expansion of the human spirit and culture. But movement from the negative to the positive requires spiritual development, and hence the appropriate forms of support and guidance. This is what the Kyoto school claims to provide.

TWO

Worldview as the Problem

*L*ET US SEEK a fuller understanding of the Japanese diagnosis of our problem.

There is a saying about certain solutions being like "rearranging the deck chairs on the *Titanic*," that late vehicle and metaphor of the modern period. In the process of sinking it would not have helped to address oneself to deck chairs in disarray, because the real problem was elsewhere and far more serious. Likewise, our problem, in Western and American culture and in the modernized world generally, is not a problem that can be solved at the level of either more permissiveness or "tough love," more individualism or stronger authority. The problem exists at the deeper level of worldview, the underlying sense of reality that both separates and unites individuals, both frees them and disciplines them, within a shared sense of vivid meaning and value. More superficial treatments of our problem may be appealing, but they are not effective; in fact, they can serve to increase frustration and draw attention away from what is really happening.

The problem of worldview can be described as follows: All human beings, except perhaps sages and the insane, wear the lenses of culture. We do not apprehend reality directly. Reality comes to us filtered, interpreted by the culture that collectively we are, and distorted by the projections each of us introduces through our ego-consciousness. A culture, from this standpoint, is a more or less commonly shared interpretation of the real; culture contains and mediates a worldview. One way to point to the essential function of a worldview is to say that it provides the meaning of and relation between the three most basic variables in human life: self, world, and God (or the ultimate conditions of existence).

In the traditional period, each culture has provided for each of its members answers as to how these three critical variables should be defined and enacted in his or her own particular life. Some religions (and the Western ideal of liberal education as well) have tried to foster for some of its members conscious awareness of the function of these variables within a particular culture, in the hope that this awareness would enable those "some" who are to be the cultural elite to choose the better over the worse from their inheritance. For most people, however, answers to critical questions about who and how to be in the world were supplied by their cultural situations, without the exercise of conscious choice.

The genius of traditional culture lay in its unconscious influence on individuals, inducing them to cooperate or act in good faith with the particular culture of which they were a part. This was accomplished through the processes we refer to as "socialization" and "acculturation." The critical message about appropriate mode of being and expectation for each person was keyed to the race, gender, and class of the individual, and implanted through early, preconscious experience. Hence we see the miraculous cooperation that constitutes culture; how it is that culture came to be both the same and different among members of any given cultural group. And critical questions were raised only by those who were located safely on the margins.

One of the most important developments of this century is people coming to conscious awareness of culture through the impact of modern values, giving rise to what I refer to as the post-traditional situation. "Modernization" brings with it values of time efficiency, instant gratification, production/consumption, and mechanical relation. Because there is a powerful, seductive lure to these values, it is hardly noticed that they displace and deconstruct traditional cultures wherever they come into contact with them.

Modern values both displace traditional values and provide a sort of perch that seems to transcend them, offering a perspective from which traditional values appear to be "old-fashioned," or tainted by assumptions that are racist, sexist, classist, or ecologically suicidal. Despite the potential value for creative change this perspective offers, however, the cultural reorientation that issues from modernization turns out to be incoherent and insufficient to the human spirit. A certain dimension of depth, spiritual significance, and being at home in an enchanted cosmos is left out of the modern package. In the midst of modern society, with its urge to critique, its technical control, and its consumption, children come to be socialized in a peculiar way. They absorb the "culture" that is mediated to them through commercial TV and the mall, rock music and computer games, the telephone and long-distance travel. For the more sensitive, this situation becomes intolerable; it fails to answer questions about self, world, and God with coherence or depth. Modern society tends to satiate the physical and psychological bodies of human beings, but it leaves them in a state of spiritual starvation and homelessness, a condition seldom noticed until it is far advanced. In response, some people accept the incoherence passively and die an inner death, "not with a bang but a whimper," as T. S. Eliot foretold;[1] others may become fanatics of one sort or another, reacting against the whimpering through denial of the situation and rigid assertion of an absolutized position.

Modernization has taken its toll on traditional societies all across the face of the earth. In fact, the modernization process, lubricated by Western technologies of transportation, communication, and war making, has brought the world together into a single world community. But this "community," consisting of shared modern values and fragments of the traditional cultures, has extreme difficulty recognizing itself, except in negative terms through crises, critiques, reactions, and limitations. Positive manifestations are fleeting—"I'd like to buy the world a Coke," "We are the world," the unanimous U.N. Resolution 760 condeming Iraq's invasion of Kuwait—and they are frequently suspect in their association with commercial interests. The present world condition, then, is one of adolescence, one in which humankind can be characterized as having the physical capacities of an adult and the mind of a child. In our time we need urgently to discover the positive and mature principles of world community; we need a global worldview.

Several historians have observed the irony that the Europe whose technologies gave rise to the present world situation was itself unable to find vitality in the larger perspective its activities had brought to birth. Hannah Arendt states this dynamic forcibly:

> [The present reality of] mankind owes its existence not to the dreams of the humanists nor to the reasoning of the philosophers and not even, at least not primarily, to political events, but almost exclusively to the technological development of the Western world. When Europe in all earnest began to prescribe its laws to all other continents, it so happened that she herself had already lost her belief in them.[2]

The great irony for the West is that it seems we ourselves have been most susceptible to the devalued world condition that our culture generated and exported to the rest of the globe, and therefore limited in our capacity to contribute to a global worldview (even though it could well be argued that America is, pragmatically speaking, the best model for world community available). Other cultures, especially those of Asia and many in the third world, seem to have developed an awareness of how modernization erodes traditional values, and have developed ways to temper its effects. But in the West the impact of modernization and the end of traditional culture has been especially painful, despite enormous material advantage. One source of the pain seems to be the guilt associated with the imposition of modern values on cultures all aroung the globe, the cultural genocide that has been perpetuated by the West. The Japanese also suggest that part of the pain arises from the fact that Western cultures are perhaps least able to tolerate the relativizing of all values, the spiritual homelessness and disenchantment of the world, and the nihilism that are the inevitable by-products of modernization. Arendt even implies that it was a cultural "loss of belief" or dis-ease that caused Western culture to generate and embrace modernization in the first place.

As a result of such factors, it has been especially difficult for us in the West to have access in any positive way to our own traditional or premodern Western values. They have been eclipsed by the rush of modernism, the ambiguity of its arising out of our own culture and the anguish of its consequences for humankind generally. When we look into our own past we tend to see only the tragic limitations of the modern project, its shallow materialism and self-destructive individualism, its chauvinism and images of exclusivity, its obsession with technique. We have great difficulty in seeing the beauty of our own tradition—difficulty in seeing our tradition at all; we tend to see only the modern critique of it (many "postmoderns" in our midst today are more modern than they know). It is much more possible for us to see (and to romanticize) other traditions.

It is no wonder that in the post-traditional Western circumstance there is so much generalized cynicism and numbing, guilt and radical lowering of human horizons. It is no wonder either that the same circumstance, its painfulness and radical insufficiency to the human spirit, sometimes induces an idealizing of the premodern past and retreat into reactionary fantasies of ways of being that no longer exist, or probably never did.

In the midst of the pain and confusion of it all, many identify worldview as the root problem, citing, for example, Proverbs 29:18 of the Old Testament: "Where there is no vision, the people perish." And there are a number of claims about the emergence of a new worldview, one that is global. One of the most powerful of these claims is the claim from Japan. The Kyoto school takes these very problems, which they summarize as the experience of homelessness or Nothingness, to be the point of departure for a new worldview.

But the Japanese claim about a new worldview is not the only one. The West is certainly not without claims to a re-visioning of worldview also. Consider for example the Claremont Center for Process Studies' description of a conference on "The Emerging Holistic Worldview":

> A holistic worldview is emerging, challenging the "modern worldview" which has dominated the Westernized world for the past three centuries. At the center of this post-modern, holistic worldview is a vision of reality as an "unbroken web" in which all things function relationally, so that their weal and woe is dependent upon the larger wholes to which they belong, and to which they contribute. If this holistic worldview becomes dominant, it will have radical, far-reaching implications for the ways in which we under-

stand and treat ourselves, our fellow human beings, our planet, and the world as a whole.[3]

Of course, it is important to notice that there are better and worse proposals on this matter of a new worldview; after all, a "global" worldview is what Hitler had in mind. Perhaps all we can say honestly at this point about the most general quality of our time is that it is a time of suspense, a time between the no longer and the not yet.

THREE

Buddhist Perspective and Zen

TO PURSUE THE suggestion of a worldwide synthesis and a new worldview arising from Japan and the Kyoto school, I want to clarify the Buddhist and Zen background of this school. To do this this I turn to a conference that had in part this very purpose: the 1986 Third North American Buddhist-Christian Theological Encounter, whose stated theme was "Notions of Ultimate Reality in Buddhism and Christianity." I also turn in this chapter, for further clarification, to works by the American Catholic Thomas Merton and by Keiji Nishitani of the Kyoto school.

The background and rationale statement for the Buddhist-Christian encounter contains a very interesting proposition:

> These North American encounters have great historical signifi-
> cance. One is reminded that Arnold Toynbee predicted that when
> future historians look at our century, they will be primarily inter-
> ested in the East-West encounter of Buddhism and Christianity and
> its impact on world civilization in the next century. Many Christian
> theologians expect Buddhism to have an impact on contemporary
> Christianity similar in magnitude to that of Greek philosophy in
> the very early centuries and the rise of science in the more recent
> centuries.[1]

The question before us at this moment is the nature of this Buddhist impact.

One of the papers that had been distributed in advance of the theologi-
cal encounter was Francis H. Cook's "Just This: Buddhist Ultimate Reality." This paper provides an essential perspective on Buddhism. Speaking as a Buddhist, Cook says that all of Buddhism can be understood in terms of the identity of *sunyata* and *pratitya-samutpada*. The former is Absolute Nothingness, radical emptiness. *Pratitya-samutpada* is the law of dependent or conditioned co-arising, "the world itself as the place where everything exists

as the result of everything else in a vast, inconceivable web of mutual conditioning."[2] To say that these terms are synonymous is to say that emptiness is fullness, absolute is relative: "Form is emptiness and emptiness is form; form is not different from emptiness and emptiness is not different from form." Put another way, "Without Buddha, no beings; without beings, no Buddha." These statements are paradoxical from the standpoint of the ego that is comprised of intellect and emotion, but not from the standpoint of "realization." What Buddhism *is* is this realization. It is the awakening and enlightenment that emerges from within a unity of paradox, a paradoxical unity. Here is the "just this" of Cook's title.

Historically, this utterly basic understanding reawakened in new form in India with the appearance of Siddhartha Gautama, the one who became frustrated with the complexity and theory of Hinduism and its lack of effectiveness in relation to the terrors of human suffering, and who sat and meditated under the *bodhi* tree until he achieved enlightenment. Initially his teaching, including the Four Noble Truths and the Eightfold Path, was taken as a way of severing ego-attachment to the world and the conditioned self, thus permitting an individual to achieve enlightenment. Early Buddhism was concerned primarily with the solitary individual and his or her release from the world of fear, ignorance, and action driven by desire (*karma*); it tended to be world-rejecting and to presume a realm of enlightenment quite separate from the ordinary.

But as the teaching spread eastward and northward, especially into China and Japan, there were significant developments in the understanding of the identity of sunyata and pratitya-samutpada. The indigenous cultures of China and Japan had different orientations to nature and natural processes. In Indian culture, the Buddhist identity of emptiness and world was taken to mean that no thing is of value since each thing is empty. But in China and Japan this essential identity led to just the opposite conclusion: "If 'empty' means that nothing has a self-existence but exists solely due to a multitude of conditions, everything has value inasmuch as it constitutes a reason for being for the other."[3] Each thing, no matter how significant or minute, comes to be regarded as of great value, because each thing is the cause of everything else.

In this appropriation of Buddhism, a two-realm view of existence was rejected. Enlightenment was understood as the ability to regard the ordinary as sacred. Cook illustrates the Far Eastern orientation with reference to a sparrow: "Hey! See that sparrow? It is the universe appearing as a small brown bird, essential nature delighting in flight, ultimate reality mindfully pecking undigested seeds from horse droppings."[4]

These developments from world-rejection to world-affirmation were even further intensified in the Japanese Zen tradition, beginning in the thirteenth century when Dogen brought Zen from China to Japan and culminating with his Kyoto school heirs in the twentieth century. With Dogen the identity of ultimate reality with the world is radicalized through the insistence that even "emptiness" must be emptied or renounced. Emptiness or Nothingness is qualified as *Absolute* Nothingness: If one knows sunyata, Nothingness, emptiness, then one also knows that it includes everything that exists. And if it includes everything, then it includes also my own experience of Nothingness—which itself must then be negated, emptied, or renounced. With this last realization, with the negation of negation, the human being comes into the full wonder of what is, the miraculousness of the ordinary—"just this." It is as though one can now experience each thing against the backdrop of the Nothingness and *as* the Nothingness, or experience the Nothingness and "what is" simultaneously, as one and the same, as not other from one another.

Through Cook and the members of the Kyoto school, it becomes apparent that the culmination of Buddhism, and the real ground of what the Kyoto school and many others on the Eastern side of dialogue have to offer, is Zen. And yet it is said frequently in some quarters that Zen is not "Buddhism." According to Cook, Zen is realization of "Just this" or that "This is it!"[5] In order to illuminate this fundamental and potentially confusing point, I need to move beyond the Cook statement and say a few things about Zen. I do this with the help of Thomas Merton and Keiji Nishitani.

Thomas Merton, a Western Catholic who is widely recognized for his profound understanding of Zen, cites Dogen: "Anybody who would regard Zen as a school or sect of Buddhism and call it *zen-shu*, Zen school, is a devil."[6] Zen refuses to be distinguished or categorized, either as a sect or a doctrine or even as a specific way of practice; in one way Zen *is* this refusal—in the service of fundamental realization. Merton says,

Zen is outside all particular structures and distinct forms, and . . . neither opposed to them nor not-opposed to them. It neither denies them nor affirms them, loves them nor hates them, rejects them nor desires them. Zen is consciousness unstructured by particular form or particular system, a trans-cultural, trans-religious, trans-formed consciousness. It is therefore in a sense "void." But it can shine through this or that system, religious or irreligious, just as light can shine through glass that is blue, or green, or red, or yellow. If Zen has any preference it is for glass that is plain, has no color, and is "just glass."[7]

Zen is transcultural metaphysical intuition—not the kind that is associated with philosophical proof through logic, but rather one that is immediately existential. It is an experience, an enlightened way of being, and one that is easily lost in the drawing back of abstraction and discursive articulation.

Merton points to the transformed consciousness of Zen by reference to "Christian expression of Zen-consciousness":

> For a Christian "the word of the Cross" is nothing theoretical, but a stark and existential experience of union with Christ in His death in order to share in His resurrection. To fully "hear" and "receive" the word of the Cross means much more than simple assent to the dogmatic proposition that Christ died for our sins. It means to be "nailed to the Cross with Christ," so that the ego-self is no longer the principle of our deepest actions, which now proceed from Christ living in us. "I live, now not I, but Christ lives in me." (Galatians 2:19–20; see also Romans 8:5–17) To receive the word of the Cross means the acceptance of a complete self-emptying, a *kenosis*, in union with the self-emptying of Christ "obedient unto death."[8]

Self-emptying is further indicated in terms of the glass metaphor, which comes from the medieval mystic St. John of the Cross: "Hence if a man can be rid of the stains and dust produced within him by his fixation upon what is good and bad in reference to himself, he will be transformed in God and will be 'one with God.'"[9] Perhaps Merton's most radical pointing to the essential self-emptying or kenosis comes in relation to another Christian mystic, Meister Eckhart, and his theme of "perfect poverty." With Eckhart the emptying is spoken of as moving beyond kenosis in the sense of providing a "place" with the self where God can act, toward the "'perfect poverty' in which man is even 'without God,' and 'has no place in himself for God to work' (i.e., is beyond purity of heart)."[10] It is only here, when God acts purely in himself, that the "true self" (like the Zen "no-self" arising from the negation of negation) appears.

Zen, then, is the deep ontological awareness or wisdom-intuition (*prajna*) of reality prior to our ego-substitution of desires and conceptualizations for reality itself. Thus it can be spoken of in terms of knowing nothing or of seeing directly. On this last point Merton cites the twentieth-century Austrian philosopher Wittgenstein: "Don't think: Look!"[11] The difficulty of Zen stems from the ego's refusal to do this in its attempt to control reality, and this refusal is especially acute in the West. Merton says: "But we in the West, living in a tradition of stubborn ego-centered practicality and geared entirely for the use and manipulation of everything, always pass from one thing to another. . . . Nothing is allowed just to be and to mean itself: everything has to mysteriously signify something else. Zen is especially designed to frustrate the mind that thinks in such terms."[12] Finally, Merton observes that in Zen, prajna (wisdom) and *karuna* (love) are one and the same, remembering the last words of D. T. Suzuki: "The most important thing is Love!"[13]

Turning now to the Kyoto school: Keiji Nishitani articulates Zen in terms of "the great death," which is necessary for the beginning of a 360-degree movement in which true freedom becomes possible.

> Freedom as it is in itself is not simply subjective freedom. Subjective freedom, which is the cornerstone of so-called liberalism, is not yet rid of the self-centered mode of being of man himself. True freedom . . . is an absolute autonomy on the field of emptiness, where "there is nothing to rely on." And this is no different from making oneself into a nothingness in the service of all things.[14]

Nishitani states that freedom—like Zen—has been extremely difficult for Westerners because the "field of emptiness" (sunyata) was avoided in the traditional period, while emptiness in the more preliminary sense of Western nihilism has been "perversely clung to" in the post-traditional twentieth century.[15] Freedom ultimately arises when one dares not only to encounter the nothingness at the base of the ego, but also to go beyond this experience and return as true self: "When person-centered self-prehension is broken down and nothingness is really actualized in the self, personal existence also comes really and truly to actualization in the self."[16]

Nishitani speaks of Buddhism as "the religion of the absolute near side,"[17] meaning that emptiness is more near to our true self than is the ego-conception of self, and is "the home-ground of the self as a self that is truly on the home-ground of the self itself, that is, the *original self in itself*."[18] Nishitani explains this key statement as follows:

> For us, this field of emptiness is something we are aware of as an absolute near side. It opens up more to the near side than we, in our ordinary consciousness, take our own self to be. It opens up, so to speak, still closer to us than what we ordinarily think of as ourselves. In other words, by turning from what we ordinarily call 'self' to the field of *sunyata*, we become truly ourselves. . . . We take leave of the essential self-attachment that lurks in the essence of self-consciousness and by virtue of which we get caught in our own grasp in trying to grasp ourselves. It means also that we take leave of the essential attachment to things that lurks in the essence of consciousness and by virtue of which we get caught in the grasp of things in trying to grasp them in an objective, representational manner.[19]

Thus it is that "the field where all things have a hold on themselves is none other than the field of Sunyata that, having passed beyond the standpoints of sensation and reason, and having passed through nihility, opens up as an absolute near side. . . . The field of Sunyata is nothing other than the field of the Great Affirmation."[20]

On concluding this initial description of Zen, perhaps it is helpful to add that another way of indicating the meaning of Zen is as "just sitting." It depends entirely on—it *is*—an experience of realization that arises from the practice of sitting or meditation. The practice of sitting is essential and prior to any articulation. This gives rise to a basic distinction between Zen thought (as the indication of an experience that is understood in its essence to be beyond thought) and the "place of thought" as we have become familiar with it in the West, in which thought seems to have become capable of containing or representing—even substituting for—the important experience in life.

FOUR

Eastern Presence in Encounter

I

ZEN INSISTS THAT to understand we must experience, and that either experience happens or it does not. So, to move closer to understanding Zen, it helps to see Zen in action. The Third North American Buddhist-Christian Encounter provides an opportunity to do just this. In his response to a paper at this 1986 conference Masao Abe, a practicing Zen Buddhist and the most prominent member of the Kyoto school, gives us a glimpse of Zen in action.

A little background is in order: At the conference there were Buddhist papers and Christian responses, then Christian papers and Buddhist responses. During the first session I was struck by a phrase that was repeated by several parties to the dialogue: "clarifying consciousness." There seemed to be agreement not only on the importance of religious development in general, but specifically on a developmental phase of emptying, of kenosis, of achieving clarity by letting go.

Another prominent theme of the conference was a repeated reference to the enormous spiritual diversity within each cultural tradition. This generated much complexity. On several occasions the value of encounter was directly related to finding from the other tradition "what you need for growth." There seemed a tacit agreement on a commonly, humanly shared pattern of spiritual development, and I thought of works like James Fowler's *The Stages of Faith*[1] and the Japanese tradition of the "Oxherding Pictures,"[2] which typify the stages toward enlightenment. The theme of ineffability was strongly present, the stance that each religious form and tradition is "but a finger pointing at the moon" and hence essentially limited. And the theme of compassion ran strong, the love of others as both the expression of and the way toward enlightenment.

II

But the high point of this conference was an exchange between Masao Abe of the Kyoto school and John B. Cobb, Jr. Cobb is a well-known Christian theologian and teacher, and retired director of the Center for Process Studies at the School of Theology at Claremont. In these capacities he has been a major convener not only of the North American Christian-Buddhist Encounters but of many other such meetings of East and West. His book, *Beyond Dialogue: Toward a Mutual Transformation of Christianity and Buddhism*,[3] has been, together with Cobb's graciousness and deep familiarity with Japanese culture, extremely significant in setting the terms of East-West dialogue—seeking not only mutual understanding, but, beyond that, mutual transformation.

At the Third North American Encounter, Cobb presented a paper entitled "Ultimate Reality: A Christian View," in which he says that differences between traditions can be understood in terms of their highlighting "different features of experience," and through which he seeks "to persuade Buddhists that belief in the Christian God can make more sense than they have supposed."[4] It is perhaps worth noting that on the other end of the dialogue, in his understanding of what Buddhists have to offer Christians and Westerners generally, Cobb has spoken of Buddhists being helpful in relation to the Western lack of "a depth of insight into the nature of reality."[5]

In terms of the persuasiveness of the Christian view, Cobb argues that "when certain features of experience are prominent, the affirmation of God's reality is convincing." Those features that he discusses in detail are truth, righteousness, freedom, and directedness. According to Cobb, belief in God and attention to these aspects of experience go together. In his paper he goes on to specify a Christian understanding of God as both immanent and transcendent, both personal and impersonal. Finally, he discusses metaphysics, or the way of speaking about ultimate reality that has prevailed in the West, and he indicates a basic problem with which this is associated.

Cobb's discussion of Christian metaphysics identifies a basic distortion of Christianity, one that was introduced with St. Thomas Aquinas. Aquinas departed from "the wisdom of Israel and Greece," which associated God with form rather than with matter, with the bringing of form (i.e., order, design, direction, law) out of chaos or the abyss. According to Cobb, Aquinas' "error," which introduced "a major source of the confusion so characteristic of Christian theology," was in departing from the original Western wisdom and identifying God with Being itself (*esse ipsum*). This had the effect of subordinating God as he was understood in Israel and Greece to a sense of spirituality that is closer to that of India, a mystical spirituality in which the emphasis on Being itself in effect places matter (i.e., what *is*) over form and design. Though this has created fruitful comparison between Indian and Western mysticism such as that of Meister Eckhart, it has caused the West to forget or be confused about its original sense of God as the creator and bringer of form.

Simply put, Cobb is saying that the wisdom of Israel and Greece emphasizes features of experience—truth, righteousness, freedom, and directedness—that center on form or design. And in his estimation this is a very different wisdom, elevating a different aspect of human experience, from that spirituality which emphasizes the sheer *isness* of what is. With Aquinas' introduction of the esse ipsum there developed a very deep confusion in Western religion and culture as a result of the mixing and blurring of the two orientations. Cobb concludes by advocating that Westerners deal with the confusion by exercising care in their enthusiasm about the wisdom of India, and "stick[ing] closer to our distinctive history and especially to our own scriptures."[6]

III

Masao Abe's response, simply entitled "A Buddhist Response," was extremely vigorous. He spoke with authority about both Buddhism and Christianity, and went so far as to say that Cobb's analysis was "weak and naive." Speaking about Christianity, Abe maintained that the confusion arises not only from the identification of the Christian God with Being itself, but also with the identification of the Christian God with form. He went on to argue that in Christianity God is (or should be thought of as being) beyond any form—in a way that is quite similar to Buddhism's sunyata.

Abe framed his response in terms of contemporary challenges to all religions by religion-negating ideologies such as scientism, traditional Freudian psychoanalysis, Marxism, and nihilism. In order to address the value of dialogue in the midst of these challenges, he proposes two crucial aspects of dialogue between world religions: (1) seeking clarification of the views peculiar to one's own tradition and allowing the different views between traditions to confront one another, and (2) being "free from the peculiarity of our own traditions in order to scrutinize the notion of the ultimate reality itself most fitting to our contemporary human predicament and the future of humanity."[7] The second aspect needs to involve "a very creative and penetrating discussion in which we must be radically critical of our own tradition so that we can re-examine and regrasp the essence of our religion from the more universal and more fundamental position," and hence "find out the truly ultimate reality for the future of humanity."

Evaluating the meeting of Christianity and Buddhism in the contemporary situation, Abe distinguishes between a "religion of faith," grouping Christianity with Judaism, Islam and Hinduism, and a "religion of awakening," citing the original form of Buddhism and Zen. Religions of faith, Abe says, are based on "an unquestioned belief in God or the divine which includes complete trust, confidence and reliance." Buddhism, as a religion of awakening, involves two necessarily simultaneous realizations: (1) the realization of true self, which is no-self or the death of the ego-sense of self, and (2) the realization of *dharma*, the true nature of reality.

Abe further develops the distinction between the two traditions in relation to the specific ways in which Christianity and Buddhism address the contemporary situation. The essence of the contemporary situation, characterized by the strength of religion-negating ideologies, he presents in terms of Nietzsche's philosophy as perspectivism, which is very close to what I have earlier spoken of as relativism. Abe argues that Nietzsche moved from the insistence "that everything related to us in one way or another is false, utterly devoid of truth, because everything is a construction through our interpretation based on our particular perspective," to the assertion of "the will to power" as the most basic cosmological principle, while admitting that even this is an artificial construct, a self-deception.

Abe goes on to say that the challenge represented by Nietzshe does not affect Buddhism because Buddhism is based on a "completely perspectiveless perspective." By this he means that Buddhism is based on an awakening which is beyond the inherent limitations of *any* perspective. Thus Buddhism comprehends and embraces Nietzsche's relativism, and goes beyond it in a direction that is very different from that taken by Nietzsche. Abe suggests that Nietzsche remained attached to philosophical and ontological concepts, or to their absence or ineffectuality, and was not radical *enough* in his grasp of emptiness. Had he been more radical he might have come to the spiritual (not merely conceptual) awakening which is the Buddhist realization of wisdom and compassion. Instead Nietzsche drew back from Nothingness, into the groundless assertion of "the will to power." Abe cites the silence of the Buddha on metaphysical questions and the ability to empty or renounce even the concept of emptiness as the crucial marks of going beyond the nihilistic or indifferent way of life (as well as transcending the way of desperate assertion) and into the "perspectiveless perspective" or "positionless position."

While Buddhism in this way has been able to meet the challenge of relativity and nihilism, Abe asserts, Christianity, at least as Cobb formulates it, has not. According to Abe, Cobb's view about an "inclusive and adequate perspective" that he calls God is "weak and naive" in the face of Nietzsche's challenge. It remains *a perspective* and thus is susceptible to Nietzsche's proclamation that "God is a sacred lie." However, Abe does suggest that a more adequate view of Christianity, including the understanding of God's being beyond all form, could meet the challenge.

The discussion that followed Abe's reading of his paper began with

Cobb's saying that he cannot find in his own experience a "perspectiveless perspective" but rather always a located position, and that there is a wisdom to Israel and Greece that is not superseded by the "positionless position." He went on to say that he worries specifically about some Western philosophers of this century who think that they can get to such a positionless position. Abe didn't say much. Cobb repeated: One is inevitably located in some position; there is wisdom to the Christian position as he had identified it, one that is not superseded by another position (or by "positionlessness"); and there are dangers to those who claim to have achieved a position "beyond positions." (By this, I think, he meant that this claim has been used in this century to justify *anything*; and that among many Westerners it has not been associated with the spirituality of radical emptiness cited by Abe, but with the mere antithesis of conceptualism—with irrationalism.

Finally an Asian man who hadn't said anything up to this point launched into a statement in a distinctly different key. He was confessional. Cobb and Westerners may not be able to understand "perspectiveless perspective," he said, but he himself can, perfectly well. Sitting there, listening, I wondered about my ability to read facial expressions and tones of voice, especially from an Easterner. Was this a pure statement of experiential truth, cutting through all previous considerations? Was it the simple confession of a believer, addressing a discussion that was somewhat beyond him? Or was it the polite but definite assertion of Japanese superiority? Do we in this man meet a kind of Asian smugness, or is this perception a projection of my own reactivity? And, come to think of it, isn't Abe really defining "dialogue" and "synthesis" in such a way that the Buddhist position *is* superior? We have seen in history the very long period of Western evangelism; do we now see Eastern evangelism in its own distinctive style? Why did the Christians at this encounter seem so passive, so careful not to assert? And why, in the midst of discussion of Israel and Greece, was there so little mention of the meaning of Jesus as the Christ?

IV

In order to seek deeper understanding of these matters, especially those having to do with "positionless position," I turn to Abe's book, *Zen and Western Thought*. Like Nishitani, he speaks over and over again about sunyata, Nothingness, Absolute Nothingness, emptiness. This emptiness is not just a concept, but a fundamental attitude or stance in life, a way of being human. Abe says that since nihilism has become very familiar to Westerners—he takes it, in fact, as our most fundamental condition—we are able to be open to the Eastern Nothingness; faced with our horrible nihilistic sense of Nothingness and the dangers of recoiling from it into Nietzschian assertion, we are able to pass into the positive form. This is Zen.

Abe emphasizes, as do all authentic spokespersons of Zen, that the actual practice of Zen is essential. To describe Zen practice, the actual attitude or stance of it, Abe presents a reflection upon the following discourse by the T'ang dynasty Zen master Ch'ing-yuan Wei-hsin:

> Thirty years ago, before I began the study of Zen, I said, 'Mountains are mountains, waters are waters.'
>
> After I got an insight into the truth of Zen through the instruction of a good master, I said, 'Mountains are not mountains, waters are not waters.'
>
> But now, having attained the abode of final rest [that is, Awakening], I say, 'Mountains are really mountains, waters are really waters.'[8]

In explicating this passage, Abe says that Zen practice involves three stages of understanding. These stages move toward an overcoming of the ego-self to an awakening of the true self. The first stage is that of the ego-self, which is characterized at its core by an anxiety and self-estrangement that arises from its splitting of reality into subject and object: I see, I know, that mountains are mountains. The ego-self seeks to overcome this anxiety and self-estrangement and attain true self through "an endless process of grasping" or "the objectification approach."[9] But this approach inevitably ends in frustration and the collapse of the ego-self: "Our true Self always stands 'behind'; it can never be found in 'front' of us. The true Self is not something attainable, but that which is unattainable. When this is *existentially* realized with our whole being, the ego-self crumbles."[10]

Realization of the futility of the grasping ego opens onto the second stage, which is one of no differentiation, no objectification, no duality of subject and object: mountains are not mountains. This is the stage of emptiness or no-self. But this stage proves to be negative and still entails a subtle differentiation and dualism, now between the differentiation of the first stage and the absence of differentiation of the second. Hence the negative second stage must itself be negated: "Emptiness must empty itself" in a "total negation of total negation."[11]

This last movement into the third stage is in fact an affirmation, a "radical return": "The realization of absolute Nothingness is in Zen the realization of one's true Self. For the realization of absolute Nothingness opens up the deepest ground of one's Subjectivity which is beyond every form of subject-object duality, including so-called divine-human relationship."[12] The movement beyond the dualism of all conceptualization enables one to come into "absolute Subjectivity" and an understanding of reality that is beyond that which has been possible in the West. Abe cites D. T. Suzuki on this: "'The Western mode of thinking can never do away with this eternal dilemma, this or that, reason or faith, man and God, etc. With Zen all these are swept aside as something veiling our insight into the nature of life and reality. Zen leads us into a realm of Emptiness or Void where no conceptualization prevails'":[13] mountains are really mountains.

Abe's articulation of the passage through these three stages involves the presentation of a series of vital paradoxes which are really variations on a single, inclusive paradox: The individual is the absolute, emptiness is fullness, particularity is interchangeability, *samsara* (the wheel of life and death) is *nirvana* (liberation), prajna (wisdom) is karuna (compassion). These are communicated through classical Zen stories. For example:

> Shih-kung (Ja: Sekkyo) asked one of his accomplished monks, "Can you take hold of empty space?"
>
> Yes, sir," he replied.
>
> "Show me how you do it."
>
> The monk stretched out his arm and clutched at empty space.
>
> Shih-kung said: "Is that the way? But after all you have not got anything."
>
> "What then," asked the monk, "is your way?"
>
> The master straightway took hold of the monk's nose and gave it a hard pull, which made the latter exclaim: "Oh, oh, how hard you pull at my nose! You are hurting me terribly."
>
> That is the way to have a good hold of empty space," said the master.[14]

The story points to the fact that resolution of paradox lies not in intellectual formulation but rather in the direct and experiential realization that what initially appeared as irresolvable dilemma is simply two aspects of a single, dynamic reality. And the key to realization or self-awakening lies in spiritual death, as "an essential element of true religion."[15]

According to Abe, realization is especially difficult for Westerners, because of our inherited forgetfulness of Being, a forgetfulness that began with Aristotle:

> In Aristotle, although the 'Being' of beings is taken up as a question, Being is grasped from the side of beings. It is looked at as if it stands 'over there' against us. Being is not grasped in itself from its own side. Just in asking about the 'Being' of beings in this objective manner, Aristotle, and Western metaphysics after him, concealed and forgot 'Being' itself.[16]

Just as he did at the conference, Abe cites Nietzsche as an instance of the implications of "forgetting" in the post-traditional twentieth century.

Despite the fact that Nietzsche appears to be radical in his nihilism, he does not actually go far enough, and is hence not yet free from the Western objectification of Being: "However basic it may be, the will to power is not 'Nothingness' but 'something' affirmatively established and thereby not free from objectification."[17]

Nietzsche rejects Christianity in general and Paul in particular because of their moralistic spirit, which stifles life and stands in the way of human naturalness. Against this, Abe defends Paul, saying that he is quite compatible with Zen:

> To Paul, faith does not suppress life; it was the living of a new life which is supported by the realization of death. As he says, we are 'always carrying in the body the death of Jesus, so that the life of Jesus may also be manifested in our bodies' (II Corinthians 4:10) and 'I have been crucified with Christ; it is no longer I who live, but Christ who lives in me; and the life I now live in the flesh I live by faith in the son of God' (Galatians 2:20). . . . On this point, Zen, which realizes birth-and-death itself as the Great Death and gains a new Life of rebirth through the realization of the Great Death, does not differ from the standpoint of Paul in essence.[18]

We can see that despite his criticism of the Western tradition, Abe finds positive resources in this pre-Aristotelian reading of Paul. He also cites in a positive frame Martin Heidegger as a post-traditional figure who "takes the issue of 'nothingness' not only with utmost seriousness, but perhaps with the most profundity in Western history."[19]

Further qualifying his criticism of the Western tradition, Abe identifies a dimension in the Western tradition which is lacking in Buddhism and Zen. This dimension is the axiological, the dimension of value:

> The idea of justice represented by the 'ought' is rather lacking, or at least very weak in Buddhism, particularly in Zen, while the idea of being and non-being, life and death, is very strong.
> The Christian idea of the one God should not be understood merely ontologically, but also axiologically. The Christian faith in the one God is more concerned with justice and love than the ontological questions of God's being. . . . In Zen the ontological aspect, the question of being and non-being, life and death, is much more central than the issue of good and evil. On the other hand, in Christianity the issue of good and evil is much more strongly emphasized than the question of being and non-being.[20]

This leads Abe to the statement that "the strength in Zen is the weakness in

Christianity and vice versa."[21] From here he concludes with the need for dialogue, "based on this recognition of these mutual strengths and weaknesses."[22]

FIVE

World Perspective

*A*LFRED NORTH WHITEHEAD makes the following statement about Christianity and Buddhism in the modern period:

> The decay of Christianity and Buddhism, as determinative influences in modern thought, is partly due to the fact that each religion has unduly sheltered itself from the other. The self-sufficient pedantry of learning and the confidence of ignorant zealots have combined to shut up each religion in its own forms of thought. Instead of looking to each other for deeper meanings, they have remained self-satisfied and unfertilized.[1]

Of course the situation is changing rapidly in our postmodern time. In order to understand our time as a time of the end of separation, and a time in which the dialogue that Cobb and Abe speak of might enable us to draw on the strengths of others, we need some large historical view. Specifically, we need some understanding of the similarities and differences between the Western and Eastern traditions. Our time requires that we risk moving out of being shut up in the particularisms of our past, to work toward a sense of unity in diversity that would enable all to relate and thrive. We need, as the Kyoto school insists, synthesis.

At this point in the inquiry, let me respond to the Kyoto school's synthesis by proposing synthesis from a Western standpoint. The synthesis that follows centers on a broad understanding of history that has emerged in the twentieth century through interdisciplinary Western scholarship. It is quite responsive to Abe's statement about the benefits of dialogue based on recognition of "mutual strengths and weaknesses."

II

To begin with similarities and the most obvious features of commonality, both Eastern and Western traditions share in the present not just the end of the modern isolation to which Whitehead refers, but also the ending of the much broader traditional period in human history as a whole, which began roughly 600 B.C. Ironically, the end of the traditional period has not meant the disappearance of the traditions, but in many cases their resurgence.

The traditions, once separated by insurmountable distance and by the enclosure of their own senses of universality and exclusiveness, began to come closer as the traditional period unfolded, due largely to technologies of transportation, communication, and warfare. But at the same time that they came closer to one another physically, they each tended to withdraw within their own societies, as Whitehead has pointed out. They accepted a secondary position of being regarded as "outmoded" and "old-fashioned" in comparison with the more "advanced" and "scientific" values of modern society. However, in our time, now that the modernist enthusiasm has been unmasked and is being deconstructed, together with its limited and distinctly Western belief in universality based on reason, the traditions reappear. They now meet on the bewildering landscape of a world situation that has been generated by the modern, technological achievements that grew out of one of these traditions, namely that of Western Europe. And they meet now in the midst of the claim that it is not just the modern period that is over, but the whole of the traditional period as well. As present, the traditions share a sense of living together in a time between times. They exist under the threat of a pervasive "life-style" of secular consumerism that proclaims the irrelevance of anything traditional, as well as wild and frequently desperate postmodern reactions against that very modern secularism, sometimes in the name of tradition.

To complexify the situation even further, we are today able to see not just the end of the traditional period, but its beginning as well. The period of tradition, sometimes referred to as the historic period, is now made other to us, such that we are able to view it as one whole thing, with both end and beginning. From this peculiar and only partially charted perspective of our time, which gives us a certain clarity to look out and back from, we see a profound sense in which the traditions share a common point of beginning as well as ending and so some deep structural similarities. There is something profoundly hopeful in the discovery of a commonly shared beginning.

Karl Jaspers is helpful in bringing this perspective into focus. Speaking about the commonly shared beginning of the traditions, he points out that there is an empirically demonstratable historical axis of common human experience passing through the fifth century B.C.[2] Forming the midpoint of a spiritual process that occurred between 800 and 200 B.C., a common pattern emerges among human groups within the cultural realms of China, India, and the West. These various groups had no physical contact with one another; Confucius and Lao-tse in China, the Upanishads and Buddha in India, Zarathustra in Persia, the prophets in Palestine, Homer, the Greek philosophers and tragedians—all remained geographically and culturally separate. Yet, despite this physical separation, Jaspers identifies a commonly shared pattern that is visible in the foundation of the great historical civilizations:

> What is new about this age [800–200 B.C.], in all three areas of the world, is that man becomes conscious of Being as a whole, of himself and his limitations. He experiences the terror of the world and his own powerlessness. He asks radical questions. Face to face with the void he strives for liberation and redemption. By consciously recognizing his limits he sets himself the highest goals. He experiences absoluteness in the depths of selfhood and in the lucidity of transcendence. . . .
>
> In this age were born the fundamental categories within which we still think today, and the beginnings of the world religions, by which human beings still live, were created. The step into universality was taken in every sense.[3]

We see, then, a deep unity beneath the diversity of traditions; we see the sense in which each tradition is a response to the same overall human condition. And this cohesiveness has very positive implications for our time as we seek an adequate principle of unification and relation, one that requires each of us neither to give up our traditions in favor of a universal agreement nor to submit to a leveling down to a least common denominator. Jaspers's empirical discovery provides the basis for, in the words of his student Hannah Arendt, "the faith that the manifold points to a Oneness which diversity conceals and reveals at the same time."[4] And this faith suggests a new world order the terms of which would be quite different from those of the traditional or historic period, one in which diversity in relationship would be a value rather than a threat.

Jaspers discusses the structural similarities between the dominant traditions viewed from the post-traditional perspective. (Perhaps he would exclude Zen and some other subtraditions, though he does not speak to this; it is the thesis of the Kyoto school that Zen must be excluded, that Zen is not "traditional.") Jaspers points out that the traditions were not only universalistic, claiming the exclusive faithfulness and effectiveness of their own ways, but they were also transcendentalistic, and thereby hierarchical, dualistic, and earth-denying. This is to say that they postulated a realm of universal reality separate from the ordinary and hence a radical distinction between the sacred and the secular in human experience that was mediated by a religiously legitimated hierarchy. This distinction entailed a derogation of the immediacy of life in the world and in the body. Robert N. Bellah describes world-rejection as a "massive fact" of the foundation of the historic period: "the emergence in the first millennium B.C. all across the Old World, at least in centers of high culture, of the phenomenon of religious rejection of the world characterized by an extremely negative evaluation of man and society and the exaltation of another realm of reality as alone true and infinitely valuable."[5] Hannah Arendt describes contemporary manifestation of this same phenomenon as "the wish to escape the human condition," and as "a rebellion against human existence as it has been given."[6]

If the fact of common origin suggests something hopeful about future world community, the world-rejection inherent in this common origin gives us some indication of our liability. It is probably not unfair to say that the chief question before the human race in our time is the question as to whether we can make the transition from the world-rejections of the traditional period to a religious and cultural orientation that is life-affirming, that regards life as a gift rather than as condemnation. And in relation to this question one must ask about the consumerism, the instant gratification, and the apparent world-embracing of the late modern and postmodern present: while this worldview does not seem to postulate another world, a spiritual dimension, is it truly life-affirming, or is it yet another expression of the urge to escape the human condition and the earth itself? The modern, along with the ancient and medieval periods, is still part of the larger traditional era; is the "postmodern" really as post-traditional as some of its celebrants like to think?

There are other similarities between the great traditions, most of which are associated with this "massive fact" of world-rejection in one way or another. Viewed from the very broad perspective that becomes available in our time, there is remarkable agreement between the independently developing Western and Eastern cultures in the historic period about the nature of the human condition. Both Eastern and Western cultures are founded on the understanding that things are not right with human beings. The human condition is understood to be one of dislocation, alienation, distortion, anxiety, restlessness. And there is agreement on the existence of a dim and innate knowing within humans about the cause of this condition, an awareness of a time when the dislocation either did not or will no longer exist, as well as some basic sense of what can be done to overcome the pain of separation. In Eastern cultures the most general term for the human problem is "karma," the mixture of fear, ignorance and desire which keeps us locked into the wheel of suffering and illusion through many births, deaths, and reincarnations. In the West the comparable term would be "original sin," that primal act of disobedience and self-assertion by which we lost innocence and rightness, and which caused God to eject us from the Garden of Eden, sending us forth into the historical world of labor, pain and judgment.

But now we must turn to the equally striking differences between the two primary traditions. If there is dramatic agreement on the problem of human life and the consequent need of transformation, there is equally dramatic disagreement between East and West in their prescriptions as to what it is that humans need to do. It is as though Eastern and Western cultures stood for an instant in agreement about the human problem, and then proceeded in precisely opposite directions to find a solution.[7] The East became intensive, and the West became extensive. The East went inward and down to the roots, seeking to extinguish the illusions of the ego-sense of reality that generate the essential human problem, developing the individual disciplines of silence and meditation. The West went outward and beyond, actualizing individuals and engaging them in the world, developing the communal disciplines of right relationship, democracy and human rights.

These observations underline the way in which traditional human cultures can be seen as essentially or in their roots to be about the matter of transformation. But we should be cautious about any neat conclusions concerning the similarities and differences between traditions; there are significant exceptions in both East and West to what I have just said. What is most compelling about the basic East/West similarities and differences, even more than the historical facts that can be cited, is their pertinence in making sense of the present meeting of East and West. Perhaps we are now engaged in distinctively post-traditional mythmaking more than in "history" in the traditional mode of supposed factuality, but there seems an incredible complementarity, a sense in which each side presents just what the other needs. Hans Waldenfels, as the conclusion to his *Absolute Nothingness: Foundation for a Buddhist-Christian Dialogue*, provides an especially dramatic statement of this complementarity:

> Enlightenment that radiates love, and love that is enlightened and gripping, condition one another. And when we have seen that, the question arises for us: Do not *the smile of the enlightened Buddha* and *the tortured countenance of the crucified Jesus* really come face to face when there is a sharing in the depths where the true self resurrects in poverty, death and absolute nothingness?[8]

Eastern culture has developed profound wisdom on the dynamics of inner life and the way in which creative change and maturation can be working in the individual, but this focus has entailed a blind spot when it comes to certain dimensions of the communal. Eastern cultures, though they can exhibit enviable cooperation and tranquility in the communal, have tended to be authoritarian, passive, or even callous in their treatment of matters external to mystical development—matters of individual rights, political and economic justice, and the search for the good (or the better) community. Western culture, on the other hand, has developed ideals of social change in the direction of equality, justice, and the sharing of political rights in the communal dimension, but it has tended to be simpleminded about what counts for maturity of the person. It is as though one culture was nearsighted and the other farsighted, with all the benefits and limitations of each condition. This difference in culture orientation is quite parallel to Abe's characterization of Eastern focus on the ontological and Western focus on the axiological dimension.

Further, each side contains an awareness that in order to be more whole it needs what the other presents. For in the Far East it is acknowledged in every viable culture that the fullness of enlightenment involves service in the world, a service which is provided not only for isolated individuals but also for the social structures that contribute significantly to the shape of individual life. But this fullness, in practice, has been achieved only rarely. Conversely, Western democratic aspirations have been acknowledged as attainable, but according to the modern philosopher John Stuart Mill, attainable only among persons who are in "the maturity of their faculties."[9] One cannot have genuine democracy, a society that is committed simultaneously to individual realization and to the common good, without maturity; without maturity the movement outward becomes either subtle self-aggrandizement or shallow "self-sacrifice," egotism in either case.

Observations about the meeting of East and West and their complementarity have very suggestive parallels in other emerging ways of speaking about what is needed for human development at this post-traditional time in history. There are at least three other readings of the present that point out that in the now-completed historic period (i.e., the period of our official and recorded remembering in either Eastern or Western cultures) we have repressed and rendered unavailable an "other" part of our own humanity, and that health and vitality now require that we reappropriate this dimension. This seems to be the message of feminism at its best, exemplified most fully in the work of Carol Gilligan: feminism does not call for female supremacy, but for recognition and inclusion, both in ourselves and in public policy, of the "feminine" dimension of intimacy, cooperation, and care, alongside the "masculine" dimension of independence, competition and rights.[10]

The need for reappropriation and inclusion is paralleled in the new literature that addresses the contrast of the "right brain," the mode of consciousness that is intuitive, spontaneous, and holistic, with the "left brain," which is analytical, future-directed, and specialized. People like Robert Ornstein and Roger Sperry[11] who speak in terms of this metaphor of two brains do not advocate the we forsake the left brain and disappear into the right, but that we learn to acknowledge and live from both.

Finally, there is the awareness raised by the work of Carl Jung, Joseph Campbell, and Bruno Bettelheim,[12] who contrast the thinking structures of the historic period with those of the prehistoric, the latter being evident in our dreams, where they appear as archetypical images common to all human cultures and the "collective unconscious." Here, too, the challenge is one of acknowledgment, reappropriation, and integration.

In all these metaphors we have the ideal of integration, a suggestion of the nature and direction of post-traditional wisdom. In each metaphor the point is that we must come into contact with what was repressed and rendered "other" during the historic period and reintegrate it into our being. It is important to notice that all metaphors of otherness are reflective of the "massive fact" of world-rejection during the traditional period. In light of this we can understand each metaphor as expressive of a more generalized dualism and dichotomizing of spirit and body, one in which the former is valued over the latter and displaced from the ordinary, while the latter is devalued and repressed.[13] In this separation both aspects of humanity are distorted, spirit forever existing "out there" in another realm in a way that renders us chronically alienated and homeless in the ordinary, and the body deprecated so that it becomes merely a tool—or a threat. What is lost is the *gift*-quality of life, the fullness of the ecstatic present as a miraculous fusion of spirit and body, the luminous actuality of complete presence and incarnation.

The work of positive reappropriation in our post-traditional period confront our era with characteristic dangers and confusions: Some individuals and groups disappear into and get lost in the repressed other. Some experience "the other" for a time and become frustrated and frightened, since they lack proper guidance and support in the effort of integration, and they rush back to dogmatically reassert the "traditional" against the ambiguities and hard work of integration. And some are so afraid of the meeting with the other that they stubbornly refuse to budge, or they define their life in a superficial manner, or go limp, or become cynical.

III

Returning to the specific metaphor of East and West, what would synthesis as integration mean from the Western side, as post-traditional wisdom? And what points need to be made about how we are able to see both the limitations of Western culture and the resources that are available from the East in the movement toward integration? I think there are three such points.

First is Nothingness. Nothingness is a way of being or a perspective (perhaps "perspectiveless") that is prior to our ordinary consciousness. Ordinary consciousness is dominated by emotion and intellect, which is to say ego, and hence limited and thoroughly infected with an ultimately self-defeating self-concern. Contact with Nothingness is contact with a more

original and deeper consciousness, one which is paradoxically most genuinely the self—Nishitani's "near side"—and at the same time the point at
which the self touches on the ultimate. This contact enables us to gradually
overcome the fear, pain, and self-concern that lie at the base of the ego; it
enables transformation of the self.

It is important to state that "Nothingness" is Nothingness from the
standpoint of the ego, not Nothingness in the sense of oblivion, ultimate
negativity, or chaos. "Nothingness" or "perspectiveless perspective" indicates a deeper view of reality that cannot be apprehended by grasping, by the
objectification approach that is inherent in the ego-consciousness of intellect
and emotion. Enlightened apprehension requires activation of a different
organ of perception, one that the ego fights in its obsession with control and
the maintenance of supremacy. Contact with the East might enable Westerners to overcome the deficiency that Cobb refers to as our lack of "deep
insight into the nature of reality."

In the post-traditional West there are many philosophical and cultural
movements that are driven by the urge to move beyond what is understood
as a traditional obsession with intellectualist "foundations," the obsession
with capturing objective reality within an intellectual formulation. These
post-traditional movements have emerged as the search for a deeper level of
perception. They include phenomenology, with its quest for the *Ding an sich*
(the thing itself), and Heidegger's attempt to recover Being; existentialism,
with its wish to move beyond the priority of essence over existence, to the
singularity of the genuine human act; the American movement of pragmatism and radical empiricism, with its aspiration to reclaim "experience"
(John Dewey), to look into the "thick" of existence (William James), or to
engage a "sixth sense";[14] perhaps even Nietzsche's nihilism and his injunction to "remain faithful to the Earth," and Derrida's deconstruction. These
movements have in common the attempt to overcome a certain abstraction,
superficiality, and logocentrism that is thought to have dominated the Western tradition. It is not mysterious that many of these movements sense affinity with the Eastern Nothingness. And perhaps with this affinity we have
evidence of a post-traditional cultural convergence.

The second point concerning limitations of the West and resources of
the East has to do with the understanding of personhood. We have seen several suggestions that the West has lacked a deep understanding of the
dynamics of individual life, and that the East is much more developed in this
dimension. Arnold Toynbee, speaking at a late stage in his distinguished
career of assaying the civilizations of the world, is quite explicit on this:

> I agree that the discovery and exploration of the subconscious
> depths of the psyche, which, in the West, started only as recently as
> Freud's generation, was anticipated in India at least as early as the

generation of the Buddha and his Hindu contemporaries, that is to say, at least 2,400 years earlier than Freud. The modern Western attempt to explore and to master the subconscious has not yet progressed beyond a naive and crude early stage. . . . I have repeatedly drawn my Western readers' attention to this historical fact, as part of my lifelong attempt to help jolt modern Western man out of his ludicrously mistaken belief that modern Western civilization has made itself superior to all others by outstripping them.[15]

Because of this mistaken belief in our superiority and the fact that humankind urgently needs to "call technology to order," Toynbee concludes that "the Western course is headed for disaster," and that "in the future, the leadership is going to be taken over from the West by Eastern Asia."[16] The reason for this shift in world dynamics is that "the Japanese command the necessary spiritual resources," since "Buddhism has made a subtler psychological analysis than any that has been made, so far, in the West."[17]

The third point to be made about limitations and resources is the place and function of the intellect. From what has been uncovered so far in this inquiry, there is the notion that Western culture has lost sight of the ontological function of the intellect. From the Eastern standpoint, the intellect by itself is a part of ego-consciousness, and is therefore subject to the contradictions and self-defeating behavior of that domain. But from the ground of awakened consciousness intellect can be a powerful tool in pointing to that which is finally beyond its ken. Masao Abe is most helpful on this, insisting that Zen is not anti-intellectual, and that the function of the intellect is to provide resources of interpretation and hence discipline for growth toward awakening.

In the West, however, it appears that the intellect has acted largely within and in service to the ego. And so it is not surprising that the intellect at some point began to take on a life of its own in the form of technology, and that finally technology comes back upon us, turns from serving our "needs" to threatening our very existence. Now we have reached the point where Eastern culture could help the West reclaim the proper function of the intellect, and thus enable us to "call technology to order."

SIX

Ram Dass, the Roshi, and Liberal Education

I

WE PURSUE INQUIRY into post-traditional wisdom, and the possibility of this wisdom being found in synthesis as integration, a joining together of elements of our humanity that had been separated or repressed in the traditional period. This seems compatible with the synthesis proposed by the Kyoto school.

Yet the voice of the Kyoto school can be heard in its stipulation that "synthesis" be not just ideational but experiential, involving something of the magnificent simultaneity of detachment and engagement that occurs in the Zen master. Arnold Toynbee points to the sort of integration we seek by identifying spiritual exertion as the issue: "This spiritual exertion, made by individual human beings, is the only effective means of social change for the better."[1] And Abe says that the future requires "*each one of us* to awaken to his or her true self, that is, each individual must break through his or her ego structure, thereby realizing original Self."[2] What do these things mean in relation to our real experience, and what is the standing of "synthesis as integration" from this perspective?

II

In the midst of pondering the nature of real experience, spiritual development or practice, and spiritual exertion, I read Peter Matthiessen's *Nine-Headed Dragon River*, his Zen journals. These are a series of meditations on the saying and doing of the primal Zen master Dogen, and contain a history of Zen that culminates in America: finally, in the present, Zen is not "over there," hidden in exotic monasteries, but here in America! The general message seems to be that "Zen" is much nearer than we think.

Matthiessen, a major interpreter and appropriator of Zen from the Western side, reports on his struggles with spiritual exertion in his own practice of Zen. A statement made to him about exertion and spiritual ambition by one of the Zen masters leaps out at me: "To be emancipated from the idea of enlightenment, he said, took a long time, and that was the true enlightenment."[3]

I sense significant clues to the nature of real experience in these points from Matthiessen. It appears, for instance, that reality in its nature is serendipitous, though the way we live, in apparent comfort and control, can keep us oblivious to this most important fact: that the messages we need for our development are given, if we just know how to look for them, if we only do not refuse them when they arise. Perhaps our initial images of spiritual exertion and achievement, of "original self" and genuine experience, are themselves part of our problem. And the answer we seek turns out to be more near at hand than we had imagined.

Still pondering one day, I was in the car, driving north in a steady November rain from Columbia, Maryland to Rochester, New York for a conversation with Zen *roshi* Philip Kapleau. In the higher elevations of the Pennsylvania mountains, icicles began to appear on road signs and guardrails.

I kept thinking about Nishitani's statements on the West's avoiding the experience of Nothingness, not going far enough, becoming arrested in its preliminary forms: What does this imply in terms of what we should do? Should we pursue the sunyata experience, should we actively seek it? Maybe this peculiar seeking accounts for part of the masochism of our culture in this era, a theme especially vivid in the works of Saul Bellow.[4] Is masochism real experience, can it lead to real experience? What is not real experience? Beyond my windshield the mountain views, which I saw only in glimpses, were strongly reminiscent of fog-shrouded, utterly spare Eastern art. Was this Zen realization in Pennsylvania?

At Columbia I had been given an audio tape of a speech by Baba Ram Dass, hippie guru of the sixties, who was back in currency in the "New Age" movement. *Nobody Special* is the title. As freezing rain and snow set in— dangerous driving, roaring trucks—I slipped it into the tape deck.[5]

Ram Dass says it all, with jokes: "Spirit is spirit"; there is one sublime consciousness to which we are all connected. There is "law" to reality, and an accompanying sense in which "everything is perfect," but this lies beyond the grasp of ego-consciousness with its self-aggrandizement and insistence on subject/object distinction. We are capable of actualizing our connection with spirit and law, but most people do not. The contradiction between perfection on one side and the harsh realities of evil, suffering and death on the other cause most people to "harden their hearts" as a way of self-protection.

Through compassion and meditation, Ram Dass continues, we are able to avoid the hardening and actualize our connection with the divine. On the spiritual path, one has many teachers. In learning to meditate, one learns to focus on being rather than on thoughts; being and thoughts are related as the blue sky is related to the clouds that continuously pass by upon it. The aim or "game" is to become "nobody special": this doesn't mean eradicating one's neuroses, but rather being able to "have them in for tea," not identifying with them.

In brief, that is Ram Dass's message. He includes many clever stories and examples, and on second thought these are very important to his overall message. He entertains, and perhaps in this way gets people started. But started at what? "Meditation," he says, with the help of "many teachers." But this is vague. What is the practice, the discipline of his method? He tells a story of swimming with John Lilly's dolphins: at first being afraid, but overcoming the fear by "flipping into intuitive" and allowing himself to be "out of mind," meaning the ego-mind.

This all sounds good; it is engaging, even inspiring. But there is something peculiar, something that makes me hesitate, draw back and think. The problem is that one could graduate rather quickly from Ram Dass's orientation and go on to all sorts of things. I think this is the same issue that John Cobb has with Western people who claim to have developed the "perspectiveless perspective": it could mean anything!

The weather eased up at Binghamton, and was clear once I got to Syracuse. From there it was a short leg west to Rochester. And there, though the encounter with Roshi Philip Kapleau involved much the same subject matter as Ram Dass's tape, it turned out to be an entirely different experience.[6]

Philip Kapleau is an American who spent thirteen years in Zen training in Japan, and was ordained to teach Zen in 1963. In 1965 he published his very influential book, *The Three Pillars of Zen*,[7] and founded The Zen Center in Rochester. Among his several other books, his *Zen: Dawn in the West* (1978)[8] is of particular significance for this inquiry. In it he speaks in a dialogue format, as he does in *Three Pillars*, providing advice and guidance to Westerners who are trying to practice Zen. Like Matthiessen, Kapleau speaks of and to the presence of Zen in American experience.

But our meeting wasn't about the books he has written. I had sent a letter to him, saying that I was working on an East-West inquiry and wanted to have a conversation with him—also indicating that my interest wasn't entirely academic.

His Zen center was exquisite, immaculate, consummately serene; it stood as a pure case of the Zen aesthetic of simplicity and suchness, a presentation of the sheer *is*ness of what is against the backdrop of the void. We were both reserved and cautious at first, but quickly fell into lively conversation. The exchange began in mid-afternoon and moved on with the sun setting over city rooftops beyond his window, as the room slowly darkened.

Briefly I told him about my project—the meeting of East and West, the search for a post-traditional wisdom. I was particularly concerned, I said, with his observations on the status of American Zen. I also told him that the inquiry I was working on was an attempt at a practice of my own discipline, that of liberal education, and that more and more I found myself convinced that practice is what is really essential.

He concurred: The practice was essential. I told him that in all honesty I was tempted to use this interview for my own purely personal purposes. For many years I had been practicing something like Zen, something like Christian mysticism, something like my own spiritual discipline or hygiene, following the path of individual development that Kapleau himself speaks to in his books. There have been external masters in my life, appearing mostly in the form of close friends and those I love, though sometimes also as strangers, and frequently for only very brief moments. Yet I've felt the absence of a single traditional master; and so I felt a desire arising, in the roshi's presence, to seize the opportunity and seek advice on my own situation. I went on to say that, since my own condition is shared by a great many people today, perhaps "using" the interview to bring this up wasn't really selfish or off the mark.

He agreed, emphasizing that one must have a teacher, that one is severely limited if one is simply picking things up from here and there. But as he said this I found this confusing, since his own books really seem addressed to the person who is practicing independently. Maybe by "teacher" he meant a discipline, one that is more completely practical than reading and listening, one that is connected to real experience. Perhaps he had delivered me a *koan*, one central to this inquiry: What is the nature of genuine authority and guidance? Is it to be found in traditional external authority, or in post-traditional internal authority that enables us to choose from among many sources or traditions?

It occurred to me to ask how he regarded religious pluralism, how he related to other paths: What did he think about the widespread "knowledge" of spiritual development which Ram Dass seems at first glance to exemplify? Isn't this knowledge potentially dangerous, leaving us vulnerable to forms of manipulation and exploitation? But somehow these questions did not get raised. In the conversation he spoke disparagingly of the state of certain aspects of Zen in Japan. He spoke of a new book he was just completing, on death, and read me a page on Socrates, asking if he'd got the citation right.[9] The reference is to Socrates' "doing *zazen*," in a passage from the *Symposium* where Plato describes Socrates' standing transfixed for a very long time. Then he remarked that life after death is not as easy as Kübler-Ross and others in the Western death-and-dying discussion proclaim, with the experience of restoration of wholeness, the bright light, the presence of loved ones. Kapleau said that it can be much harder after this initial transition. He reported his own recent experience of working with people planning to commit suicide; he spoke of the inability of people today to with-stand pain, their lack of belief in the future, and the prevalent materialism even in people's feeling about their own existence. This struck me as a signif-icant comment on the observations made in the East-West dialogue about Western lack of deep insight into the nature of reality.

Roshi Kapleau turned on the light on the table between us and we stood up. He gave me a tour of the center and invited me to return for a workshop.

III

Between New York and my home in Michigan, the drive through Canada was fast across a spare landscape. I found myself in the middle between Ram Dass and Kapleau. Ram Dass's expressed position makes sense theoretically: There is one God and there are many ways to Him/Her. But I see that the consequence of this position in terms of practice can be incoherent or disas-trous. Any way or no way follows, or perspectivelessness in the dangerous sense. Kapleau and his Zen center, on the other hand, have the beauty of tra-dition, the advantage of a very specific way of practice; discipline, authority and structure are all given. At first blush it would seem that Ram Dass's lis-teners would have to invent these structures; but such aids to enlightenment cannot be invented or chosen properly until one has achieved enlighten-ment! Another danger of the eclectic do-it-yourself approach, one we are familiar with from America's experience with cults, is that of choosing a master, someone who would provide discipline, authority, and structure; what if the master turned out to be a Charles Manson, a Jim Jones, a David Koresh—or merely a clever entertainer?

Yet in actuality I stand with Ram Dass, with whom I am uneasy, and with Matthiessen, with whom I am more comfortable: like it or not, I am a post-traditional person. I began picking and choosing from among the world's spiritual resources at a young age: from this book and that minister, from this revelatory experience and that moment of relationship. What authority, discipline, and structure I have has been largely of my own inven-tion or choosing. I first learned to meditate through the fortunate but "acci-dental" presence of Buddhist monks who happened to be in exile at a center associated with the college I attended. Nor do I claim any special excellence in my picking and choosing; it has been mostly by the "muddle method" and through the raw urge to spiritual survival in the wasteland of post-tradi-tional secular society.

Like so many people in the world today, my tradition was exchanged for automobiles, modern homes and medical advances, without our gener-ally well-intentioned ancestors really being aware of what lay in the bargain. Now all of us have a longing for tradition, but find none that is really ours. I am a post-traditional person and an American, one of many who inherits not a single tradition but a sort of thin twentieth-century tradition of many traditions.

When I read a piece in *The New York Times Magazine* about the Catholic theologian David Tracy,[10] what I am trying to say becomes all the more clear to me. Like Cobb and Kapleau, both of whom I admire greatly, Tracy is wrestling with a tradition. But I am different from these people in that I have no such solid ground from which to begin. Paul Tillich said that the "protestant principle" requires a "catholic substance."[11] I see that the Protestantism that is part of my own inheritance has run out of things to protest against, or perhaps it has run too far from a substance against which to define itself, and for this reason it has lost its zest. I find it somewhat peculiar, given the fact that I have been more "radical" or "liberal" than most Protestant denominations, to see my own suggestion that Protestantism has lost touch with its tradition, and the implication that it is in need of the very work of reappropriation, now in a world context, that I have discussed earlier in relation to individuals. In any event, it seems no coincidence that most of the vital work today in Western theology—and in practice—is occurring within Catholicism.

These last thoughts bring me back again to the question: Where do I stand? I stand in the company of post-traditional people like Ram Dass and Matthiessen. I cannot, despite intense desire to do so, accept the roshi's invitation to come and practice Zen; at least not now. I cannot, like Peter Matthiessen, become a humble student of another tradition, but must continue in and clarify my own orientation and learn how to be more fully faithful to it. To travel elsewhere now would be escapist.

IV

As I ask myself the hard question as to the content of my post-traditional orientation, one at odds with both Ram Dass's eclecticism and Matthiessen's willingness to join another tradition, three elements become visible. The first is the twentieth-century tradition in the West of many traditions or a tradition beyond traditions (perhaps analogous to the Kyoto school in Japan). In this century there is a rich body of literature and wisdom from Western people who have struggled as I struggle in post-traditional cultural confusion.[12] Karl Jaspers, for example, speaks of movement through a zone of disorientation and into the development of a new kind of humanity, a "new nobility" and genuine world citizenship.[13] I now see that much of my post-secondary education has been focused on this post-traditional drama, and on the emergence out of it of a world ethic and spirituality—something very closely related to a postmodern, "holistic" worldview that is discussed by the Center for Process Studies and other groups. This realization also helps me to understand my enduring love for and fascination with America, from its beginning an "experiment" organized around the notion of a "republic of mankind."

The dim but persuasive perception that there is available to us a post-traditional way of both personhood and culture is crucial. Within this perception Ram Dass's seeming eclecticism is not the only option, nor is converting to another tradition. However, this new way is hard to see, barely articulated, not much institutionalized; and most important, it requires a great deal from us, since it entails precisely the "spiritual exertion" to which Toynbee refers. I come to see that making this option of a healthy post-traditional spirituality more fully and more widely accessible is in fact at the very center of my vocation.

A second element in my orientation, one which is closely related to the first, is the pick-and-choose, muddle method I have perforce followed in my own life. Circumstances have made it necessary to develop a discipline of invention and choice. And this development has been "from below," from the ground up, within myself and within the intimacy of friendship, for culture "from above" has proved either incoherent or absent or unreliable in our time. In this generation all of us have needed to be our own masters and to find masters within the web of our relationships, groping together toward the achievement of ourselves, struggling from beyond the definition of adulthood that we received from the culture. Through trial and error and by the grace of friendship we have been taught what works and what doesn't, what sources are sustaining and what are only superficially exciting, what choices lead to human thriving and what lead off in curious or dangerous directions. Through friendship we have been taught how to position ourselves so as to be ready for the serendipitous. Functioning something like the early Christian congregations, the small face-to-face groups in which we have "grown up" have supported us to pursue a barely articulate vision of "humankind come of age." We have done this in the midst of social and cultural decadence and keen awareness of the various threats to the future of human life. Our congregation has not been any "special" sort of community, but the world itself, a community of human beings engaged in something like what Dietrich Bonhoeffer called "religionless Christianity."[14]

A third and final element of my spiritual orientation is liberal education. Viewed from the perspective of this inquiry, it is amazing how little my own schooling attended to practice (*praxis*), at least in the explicit way I mean it. The educational premium was almost exclusively on the mastery of content, and I suppose one could argue that it was assumed that matters of application and implication for action, vocation, and the living of a life were best left to the conscience of the individual student, even if that student was preparing to become a teacher. But I do not think this assumption holds; and neither did the so-called campus rebels of the sixties whose rebellion centered on this very point of educational practice and participation, or the advocates of "alternative education" in the early seventies (like the advocates of "progressive education" in the thirties) who in their best moments insisted on reform in the direction of an integration of theory and practice.

As a member to some degree of both of these groups, and as one who is now teaching within a "traditional" structure, I continue to have faith in the transformative power of liberal education as a practice. Out of direct experience with my students and colleagues I have evidence of the capacity of the Socratic method of dialectical inquiry to enable us to turn around from the shadows of illusion, to move out of the Platonic "cave of ignorance" and into the light of being fully human. My experience has been that this essential turning around through liberal education, from illusion to reality, can happen within a fairly wide range of institutional and pedagogical options; so what is fundamental to the practice of liberal education is somewhat elusive. David Bromwich has made this point in an illuminating way:

> Another name for the subject of debate about the humanities today is "liberal education." The phrase is still in common use because it has a sound that is flattering to Americans. But, in practice, the thing has never been as common as the phrase. The process it names cannot, in fact, be formulated as an official policy or embodied in a state curriculum, for it describes a tacit way of thinking and acting in a moral community. A liberal education tries to assure the persistence of a culture of responsive individuals—people who, in the course of the long experiment in learning, will have discovered the habits of attention that will make it possible to be at once thoughtful and critical citizens.[15]

Is this "attention" the same as "real experience"?

In relation to basic Western educational *experience* from secondary school through the university, in relation to the occasions and conditions of thought and action that lead to and sustain this experience of attention or attentiveness, most arguments about curriculum and discussions of the philosophy of education and "science of learning" are pale at best, frustrating distractions at worst. Though these discussions and the endless commission reports they generate sometimes contain statements to the effect that finally everything depends on the practice of the teacher and the immediate conduct of the classroom, they mostly slide off this point into statements that are either merely theoretical or concern themselves with shallow technique. Liberal education, not just as information but as transformation, is missed in either case. What is missing is the sense in which, as Whitehead says, "the essence of education is that it be religious."[16]

But what is that elusive center of practice in liberal education, this attentiveness, and in what sense is it religious? Bromwich, again, this time through his citation of Michael Oakeshott, helps me see:

> Perhaps we may think [of the components of a culture] as voices, each the expression of a distinct and conditional understanding of the world and a distinct idiom of human self-understanding, and of the culture itself as these voices joined, as such voices could only be joined, in a conversation—an endless unrehearsed intellectual adventure in which, in imagination, we enter into a variety of modes of understanding the world and ourselves and are not disconcerted by the differences or dismayed by the inconclusiveness of it all. And perhaps we may recognize liberal learning as, above all else, an education in imagination, an initiation into the art of this conversation in which we learn to recognize the voices.[17]

Conversation *is* the practice: something I was practicing with Kapleau, even while thinking of myself as traditionless! I would only add to what Oakeshott says that conversation is that mode of human interaction in which truth in the Greek sense of *a-letheia* occurs, truth as dis-closure, the un-veiling of reality—and of truth as real or authentic experience. It is in this sense that the practice of dialectical inquiry that is liberal education becomes religious: through the conversation, through participation in the "moral community" that cultivates "habits of attention," we come to touch both reality itself and our deepest self, and the point of contact between the two. "Attentiveness" indicates the moment in which this occurs.

These considerations of educational experience and the dialogue with Bromwich lead me to a change of mind about my own education, and to modify my view of myself as a person without tradition. My education *did* involve practice; but, perhaps like any other person practicing a traditional discipline in the midst of post-traditional confusion, I have not until now fully identified, understood, or valued my own practice. I now see that this discovery of my own tradition and practice solves the koan or riddle about tradition that was posed by Kapleau and Ram Dass. For in genuine conversation authority is neither exclusively external, as some suppose "traditional" authority to be, nor exclusively internal, as some suppose the "new" or post-traditional authority to be. Rather, it consists essentially in the linkage and simultaneity between the external and the internal; it consists of a joining of the two in which both aspects are not only preserved but enhanced. This union is what appears from our post-traditional standpoint as the secret of authentic authority and the genius of real conversation.

But the fullness of conversation or liberal education is very hard to see and sustain if one is wearing the lenses of the modern Western mind-set, the mind-set of Cartesian dualism and mechanism, with its virtually hydraulic model of relation, its simple push-pull vision. This mind-set can grasp the claims and need for external authority; it can grasp what has come to be called "traditional" education in the ongoing debate of my profession, the approach that emphasizes teacher as deliverer of subject matter in which the student is a passive receiver of inert information. The modern mind-set can also grasp the opposite or antithesis of the "traditional"; it can formulate an approach that presumes the internal authority of the student, the approach that is variously called progressive, student-centered, innovative, or sometimes alternative education. But to conceive transcendence of this dichotomy (one that seems to constitute most of the educational and cultural history of this century), to create an approach that unifies elements of each in a mode of relation that lies beyond their opposition, is impossible in the frame of the modern laissez-faire mentality. The fruits of liberal education as the practice of disciplined conversation, and conversation as a mode of transformation, may be experienced from time to time in the classroom because of fortunate combinations of teachers, students, and texts. However, without adequate ways of speaking about this mode, and hence without ways of discipline and institutionalization, the fullness of authentic conversation remains a memorable exception to business as usual. Herein lies the problem with my tradition in the post-traditional wilderness.

Returning to the general themes with which this chapter began, we can conclude that practice or healthy spiritual exertion has to do with identifying and nurturing our real experience. And it appears that tradition is necessary in order for genuine practice to function. So the synthesis or post-traditional wisdom we seek certainly does not exclude tradition. Whether we can choose our tradition, or finally must submit to the discovery that it has chosen us, whether we find it surprisingly near or amazingly far—these all remain as questions. One thing, though, seems clear: we need tradition in order to become fully attentive in the present.

SEVEN

L.A.:
Searching for Post-traditional Wisdom

GENUINE INQUIRY IS a conversational back and forth, not simply isolated construction of theory. And this requires digestion, integration with practice and consequences for being, not just for thought. Real inquiry is necessarily "personal"—a term, like "the ordinary," that is much in question today.

As my family and I flew into Los Angeles one dazzling winter day, a remark of Masao Abe's came to mind: "The true investigation of the self is always the investigation of the world and of history."[1] He would agree that, within the context of healthy practice, the reverse must be true as well.

Our ostensible reason for going to L.A. was a reunion of my wife's extended family, but we had other plans as well. Since we have long been interested in whales and dolphins and the general idea that it may be we humans who are the "missing link" in evolution, we wanted to take a whale-watching voyage. And we all wanted to see Hollywood, and the beaches—we'd heard Laguna Beach was ideal. I also looked forward to a conversation with John Cobb.

As the plane left our city and began its climb over the eastern shores of Lake Michigan, I had a strong but nonspecific sense about the importance of seeing Cobb: perhaps he is the same as Kapleau, I thought, namely traditional, except that he stands in my own tradition. Even with no family trip, I probably would have gone to see him. And L.A. itself is a major context for the actual meeting and living together of East and West. L.A. can be seen as the very belly of the post-traditional beast; I have heard some of its more chauvinistic citizens even claim that they are now living in the twenty-first century! It seems essential that an inquiry in search of post-traditional wisdom involve the field exploration of direct encounter. How strange, I mused, that Cobb lives in this place.

The matter of field exploration puts me back in dialogue with Peter

Matthiessen. His *The Snow Leopard* is a major contribution to East-West dialogue, and not just ideationally, but also on the experiental grounds we seek. In the course of his narrative, Matthiessen searches Tibet for the Lama of the Crystal Monastery; the journey is exotic, and Matthiessen's expectations are high.[2] When he finally finds the lama it turns out that this ideal figure is painfully crippled but remarkably happy: "Of course I am happy here! It's wonderful. *Especially* when I have no choice!" Matthiessen takes this as a statement of the heart of Zen, of the fullness of Zen as appreciation of the ordinary, as "the wholehearted acceptance of *what is.*"[3] This realization breaks a spell that Matthiessen had been under, a spell of the extraordinary and the exotic, and it enables him to resolve the koan which had been given to him by his own roshi before departing New York: "Expect nothing."

I did not fully understand my expectations on going to L.A.—the very reverse of Tibet in so many ways; but like Matthiessen, I felt compelled by my inquiry to make the journey. I suppose that my koan is: What, where, is post-traditional wisdom? It occurred to me that Peter Matthiessen's experience might suggest how or where this wisdom could be found: in the ordinary. But where is the ordinary in L.A.?

Looking up from the earth in our era, one observes that jet planes leave tracks in the sky. Sitting in the plane one notices that we leave tracks on the earth as well. From up here we see vapor cloud shadows cutting across lines made by farmers, builders of roads, and Mother Nature: shadows of a newer grid of connectedness which overlies an earth above which distant air travel has become quite ordinary.

Flying low over a mountain resort we approached the Ontario airport and entered Southern California, "Socal." Warm, sunny days, cool nights; we transplants from Michigan in January were receptive to its climate. We toured Universal Studios, on that fanciful hillside where the "reality" of TV and movies is invented. Then we conducted our own improvisational tour of Beverly Hills and Hollywood: Ferraris became commonplace, and the opulence was astounding, while a seamy underside began to be visible by the time we reached the intersection of Hollywood and Vine.

The subject of earthquakes, and the possibility of "the big one," entered our conversations with the residents of Socal. As with the threat of nuclear war, the big one is somehow walled off from daily functioning. But the presence of strangers seemed to evoke talk of it; it is part of the mythology of the region, a strange secular apocalypticism (or perhaps some manifestation of ancient—or new—Earth-worshiping religion). Falling asleep one night I had a half-dream vision of Socal as a thin and improbable zone of life existing by a mysterious grace, between geological dangers from below and nuclear dangers from above.

We had lunch with the other tourists on the *Queen Mary* in Long Beach, and shared an agreement that after seeing Hollywood, the world's largest airplane, Howard Hughes's *Spruce Goose*, was not terribly impressive. Setting out down the Coast Highway, what was impressive was Laguna Beach. Paradise. And it continued, on down the coast to La Jolla and San Diego, where the whales were just beginning to run off Loma Point. No wonder these places are becoming overcrowded.

Also within easy reach from our hub in Claremont were the mountains, the low desert, the high desert, Palm Springs and the Joshua Tree National Monument. What could it mean that we traveled to all these places, that this huge bundle of striking impression passed through our senses and entered our beings? How strange this enormous gulp of experience is, when considered from the perspective of human history. Sitting in my Michigan study later, in the midst of a new workweek, it all seemed more remote than a dream. We were there. Where? And ordinary?

On the plane coming home I looked out the window and back. We were well into the Great Plains. Back behind us stood the Rockies in the distance at the western edge of a vast flatness, rising from north to south as far as you could see. Beyond those mountains were deserts and more mountains, then the coast and the Pacific abyss; standing on its rim just the week before, I'd heard a fellow talking about joining an upcoming sailboat race to Hawaii and back; it sounded so easy, so ordinary for him.

But what about the meeting of East and West? We saw many Asians in L.A., many of whom were tourists like ourselves. At one stop on the Universal Studio tour I became acutely aware that America was being presented to foreigners by Hollywood—and *as* Hollywood; and I became annoyed with the show-biz orientation and the seriousness with which it was being taken by such sophisticated-looking Japanese people. I searched their faces for humor or wryness, perhaps a trace of cynicism or judgment, but found none. Certainly here in the entertainments of consumer society, where "experience" itself is part of the stuff of consumption, is a mainstream form of the meeting of East and West. In one sense I see that L.A. is all entertainment, pastime, titillation, synthetic experience. And yet, though as an American I resist, I must admit that L.A. is indeed a high temple of American culture, even the hometown of one recent president.

In like fashion we also see in the melting pot of L.A. a meeting of left- and right-brain orientation, masculine and feminine, and elements of the prehistoric and the historical periods; but these are as mixed and ambiguous here as the meeting of East and West. Celebration of "body" is evident everywhere, but in L.A. we see merely the reverse of the spirit/body split of the traditional period: instead of a spirit above and prior to body, in L.A. we see the sensationalism of body without spirit. No synthesis, but merely the reverse of what had prevailed before.

More numerous than the Asians in Socal were the settlers from the south, the Spanish-speaking people. I heard someone comment recently that the relevant distinction in the world is no longer East/West, but now North/South—the developed, industrial Northern Hemisphere versus the undeveloped and developing third-world Southern Hemisphere. Several white and black citizens of L.A. observed to me with a certain foreboding that their Spanish-speaking compatriots will take over the whole Socal region in the not-too-distant future.

America has become what some of her founders had envisioned, a "republic of mankind," though not at all on the terms they had in mind. They could not have imagined L.A. What did they imagine as the future of their experiment? And L.A. seems to embody the worst and the best of what America has become, all mixed together. On one side, America's modern project of liberating the masses and trusting individual initiative has led to another decadent empire, maybe the last of the traditional period, straddling precariously the gap between the traditional period and what lies beyond. Perhaps it will crack along the San Andreas Fault, break off and fall into the sea, not because of any earthquake from below or blast from above, but because of the weight of an unrestrained consumerism which seduces all peoples on the earth to come and be entertained.

But right alongside this horrific possibility stands the magnificent diversity of L.A., its unity in diversity; it reminds us of America as the best model of world community we as a world have, in its capacity to hold such a broad diversity within a unity, however shallow it may appear. It must be the grace of this mysterious unity, one that is surely deeper and other than mere entertainment, that holds together this westernmost coast. How different the world would be if America could see and be responsive to what L.A. is in this positive sense—a republic of humankind, a unity that celebrates diversity and a diversity that builds unity. But as though behind movie-set facades, the best is so well hidden: What, I wonder, is the opposite of a riot? My intuition is that there is present in L.A. a form of unity which is deep and positive, if only it could be called forth.

Here, it seems to me, is an essential feature of post-traditional wisdom: the ability to envision and participate in the kind of relationship in which unity and diversity are not opposed but complementary. It is in this sense that America is great, despite conspicuous failures, and will continue to be great—if we can avoid the temptation to give up such a vision of worldwide republic altogether in favor of entertainments.

In the midst of our vigorous tourism and family visiting, I spent one afternoon with John Cobb.[4] I sought his advice on the East-West project, needing someone with whom I could discuss as freshly as possible the broad contours and most basic questions of my inquiry. I needed encounter with someone with whom I share the bond of tradition, and hence that communication which lies beyond the idiosyncrasies of personality and life circumstance.

He listened fully as I described the project and its progress to date. His first remark was to the effect that given what I say concerning this project and in my other work, I am certainly not post-traditional, at least not in the sense that Cobb associates with the term. "Post-traditional," in his understanding, connotes those feminists, minorities, and other interpreters of civilization who see the whole of the traditional period as ill-founded, misguided or otherwise in need of rejection, as fundamentally sexist, racist, or founded on values that lead to technological determinism and ecological suicide.

I discover that "post-traditional" means something different for me and for Cobb. To me it signifies a time in the twentieth century when humans have ceased to live within one enclosed tradition, when the meeting of traditions is inevitable and somehow positive, despite appearance to the contrary; and a time when the essential human drama involves moving beyond the morass of modernism and relativism (and beyond the concomitant threats of either reactionary or fascist "solutions" to the tensions of this period) into a worldview that is adequate both to our separate pasts and to our common present and future.

John is right: Although I have very serious problems with the Western tradition since Aristotle, and even more so since Descartes, still it contains something to which I appeal. For me, the "post-traditional" must not exclude tradition, must not include committing the arrogance of thinking we can be done with it or the insensitivity of thinking it all negative. I return again and again to Socratic encounter and the Greek *polis*, to the Hebrew notion of right relationship and the Christian vision of compassionate presence for others, to a unity in diversity that is vital, even redemptive. And my intuition is that both the revitalization of tradition and the post-traditional wisdom we Westerners are seeking is to be found not in a better doctrine or way of thinking, but rather in a way of being and doing that is somehow associated with the body of tradition. Perhaps our post-traditional dislocation and homelessness puts us in a position to apprehend the significance and presence of such figures as Socrates and Jesus in a way that has not occurred for a very long time.

Cobb and I moved on to discuss the question of genre, the struggle with the relation between forms of writing and consequences for practice. I cited Madeleine L'Engle's *A Circle of Quiet*[5] and Martin Buber's *I and Thou*[6] as works that speak not only to the intellect or the reader's code of belief, but also to the whole person in his or her real life process, in genuine experience and practice, in the radiant ordinary. John was responsive to the works I mentioned, but pointed to some writers and artists who have rejected the discursive mode and become unintelligible as a result—unintelligible to him at least, he said modestly. We agreed that the effort to transcend or go beyond the limitations of the strictly discursive orientation is important but very tricky.

After the conversation we stood for a time on his front porch and that topic unique to L.A., the earthquake, came up. John told me a story of waking in the night to a moving bed and his wife's asking with urgency, "What's that?" John, brought up in Japan, had replied: "Oh, don't worry, its only an earthquake." Walking to my car, I smiled to myself when I saw the parallel between John's story and the lama's words to Matthiessen.

Driving away, while being aware of the hugeness and wildness of the mountains to the east, I had a strong experience of "perspectiveless perspective," an experience of seeing the world with Zen: Realization consists in "clarifying consciousness," becoming "clear glass." This mode of being develops through the sunyata experience of Absolute Nothingness or "absolute subjectivity," with the awareness that this "perspectiveless" consciousness is more near to genuine self than is ego-consciousness. And yet perspectiveless perspective cannot be grasped or achieved, or sustained; even the "enlightenment" of this awareness must be renounced. Only after this seemingly impossible radicalization of Nothingness, giving up even my experience of Nothingness, does it become possible to enter the lucidity of "accepting what is," "expecting nothing," and living in the radiant ordinary. In regard to this way of being, it is of consequence that Matthiessen's lama was crippled: the realization to which Zen points happens in no particular part of the self, but as a "360-degree movement of return" of the whole being, to full in-carnation, em-bodiment—limitations included, affirmed; not "in spite of," but wholly affirmed. "The mystical" is fulfilled and rendered invisible in the movement of return. The "non-religion" of Zen does not reject the earth, as do most traditional religions and cultures, though it recognizes the particular mysticism of "then there was no mountain" as a phase along the way. In its fullness, Zen is earth- and life-affirming, non-dualizing, non-dichotomizing. As such it is offered by the Kyoto school as a model for the future.

I realized later that there was an irony in my having this experience after the conversation with Cobb, someone who apparently does not share this way of seeing. After all, it was Cobb, back in Indiana at the Buddhist-Christian encounter, who told Masao Abe that he could find no such perspective-less perspective, and that insofar as he could it was associated in his mind with dangerous people and movements.

Cobb emphasizes locatedness. Yet in the experience I was having at that very moment, driving away from my conversation with him, perspective-lessness and location were not opposed. Perspectivelessness was at the same time locatedness, the fullness of the ordinary—right there in L.A.! Stated another way, it was an experience of "real experience" as simultaneaous with perception of the miraculous quality of the world as it actually is. Out of the practice of genuine conversation I experienced a profoundly refreshing openness: it was as though the encounter had somehow cleared away what is inessential or merely egotistical in my experience, opening a channel to genuine self; as though the conversation had put me in touch with the source of my real embodiment which was no distance whatsoever from where I was in immediate, "ordinary" experience.

Could it be that underneath the differences between Abe and Cobb, Zen and the West, perspectivelessness and perspective, there is a deeper point of commonality?

The koan I took to L.A. was: What and where is post-traditional wisdom? Does the experience and intuition of a deep commonality, something even deeper than tradition, suggest an answer? If so, how are we to name and to know this sense of deep commonness? I propose that we name it "return"—return from expectation, dualism, egocentrism, displacement, entertainment—where the mark of true return is that elusive and yet utterly self-evident quality of full human presence.

PART TWO

REDISCOVERING THE WEST

Truly, my life is one long hearkening unto my self and unto others, unto God. And if I say that I hearken, it is really God who hearkens inside me. The most essential and deepest in me hearkening unto the most essential and deepest in the other. God to God.

Etty Hillesum

Who is God? Not in the first place an abstract belief in God, in his omnipotence, etc. That is not a genuine experience of God, but a partial extension of the world. Encounter with Jesus Christ. The experience that a transformation of all human life is given in the fact that 'Jesus is there only for others.' His 'being there for others' is the experience of transcendence. It is only this 'being there for others,' maintained till death, that is the ground of his omnipotence, omniscience, and omnipresence. Faith is participation in this being of Jesus (incarnation, cross, and resurrection). Our relationship to God is not a 'religious' relationship to the highest, most powerful, and best Being imaginable—that is not authentic transcendence—but our relation to God is a new life in 'existence for others,' through participation in the being of Jesus. The transcendental is not infinite and unattainable tasks, but the neighbor who is within reach in any given situation.

Dietrich Bonhoeffer

I am subject to a divine or supernatural experience. . . . It began in my childhood—a sort of voice which comes to me. . . . In the past the prophetic voice to which I have become accustomed has always been my constant companion, opposing me in even trivial things if I was going to take the wrong course.

Socrates

EIGHT

Standing Our Ground

I

WE ARRIVE AT a point of transition in the inquiry. We have moved from focus on the Japanese claim about the character of the present world situation and perspectiveless perspective to the more general search for post-traditional wisdom. And we have pursued the idea that the wisdom we seek is to be found in integration, in the inclusion of that dimension of humanity which had been "other" in the traditional period. Further, we have gathered some strong clues from Zen and other sources as to what it is that needs to be brought in and integrated.

But now the question arises: integrated into what? What exactly is that Western orientation into which "the other" might be included? One of the peculiarities of our era is that people are sometimes more aware of what needs to be included than they are of what it is that it needs to be integrated into. To pursue this question, I start from two statements from others who have traveled down and provided some maps for the very same road we are traveling. These statements are reflective of this stage of our inquiry and of the larger process of spiritual development that it represents. The first is from Winston King, translator of Nishitani's *Religion and Nothingness*. He states the essential problematic of Nishitani's work as follows: "The West has nowhere to go but in the direction of the Eastern (Buddhist) ideal, but it cannot do so except from its own Western (Christian) premises."[1] The second is from Paul Tillich:

> The way is to penetrate into the depth of one's own religion, in devotion, thought and action. In the depth of every living religion there is a point where the religion itself loses its importance, and that to which it points breaks through its particularity, elevating it to spiritual freedom and with it to a vision of the spiritual presence in other expressions of the ultimate meaning of man's existence.[2]

In order to move ahead, we need to locate the Western premises, the depth of them, and we need to move in the direction of penetration and breakthrough. This is necessary to achieve the integration we seek, instead of a mere mixture of fragments from various traditions, floating in the thin air of our era. We need grounding.

Identifying the direction of inquiry enables us to bring into perspective one of the limitations of what was achieved in Part I of the inquiry. Part I established an orientation to the world situation and the goal of integration, and even provided some sense of what needs to be integrated and of what would constitute post-traditional wisdom. But these discursive considerations remain at some distance from deep experience and from the concrete actuality of practice. Even though we have developed some sense of the importance of experience and practice, and of conversation in the tradition of liberal education as the practice of this inquiry, our considerations of these so far are limited. Their theoretical or ideational vividness could be deceptive, perhaps especially to Westerners, who seem to be satisfied too quickly with merely ideational resolution: in the deception of false closure and false experience, the dimension of depth, of actually living what has been discovered rather than only thinking (or feeling) its impact, is missing (even as "the other" appears to be included).

This deceptiveness of superficial or false experience is perhaps most dramatically evident today in the effects of contemporary media, especially commercial TV, effects that are probably not characteristic of Western people in particular but are inherent in the media themselves. The contents of electronic media are very close in one sense, as the whole world appears quite vividly right in our homes. But at the same time those contents are rendered very distant in another sense, as we become desensitized to the realities behind the very "realistic" photographic images of events that are constantly paraded before us. This phenomenon of skewed closeness and distance is related to the "entertainment" orientation I encountered in L.A., and to the incessant bombardment of images as a general quality of our time. We are tempted constantly to settle for dramatic or inflamed surface rather than penetrating to the depth of anything.

There is a limit to the usefulness of the ideational and the imagal, even a point of diminishing returns and deception. Having reached a limit in our hearing of the Kyoto school's claims and surveying our new global circumstances, then, we must now alter our stance and direction. I propose that we heed the advice of Nishitani and Tillich and turn to the West. Against the temptation of premature closure at the level of the superficial, whether it be in idea or image, thought or feeling, we need to locate and consider the deep substance of the Western tradition, with particular attention to the meaning therein of practice.

But I am in no way proposing that in this undertaking we can or should retreat from and close the door on East-West dialogue and the world situation. Many in our culture, especially the neoconservatives and fundamentalists, respond to the imperative of our moment to recognize and reclaim the greatness of the Western tradition by doing just this. This move seems to me as false as the superficial integrations that the neoconservatives and fundamentalists frequently criticize; it is a denial of our actual situation and the pretense of an isolation and simplicity that is no longer possible. What I am proposing is something that is necessarily more demanding and ambitious: that we stay on the actual ground of the post-traditional situation and turn our focus. This means that we must remain in the encounter with the East and attend to integration at the same time that we inquire as to the vitality of the West. The transition is a subtle one, and one that is necessarily more delicate than simply leaping out of the encounter and the actual situation into exclusive concern with the West. Still, our focus in this next stage of inquiry must be directed to the West, in the hope that this can lead us to an integration that is deep and practical.

II

How, then, are we to proceed in our search for the West? How is it possible to remain in the East-West encounter, on the ground of our actual situation, and, at the same time and as part of the same act, also search for the depth of Western premises?

John Cobb, I think, helps us gain our footing and begin to move in such an inquiry. He does this through his method of "dialogue" that leads "beyond dialogue" to "mutual transformation." Let us look at what he means by this, how his approach and "position" enables us to achieve a deeper understanding of the ground upon which we stand, and also enables us to rediscover the West as our true ground, rather than as the groundlessness of the mere mixing of fragments.

Cobb speaks from a standpoint that is both post-traditional and Christian, though what he says applies as well to Westerners whose orientation is Jewish or Hellenic rather than specifically Christian. In his book *Beyond Dialogue: Toward a Mutual Transformation of Christianity and Buddhism*, he begins by saying that "an inescapable feature of Christian self-understanding is the recognition that we share the world with people of other religious traditions."[3] This was true during the first centuries of the Christian movement, when it shared the world of Hellenism and drew heavily on Neoplatonism for its articulation and self-understanding. It becomes true again in our own century because of the emergence of global civilization and the resultant necessities of living together and "cultivating a global memory"[4]—Cobb's term for integration. Between the early times of the formation of what has become the Western tradition and our time today, the

Christian response to other traditions has been primarily one of assuming its own superiority and seeking to convert, either by persuasion or by more forceful methods. Recognition of this fact now constitutes a source of guilt that colors relations with other traditions in the present.

In our century "dialogue" has emerged as the principle by which Christians relate to and share the world with the other traditions in a way that is different from the traditional way of simple judgment. But Cobb points out that there is a great deal of confusion as to what "dialogue" means, beyond the understanding that it lies somewhere between imperialism, maintaining a covert sense of superiority, and relativity, seeing Jesus as merely one savior among many. After reviewing the history of understandings of dialogue, which range from imperialistic to relativistic, Cobb seeks to offer a more adequate way of conducting and thinking about the exchange between Christianity and other traditions.

Cobb's thesis is that "the goal is to go beyond dialogue," that "authentic dialogue will necessarily carry us beyond itself."[5] What he means by this unfolds from his understanding of authentic dialogue. It must begin with and have as its first element some fairly clear reason as to how the encounter with another tradition could contribute to the "purgation and transformation" of Christianity. This reason will vary with each encounter: with Jews, Christians must come to terms with their own anti-Judaism; with Buddhists the catalyst must be Christianity's lack of "a depth of insight into the nature of reality."[6] Despite different reasons for each encounter, all encounters have as a common reason the need to incorporate into the effective historical memory of Christianity the history of the other tradition, contributing to the genuine universality of Christianity and the cultivation of "global memory."

The second element of dialogue, for Cobb, is offering to the other tradition "what we believe to be true and valuable in our own tradition": "Dialogue has a missional goal. That Christians hope to make a difference in others through dialogue should not be concealed."[7] Cobb emphasizes that this influence on the other tradition is addressed to religious communities, not to the conversion of their individual members. With this second element Cobb stresses that the purpose of dialogue cannot be only to edify and improve Christianity, but to offer something to the other tradition as well. We must enter dialogue with some sense of what is persuasive and beautiful in our own tradition, with some sense of its dignity, with the awareness of that within our tradition we do not wish to deconstruct.

If dialogue that includes these two elements is successful, it will necessarily move "beyond dialogue," to the "mutual transformation" of both parties. This will lead to a "transformation of respective historical memories,"[8] as each tradition includes the memory of the other and thus becomes more fully universal. The result will be a dissolving of the present sharp lines of distinction between traditions, but not an obliteration of the difference between them; there will emerge "a very different Christianity from any we now know."[9]

Cobb goes on in the rest of his book to clarify and give content to the movement beyond dialogue which he says is already occurring between Christianity and Buddhism. He is speaking about the specifically Christian response to the same circumstance of mingling traditions I have described in Part I under "Worldview as the Problem." Given this, let us return to the post-traditional situation to see how Cobb's approach helps us to continue and extend themes already active in the inquiry, specifically in the direction of identifying Western presence in our new world situation. Perhaps the specifics of his suggestions about "a very different Christianity" will become pertinent later; for now, what is helpful is his demarcation of the ground on which we can proceed.

III

Once, people were born, lived, and died within a single culture. Cultural otherness was not recognized as a problem. For more than two thousand years the world had been organized around corporate senses of identity that were exclusive, that assumed that "our" group stood at the center of history or the cosmos, and that all other groups therefore were either uncivilized, striving to become what we were, or enemies. Given the prevailing reality of geographical isolation, this cognitive arrangement more or less worked in its time; its credibility depended on the success or isolation of each cultural group. Geographical isolation made it possible for a culture to interact with others by judging, colonializing, making war, or simply moving on—denying otherness in any case. But this will not do any longer. The geographical isolation has ended and the frontier is closed. There is no place left to go on this earth; oceans no longer provide insulation as they once did, and the instruments of aggression have become too lethal. Those who once were strangers have become the people we live with, and the earth can no longer be regarded as a field on which we project our images of superiority, a place where the earth itself becomes "other." Because of the end of geographic isolation, we must now confront otherness as real *within* our worldview, not as something that can be denied or held off at the boundaries by labels or warfare.

This closing of historic options is profoundly shocking. It provokes what can be seen as the most general cultural problem of our post-traditional era, the problem of otherness. This is a problem that appears within ourselves as well as "out there" in our world; it seems no coincidence that we have become aware of "the unconscious" as other within ourselves at just about the same time that we become aware of the cultural other. What must it mean if we take other cultures seriously, recognize their integrity, their capacity fully to house a human life? Does that mean they are better than ours, or as valid as ours? Does it mean that all cultures are equal, striving for the same goals of human actualization—truth, beauty, justice, goodness? If so, then what is the perspective from which this observation is made, and what does it imply about our ability to be engaged in any particular culture and process of transformation? And what about the cultures that are obviously demented, the "culture" of the Third Reich or other regimes that deny human rights?

The overriding theme is a "Catch-22" or what Gregory Bateson calls "double bind," a basic condition of our time: there are two choices; neither of them works; and we must choose one. One choice is that culture is absolute: there is one right way, other ways that are less right, and many that are wrong. The other choice is relativism: each is as good as the other, none is better, and "best" is a judgment that depends entirely on one's perspective. The absolutists assert, and are insensitive or even vicious. The relativists wallow dangerously; some of them cannot stand the ambiguity after a time and more or less arbitrarily convert to some form of absolutism. Absolutism/relativism, objective/subjective, unity/diversity: there are many forms in which the either/or quality of our time is manifest.

There are several Western responses to the basic Catch-22. Most can be seen as patently unhealthy or undesirable when they are brought out and examined in the light of day. Perhaps the most widespread response is going limp or psychic numbing—what T. S. Eliot described as the world's ending with a whimper. With the numbing there is an inner death to the deeper questions and sensibilities in life, and a consequent shallowing of relationship, appreciation, and expectation. This mode of accommodation is frequently accompanied by a materialism that can gather all kinds of comfort and convenience around itself, masking its essential emptiness and the fact that superficial images of individual "survival" constitute its highest ideal. The numbing is also associated with a focus on individual selfhood, at the level of what the Kyoto school refers to as ego-self and what some Westerners have come to call "self-psychology." Many of our great social thinkers in recent decades have described the psychic numbing response: we see it in Robert Jay Lifton's "protean man,"[10] in William Whyte's "organization man" and David Riesman's "other-directed" personality type,[11] and in much of the recent writing and cinema on narcissism and the sociopathic individual.[12] These understandable accommodations to the overwhelming challenges of our era are extremely disturbing to traditional assumptions of personhood involving a core self, conscience, and personal integrity.

A second response to the dilemma of our era is reactionary: the cultural situation of either/or and the decadence of the response to it described above are both perceived as untenable. Escape is sought in the past. A previous cultural and religious situation is identified as ideal, and an effort is made to go back to it. The problem with this accommodation is that the previous ideal is not brought to the present; rather, the present is denied in the attempt to escape. In denial essential realities of the present are not dealt with, including possible solutions and vitalities that would enable us to move beyond impasse. The reactionary response, moreover, involves both personal and social constriction, and hence a loss of flexibility, of openness to the other, of the ability to be present. While the psychic numbing response is relativistic and fluid, the reactionary response entails an absolutism of retreat and rigidity. America has had considerable experience with both of these accommodations in recent times.

Another response, related to the reactionary, is that of cults and fascism. More radical than the reactionary response, the recoil against the confusion, shallowness, and decadence of the present can take the form of escape into *both* an idealized sense of the past *and* some equally idealized vision of the future. Here frustration with Catch-22 becomes so severe that escape is sought not only from the present, but from history altogether. The convert recoils into an ideology that fixes on elements of a prehistoric or mythic past, and mixes this prehistoric content with a fantasy of what is to come. This escape from and attempt to control history through access to supernatural forces that are thought to stand above history is encapsulated in the cult or in fascist ideology, in which the present is related to strictly in terms of what the ideology and its enforcement require. "Insensitivity" and "failure of openness" are terms too mild to describe the destruction of the present that occurs in this accommodation.[13] We have to hope that the exposés of the cults and the reminders from Elie Wiesel and others about Nazi Germany have served to warn us of this pathology.

One last response to our circumstance must be discussed before moving forward to what I see as a valid resolution to the Catch-22 riddle or koan of our period. This last response is the way of "many paths up the same mountain," a phrase which was coined by the Indian master Ramakrishna a century ago. In brief, this way observes that all cultures and religions are striving to union with one God, and that underneath their differences there is a shared understanding of the human condition and what is to be done about it. Aldous Huxley's *The Perennial Philosophy* and Joseph Campbell's *Myths to Live By* are two very persuasive presentations of this position, as are recent works by John Hick (*God Has Many Names*), Paul Knitter (*No Other Name?*), and Huston Smith (*Beyond the Post-Modern Mind*).[14]

The "many paths" response is satisfying in some ways. It neatly solves the riddle of otherness by affirming both unity and diversity, both the absolute quality of God and our relative efforts to achieve union, both objective and subjective realities. The key to this affirmation is the acknowledgment of the ineffability of God, that God always remains greater than religion. The top of the mountain is mysterious and not susceptible to complete formulation by any human symbol system, but we are assured that the variety of religions are pathways up the same mountain. The old story about the blind men and the elephant makes the same point: we all touch the elephant at different places; hence the unity behind the superficial disagreements in our theologies—you may be describing an ear while I describe a leg, but it is the same beast!

Yet there is one very serious problem with this orientation, a problem that is shared by syncretic approaches to religion and culture that seek "synthesis" as a hypostatized combination of ideas or images from various religions, rather than as a vital practice. The problem can be stated as an ironic question: If it is observed that all religions are seeking the transformation of humankind in the direction of union or right relationship with God, then where does the observer of this fact stand with respect to the immediate and practical matter of his or her own transformation? From the standpoint of most traditional religions the primary reason for their existence is not adequacy of doctrine or intellectual formulation, but the actual *practice* of the religion, the worship, the sitting, the yoga; the religions of the world agree on our need of transformation. Though the taking of the "many paths" approach can be extremely satisfying to intellect and feeling, it can also be a distraction from practice; it can even be regarded as a clever avoidance, or as the typically contemporary way of alienation from any actual process of transformation. If the point is development and transformation of our actual lives on earth, then observations from the moon or outer space may be attractive, even inspiring, but they also may lead us away from the very thing that we most need to do, which is right here in the particular. This is the ambiguity that arises from the transcultural awareness of our era and the marvelous availability of the world's cultural and historical riches: spread out before us are the inner secrets of the world religions, as symbolized by the photograph of Planet Earth from outer space, but the very capacities that give us access may also make it impossible for us to become engaged. The irony of availability, an irony that is perhaps most fully visible in the work and influence of Joseph Campbell, is that so much of the human past and present is available to us now, but it seems to make so little difference; what we see and know in breadth seems to compromise our touching in depth.[15] At best, the "many paths" approach is a stage along the way; at worst it is mere entertainment.

What, then, is the healthy Western response of our era? And how does it bear on John Cobb's movement beyond dialogue to mutual transformation?

It seems to me that in the genuinely creative, artistic, and philosophical work of our period another response to the basic cultural Catch-22 appears. It flickers in and out of the endless barrage of information and image with which we are assaulted. The healthy response is challenging and difficult for us because of its two basic conditions: first, it requires a certain growth or maturity from us to even *see* it (recalling, perhaps, the spiritual adage that the higher consciousness knows the lower, but the lower does not know the higher). Second, it requires that we come to understand the proper function of the intellect within a human life, and thus also something of what lies beyond the intellect, something of the fully human that we ask the intellect to serve.

IV

A great deal could be said about these two conditions and the senses in which they entail going beyond basic assumptions about the living of a human life that have dominated the modern West. This "going beyond" makes articulation difficult, even dangerous; both Nietzsche and William James were concerned with this "going beyond," and it is a fact that Hitler read Nietzsche, and Mussolini read William James. But for now it seems most appropriate to attempt a fairly simple description of the creative response to our time as I envision it, and to show how Cobb's work can be seen as an instance of this response. This creative response has four components, which need to be taken together as a complete set; each of the components taken by itself in isolation corresponds to one of the unhealthy responses I have identified above. The components can also be seen sequentially as a developmental process through which people move through and beyond the Catch-22 of our era.

Reappropriation of One's Tradition

Traditional religions were and are absolutistic. When it becomes necessary for them to take seriously the integrity of other cultures and religions, adherents to the traditional religions confront the specter of relativism and the Catch-22 situation. Relativism becomes a problem, as in the psychic numbing response; in the guise of the "many ways" responses, it can be considered as a phase.

We begin to move beyond the outer space of relativism when we are able to acknowledge and affirm our earthbound condition, and, as part of doing this, begin to reappropriate our traditional origins. This can occur when we realize that we are inherently and unavoidably people of some particular tradition, embodiments or fruits of a live thing that spans time and generations—in short, a tradition. No matter how distasteful we may find our past, we are driven to accept that it is inescapable. We do not live in thin air, but on the earth; we body forth some particular past, one that is inevitably problematic in some respects. Neglect of this fact, or the attempt to deny it, accounts for many of the characteristic problems in the twentieth century: unconscious repetition of past mistakes, naive attempts to "start over," and projects that seek to grasp history itself and remake it according to someone's plan in the present. Tradition, like a tendon, binds the flesh of the present to the bone of the past; without it we flap and flail, unable to find coordination or direction.

Cobb in effect specifies the two crucial marks of a healthy reappropriation of our tradition. They are simple: the task of appropriation and the movement beyond relativism is completed when we are able to identify (1) what is problematic or incomplete in our tradition, and also (2) what is magnificent, what we can advocate and offer to others. The reactionary movement of denial that seeks reappropriation of tradition clearly fails on the first point, rigidly or defensively refusing to acknowledge any sense of problem; and it seems equally clear that it is not possible in this posture to have the perspective necessary to speak with any persuasiveness, thus failing on Cobb's second point as well.

Affirmation of Ineffability

This component appears to be the opposite of the first, though it actually provides the broader context in which it is possible to live beyond the reactionary orientation that, like relativism, may be a stage. Having achieved conscious connection with one's own traditional past, it now becomes necessary to appropriate the core insight of the "many ways" approach, an insight that can lead to trouble if it is taken by itself, in isolation from the other components.

Affirmation of ineffability entails the realization that any symbol system is finite, that God and reality always transcend our capacity for articulation or worship. As some Buddhists say, the symbol must be understood as a finger pointing to the moon, not as the moon itself. This mistaking of the symbol for that to which it points is the classical Western definition of idolatry.

Paul Tillich says that the fullest language is that which is "transparent to the ultimate."[16] This is interesting because in these terms the better symbol would be a window, and the best would be nothing at all. But "nothing" in Western terms, exempting perhaps the mystical tradition, could not be something, would not be a symbol. Humankind is driven by experiences of the unspeakable, of that which lies beyond all categories and language. However, just because these experiences *are* so important, we must speak about them, or dance, or bow, or—somehow *respond*, if only to ourselves, in order to *remember*. But precisely at the moment we have remembered, much less spoken to others or created a church, we are in danger of idolatry and hence of the reactionary move.

Realization of this fact of human symbolizing as affirmation of ineffability leads us to a respect for and openness to others. At the very least it counsels a certain modesty about the authority of our own tradition, the kind of modesty that was exhibited, for example, by Billy Graham's rejection of "moral majority" chauvinism in the 1970s in his statement, "America is not God's only chosen land." Beyond this it implies that God, Reality, is present and at work in other traditions.

Attention to Development

If the second component leads to openness to others, the third establishes the full importance of this openness. As beings on earth we are incomplete, unfinished, and in process; and our traditions, when they are lively, are modes of transformation which may themselves be in transformation. Here is another helpful insight provided for us by the "many ways" view of traditions from the perspective of outer space: there is deep agreement among the various traditions that humans are in need of transformation, redemption. They agree that the fully formed human being does not simply unfold out of the natural process as do other forms of life, but that humans require intervention and work of some kind.

This recognition of *development* is perhaps especially difficult for Western Judeo-Christian thinking to grasp, with the "all or nothing" tendency that is present in much of our history: one is either saved or not, among the elect or not, within the covenant or not. In the either/or habit of thought and the focus on a partial truth, perhaps we have an accounting for the cult phenomenon and the fascist obsession with rushing through a painful developmental stage while claiming to know more about "historical necessity" than is the case. Perhaps the cults and fascism represent, among other things, the sudden rediscovery in Western culture of the significance of humanly directed development. In the cults and fascism this voluntary development of individuals and groups is confused with traditional understandings of development through the direction of a transcendant God. Although it is a much longer story, maybe it is sufficient to say here that there has been an uneasiness with the idea of development in the West, an uneasiness that has sometimes been expressed as attempts to "play God" in the determination of individual and group development. The struggle to overcome this uneasiness may account for the positive attraction that those Eastern religions explicitly concerned with development hold for Western people.

Capacity for Dialogue

Finally we come to the actualization of a human capacity for a certain kind of relationship as a way of development. The specific relational capacity I seek to articulate, as the fourth component of creative response in our era, one that includes and unifies the previous three, is that of our becoming able to be simultaneously *definite* about who we are and what we stand for, and *open* to the other. Or, in John Cobb's language, we come upon the dialogue that is "beyond dialogue," upon "mutual transformation": the kind of mutuality that is transformative and the way of transformation that requires mutuality.

It is here, in the domain of the relational, that the limitations of our Western intellectual tools for communication become most acute. For speaking about this way of relating takes us beyond the mechanical or hydraulic model of relationship based on Newtonian physics that has prevailed in the modern West. We arrive at a certain kind of relatedness as religious practice in which "synthesis" can be regarded as living dialogue, a source of actual energy and significance, rather than as a static end-product of intellectual formulation.

Cobb's saying that there has been no adequate "theology of dialogue"—no adequate interpretation, discipline, or way of nurturing this kind of relationship and development—can be misleading. In fact, a strong case can be made for the fact that dialogue as Cobb describes it, and "conversation" as we have seen it earlier in the inquiry as intrinsic to the Western ideal of a liberal education, is precisely what is great in the Western tradition. And not to overlook the obvious, Cobb's book, and his "position" generally, is itself a major contribution to a theology of dialogue. Cobb's work can also be regarded as a resource for the developmental movement through the stages I have described, and beyond the accompanying dangers of relativism, reactionary movements, and cults or fascism.

What needs to come next in our inquiry is a more direct investigation of dialogue as that which is essential to the West, to its beauty, persuasiveness, and dignity, and of the suggestion that "penetration" of the Western tradition results in our being located in the present within the mode of "dialogue that leads beyond dialogue to mutual transformation."

NINE

From Dialectic to Feminism

I

NOW DIALOGUE EMERGES as a crucial term. Both Abe and Cobb have identified dialogue as essential to the positive potential of our era. Our inquiry so far suggests that dialogue provides a way of spiritual development that enables the traditions to move beyond their respective historic limitations; and also that dialogue gives us access to what is genuinely great in the Western tradition. The religious significance of dialogue from the standpoint of the traditions of the East is a question: Where, in the tradition and subtraditions represented by the Kyoto school, is dialogue found, and how is dialogue to be valued by Eastern peoples as they reappropriate their own traditions in the present?

From the standpoint of the present inquiry, it seems appropriate to seek an answer to the same question from the Western side: Where and how in the West is dialogue valued, and what might this mean in terms of our being in the present? In pursuing an answer to this question, I turn in this chapter to a recent work that presents dialogue as dialectic, from the Greek side of the Western inheritance. I turn to Jon Moline's *Plato's Theory of Understanding*.[1]

Moline argues that what is magnificent in Western civilization is the discipline of discussion, the art of "dialectic" in Socrates' terminology. He demonstrates this through his reading of Plato:

> Two human abilities are remarkable perhaps above all others. The first is our ability to carry on discussions with one another. The second is our ability to turn the first upon itself, to reflect on and discuss critically our own discussion. . . .
>
> Plato's philosophy was founded, first and last, on the requirements of discussion . . . an art or discipline, holding forth the promise of wisdom or understanding. He wished to explore fully what makes such disciplined discussion possible.[2]

In relation to our present situation Moline says that it is difficult for us to take the synoptic (i.e., "seeing the whole together") approach of Plato, and hence also difficult to see the profound significance of discussion. This is owing to the dominance of "recent interpretive orthodoxy," which is rooted in what he calls "verificationism": "Verificationism's paradigm of inquiry is the quest for certainty. Its methods are restricted to what are conceived to be ways of showing that a given proposition is certainly true."[3] This demand for intellectual certainty is associated with the eclipse of Socrates and Plato by Aristotle's concern with logical, deductive demonstration. The same demand has led to the elevation of intellectual/cognitive knowledge over all others, and to the fragmentation and specialization of knowledge, to an "intellectualist bias." As a result, the greatness of our tradition, philosophy as "the love of wisdom" (*philo-sophia*), is hardly visible as an option today.

To reclaim the greatness of dialectic, Moline proposes to adopt Plato's synoptic method of "walking around and examining from all sides."[4] The center, that which is walked around and described from various angles by Moline, is a single Greek concept, *episteme*, usually translated as "knowledge," or sometimes "wisdom" or "spiritual awareness." Moline says that "understanding" is the best we can do in the English language, and he says that we may not presently have any adequate symbol with which to point to the crucial reality of episteme, a reality we may have totally forgotten. The problem in terms of our language is that Plato was speaking of a state that had "both articulate intellectual characteristics and powerful motivational ones,"[5] while in our language/world we separate intellect and emotion: "Neither Socrates as Plato describes him nor Plato himself intellectualized the explanation of behavior any more than they emotionalized the explanation of intellect. They simply had little use for distinctions between intellect and emotion."[6]

The specific angles from which Moline seeks to describe the "understanding" of Socrates and Plato are dialectical, psychological, semantic, and ontological, and these angles are themselves the subjects of a number of chapters of his book. The point, in brief, is that "understanding" can only be acquired through "dialectic" or discussion. We must articulate our view of reality, try to describe "the good,"[7] and interact with the articulations of others by asking questions and giving answers to actualize and arrive at understanding. The essence of dialectic or genuine discussion is presented in terms of the characteristics of a certain kind of human encounter. These characteristics consist of a series of "constraints" on the questioner and the answerer, together with certain "conditions" that are to be shared by both. These are so central to Moline's presentation of what is essential to the Western tradition that they must be cited in full:

Constraints upon the answerer:
1. The answerer must agree to take up the role of answerer and must

agree to answer whatever questions are put to him unless the sense of those questions is unclear.

2. The answerer must not stand in the way of taking up questions in the order likely to leave the fewest loose ends.
3. The answerer must say what he sincerely thinks even if he realizes that it contradicts what he said earlier.
4. The answerer must say what *he* thinks. Outside authorities are not relevant. Their views may be given only if the answerer takes full responsibility for their defense on his own.
5. Answers must be succinct, not speeches or rhetorical performances.
6. The answerer must express as clearly as possible what he means.
7. The answerer must express his view as accurately as possible in order to give an account of precisely what he promises to give an account of, neither more nor less.
8. The answerer must accept dialectical refutation gracefully as a benefit and a purification.

Constraints upon the questioner:
9. The questioner may not put two questions in the guise of one.
10. The questioner must ask questions with a view first to the orderly completion or safe delivery of the answerer's account as he had conceived of it and then to the fair and sufficient testing of it.
11. The questioner must follow the answerer wherever he and the account lead.
12. Above all, the questioner is to point out which answers are inconsistent.

Conditions which bind both:
13. Questioner and answerer must not fall into the habit of snatching at each other's words with a hasty guess as to the speaker's meaning, completing them in their own fashion and not as intended. Questioners in particular are to remember that they may not be grasping the intended meaning aright.
14. Neither questioner nor answerer may proceed . . . by making merely verbal distinctions and classifications. Conventional nomenclature is not to be the final arbiter in distinguishing and classifying. . . .
15. Both questioner and answerer are to seek the truth, not debating points.[8]

This striking list of constraints and conditions can be seen in what are for us the rather formal and culturally distant Socratic dialogues from which they are derived. In a less formal and more immediate way we can see these characteristics of genuine human encounter present in our own best relationships.

And here, it seems to me, in a certain way of being with others, not in some doctrine or set of intellectual conclusions, is located the best of what the West has to offer. It is in this vital context that we are able to discover the "answers" that enable us to develop toward our fullest capacities. Moline's articulation is certainly very direct and clear, and we could discuss at great length the characteristics he presents as they are manifest in our experience of certain relationships.

Moline goes on to point out that the practice of this kind of interaction has the effect of bringing to maturity and goodness both the person and the community. In the person, practice of dialectic fosters "a condition of the psyche in which it apprehends reality in a special way and has its behavior automatically reordered."[9] The reordering involves harmonizing what were for Plato the three parts of the soul, usually understood as "reason," "spirit," and "appetite." This harmonizing entails overcoming painful imbalances through submitting one's whole being to the guidance of reason, reason that pacifies the other parts, and enables them to serve their rightful functions; "reason" in Plato's use of that term, it should be added, is quite different from the much narrowed definition it came to have in later Western experience.

Moline maintains that because the community is isomorphic to the individual—that is, because they have the same form—the practice of dialectic will also lead to a community or world that is both peaceful and just. This may seem initially a peculiar idea, one we associate today with people who refuse to become involved or related until they "get it together" personally. But this very notion of isomorphic relation between individual and society, and faith in the transforming power of discussion, are at the root of our idea of democracy. In the ideal democracy both public policy and civic well-being come from discussion. The American tradition of valuing the independent sector of voluntary associations is probably the most accessible example of this idea of isomorphic relation (though one that is still very removed from the day-to-day experience of most people in this culture today). In this vision of the relation between the individual and the social, personal development does not occur in isolation, as it seems to for so many today, but is public in the fullest sense.

Moline describes the view of reality that corresponds to the transforming power of dialectic. As we develop understanding through dialectic we come to participate more and more fully in an "extrapsychic reality,"[10] which is associated with Plato's famous theory of "the forms." In our very best moments we become a channel through which the pure energy of "the good" flows. But this good, the form of the forms, cannot be captured or contained in *any* intellectual formulation; it exists beyond the intellectualist urge, both in its essential reality and in our practice of dialectic. The good itself, the form of the forms, remains ineffable. We cannot develop fully as human beings without an articulation of the good or reality itself; but in order to engage in dialectic and receive its transforming power, we must go beyond these articulations, into the moment of dialectical encounter. Moline argues that the idea of reality as constituted by forms, their appearance in varying intensities and mixtures, and their apprehension through contemplation, is one that is ontologically and epistemologically necessary to support the practice of dialectic—not the other way around, as most interpreters of Plato in Western history have wanted it to be.

One reason I find Moline's work compelling is that it resonates with what I have tried to say in other places and how I have tried to teach. In my previous attempts to articulate the greatness of the West I have stressed that "relatedness is the locus of the ultimate."[11] By this I mean that there is a certain way of being with others that involves two vital paradoxes. The first is that of simultaneous definiteness and openness: I can only enter into the fully human relationship when I am definite in who I am, what I think and stand for, not when I am merely available or protean; and, at the same time, I can only enter fully when I am open to the other and to what is revealed in relationship, not when I am doctrinaire or rigid. The second paradox is that of self-development and other-development: the best thing I can do for myself is to participate in a relationship of genuine concern for and with the other, and the best I can do for the other is to be fully myself.

To live creatively with these two paradoxes, we must find a form of human association or being together that is transformative. There is a way of being in which it is possible to actually live these paradoxes and have access to the energy that flows through them, rather than stand outside of them as vexing contradictions. The form of association through which this becomes possible can be spoken of as the temple or holy place, the locus of salvation, of enlightenment, of that which we as humans most fundamentally need. It is this relational locus that Moline is pointing to in his reading of Plato as grounded in the kind of discussion that holds forth the promise of wisdom. And we can relate this vital locus back to Cobb's dialogue that leads beyond dialogue to mutual transformation.

With Moline, then, it becomes possible to conclude that the wisdom of the West, at least on the Greek side, finds its foundation in this sense of a certain kind of relationship. To me, this bears an interesting parallel to the Hebrew emphasis on being in a state of "right relationship."

But how hard it is, as Moline and others remind us, for us to have access to this wisdom today. It tends to be buried under the preference that has prevailed since Aristotle for the kind of knowledge that is logically certain and strictly deductive from settled first principles. And the modern development of the Cartesian worldview has entailed an understanding of relationship based on mechanics, even hydraulics: any doing for the other entails "self-sacrifice," while any doing for oneself is thought to be necessarily at someone else's expense. About as close as we come to the pre-Aristotelian wisdom is the contemporary term *synergy*—the kind of relationship in which there is simultaneous growth and benefit for all parties to relationship, the kind of relationship which gives more energy than it takes. But of course it is very difficult to experience this kind of relating if we are preoccupied with the priority of intellectual certainty, purely logical ways of knowing, and the mechanistic, push/pull view of the universe that was given formulation by Newton and Descartes.

My critical response to Moline is hardly a criticism. It is the practical question: How do we actually engage in dialectic in the world of today? I have argued that we can do this, that we in fact must do this, in and through the conversational practice and attentiveness intrinsic to liberal education. And yet the idea of dialectic seems so distant from our world, a world that has largely lost the language by which to conceive this vision, the institutions by which to nurture and support it, and the philosophical and artistic reminders as to how it opens onto the fullness of human being.

II

How far our world has moved away from dialectic and conversation was brought home to me one day when a colleague appeared in my office in despair. This particular colleague is a teacher and a public person, one who is profoundly serious about the practice of liberal education; he has served on university committees for many years in a way that has caused him to be described as a "moral center," a consistent voice against "politics" in the low sense as mere acquisition of "turf." He has stood for "the public" as the open and free space in which human beings can be present to one another in the full complexity of their similarity and difference, in the relatedness of dialectic. The focus of his despair on this particular day was not the limitations of students, as is so frequently the complaint of faculty today, but rather the university itself: what it has become, how it has moved from the genuine politics of conversation and the public of learning community to a relativistic chaos, a "war of all against all," a situation in which the public, in the essential sense of this word, is all but completely lost.

He had with him two books. One was Barbara Herrnstein Smith's *Contingencies of Value*, published by Harvard University Press. My colleague pointed with astonished urgency to her central thesis about "the inexorability of economic accounting in and throughout every aspect of human—and not only human—existence," and her argument against "the recurrent impulse to dream an escape from economy."[12] To this author that escape is impossible; the university—and the world—are essentially about the economics of separative individualism and exchange.

The other volume was Ellen Rooney's *Seductive Reasoning*, published by Cornell University Press, with its aspiration "to be an instance of anti-pluralist practice, to break with pluralism in the very act of disclosing its ideological ground."[13] Her point is that "pluralism *produces* seductive reasoning, that is, produces reason as a universal seduction. Pluralism defines reason itself as the assumption of the theoretical possibility of general persuasion."[14] Her argument is against the "seduction" of reason and for an "emphasis on the gesture of exclusion [that is] based on a critical awareness that historically irreducible interests divide. . . . "[15] She gives an example of what this amounts to from a classroom in which students refuse to take a text seriously. At first the professor chastizes them, but then "acknowledges the force of their 'frivolous' reading and their indifference."[16] To this my colleague responded with a horrified exclamation: "We are guilty of 'universal seduction' by making students read well enough to understand a text?!"

My colleague went on: These authors are examples of what David Bromwich refers to as the "culture of suspicion" that is taking over higher education and culture at large. The culture of suspicion rejects both the conservative "culture of assent" and the liberal or Enlightenment ideal of persuasive reason: "Faced with a choice between the conservative belief that culture is sacred and the liberal belief that it is a common possession of some utility, the truly suspicious reply that it is always partial, always compromised."[17] My colleague pointed out that Smith and Rooney are established figures, writing under the imprint of old and prestigous publishers, writing books that are unabashedly anti-humanist and anti-Enlightenment.

In relation to this disturbing new culture my colleague identified a passage in which one of the authors confesses that she herself is the product of recent university life, characterized by "wide-ranging political agitation from the left in concert with disciplinary upheaval, the fall into theory, and a number of consciously politicized critical and theoretical movements."[18] As such she has had no experience with the liberal culture that Bromwich seeks to revive and extend, with what he calls the paradox of a "nonrestrictive tradition," "a tradition that is not the property of any party," one that is the necessary presupposition of a liberal education:

A tradition on this view, far from being fixed forever, may be shaped by the voluntary choices of readers and thinkers. Indeed, it exists not only as something to know, but as something to interpret and reform. But a difficult paradox holds together the idea of a non-restrictive tradition. Before it can be reformed intelligently, it must be known adequately; and yet, unless one realizes first that it *can* be reformed, one will come to know it only as a matter of rote—with the result that the knowledge of tradition will seems as unimaginative a business as the knowledge of an alphabet or a catechism. Difficult as it is, the liberal understanding of a tradition was for a long time promoted by American politicians, shared by public servants, exemplified by artists, critics, and freelance citizens. The process of sifting the tradition still continues, or we would be dead as a society. Our agreement that it ought to continue, however, is weaker now than it has been for several generations.[19]

What we see with Smith and Rooney, then, is a forgetting of and hence a failure to transmit the essence of tradition in this nonrestrictive sense. In the absence of any other coherent sense of tradition, education and culture are both reduced to interactions of self-interest and irresolvable conflict, descending to the low level of "might makes right," reflecting "the growing distrust in America of any common discourse."[20] Amidst the clashing of interests, there is no room for nonrestrictive tradition, something shared that can be interpreted and reformed. In such a climate, even when nonrestrictive tradition does appear for a moment, it is quickly reduced to a function of the interests of the one who brings it forth into the space of interaction.

III

Some integrative feminists, like Caroline Whitbeck, have sought to show us what we need to do in order to move beyond the laissez-faire individualism that is oriented to self-interest alone, and that is so frequently mistaken for "liberalism" today.[21] She argues that "Western thought" is so thoroughly tainted by "dualistic opposition," the generalized assumption of opposition rather than relation, that we need a new ontology,[22] a new understanding of Being itself and hence of how humans can participate in the fullness of life. The problem of dualistic opposition is visible in the primary social forms of patriarchy itself, and also in the rebellion of individualism, which "retains the same opposition of self to other" since it is generated by people "whose primary experience of domination was at the hands of a father or monarch," and "leaves untouched forms of domination other than domination of the sons by the father."[23] According to Whitbeck, a new ontology must arise from the specifically and fully human *practice:* "The practice that I consider to be the core practice is that of the (mutual) realization of people."[24] Movement to a new ontology requires that we change our understanding of relationship from one that assumes the radical difference between human beings, with the corresponding ethic of rights, conflict, contract and competition, to one of the "relation of analogous beings."[25] The ethic of this new view is more complex and demanding than the relatively simple, even mechanistic ethic of rights; the ethic of relation entails a "multifactorial interactive model" that emphasizes the "responsibility for" and "the practice of mutual realization."[26]

That an ethic of mutual realization—or we might say of synergetic relation—both entails and requires a new ontology, and a nonrestrictive way of receiving and relating to tradition, is well indicated in the following statement from Ruth Nanda Anshen:

> Our Judeo-Christian and Greco-Roman heritage, our Hellenistic tradition, has compelled us to think in exclusive categories. But our *experience* challenges us to recognize a totality much richer and far more complex than the average observer could have suspected—a totality which compels him to think in ways which the logic of dichotomy denies. We are summoned to revise fundamentally our ordinary ways of conceiving experience, and thus, by expanding our vision and by accepting those forms of thought which also include non-exclusive categories, the mind is then able to grasp what it was incapable of grasping or accepting before.[27]

Once again, the strenuousness of a new way of being comes into view, and the way in which it requires deep revaluation of the inherited past.

In order to have dialectic or conversation we must integrate that which our ancestors in the traditional period made other, that which they suppressed, repressed, and oppressed. And in order to integrate we need to move beyond the "intellectualist bias" of Aristotle and "the logic of dichotomy," which is founded on opposition and exclusive categories. We need to overcome world-rejection and reclaim the "body" of "mutual realization," the fullness of genuine relationship. We must have *both* separation and attachment, definiteness and openness, distance and closeness, independence and intimacy, male and female. Out of the instability of our era it is revealed to be impossible to have either one in any real sense without having the other at the same time.

Yet the way of dialectic or full and real relationship is so remote from the world as we actually experience it today. In the midst of the clamor and din, the conflict and threat of our time, the creative alternative is so very difficult to identify and hold on to.

TEN

A View on the Western Drama

WE ARE WORKING with the following possibility: that dialogue, and dialogue as dialectic or the fullness of conversation, points the way toward what is great in the Western tradition and what is required for revitalization in the present. This greatness is centered in the fully human encounter, in a way of being in which relatedness is the locus of the ultimate. And yet the meaning of this is not yet clear for us, either intellectually or in terms of our own practice and experience. Why is this so?

Part of the difficulty in achieving clarity is that in the actual unfolding of the Western drama, there have been profound obstacles to the dialogical way of being. In the inquiry to this point we have identified three chief obstacles that are tightly intertwined, forming a sort of knot of inhibition against recognizing and sustaining the relational greatness at the heart of Western tradition. First, there is the observation from Cobb and others that the West has lacked depth in its view of reality and therefore of the inner dynamics of the human being. Second is the prevailing Western tendency toward displacement of those aspects of life that are spiritual through intellectualization, the locating of meaning and value in systems of thought and belief that have been given priority over authentic experience and encounter. The third obstacle is the cultural tendency toward opposition rather than relation, dichotomy rather than complexity, and exclusion rather than inclusion—an either/or mentality that alienates people from the richness of actual experience.

Given these obstacles and the problems and perplexities that are associated with them, at this point in our search for the greatness of the West as a living ideal that can be present in our actual experience we must reach for a broad historical perspective. We need to reconsider the Western tradition from the perspective of our time and place, from the ground of our present situation. What follows in this chapter is such an attempt. The aim of this essay, this attempt, is comprehensiveness rather than detail; it it an exercise in cultural aerial photography. With such a perspective, one that many in the academic world of today seek to avoid, we run the risk of committing the very intellectualization that has been identified as a major problem! Still, it seems worth the risk to try to appropriate Western experience as one whole thing, as a stream of cultural disposition containing possibilities as well as obstacles, possibilities that may be able to flow into and vitalize the present. Perhaps the risk of intellectual displacement can be avoided if we require the intellect to serve the function of appropriating those possibilities that are truly vital, that enable us to live more fully.

It is in the nature of tradition itself that again and again in each generation the human drama must be retold, the story of what possibilities and obstacles we inherit and what we must do to become fully human. There is no such thing as "handing down" tradition, no simple act of transmitting the vital information—as though it were on a computer disk. It must be appropriated, *taken*, wrestled from the abstract or merely chronological past by the urgent need of the present. The paradox of tradition is that it only achieves its luminous reality as it becomes an essential element of the moment that is genuinely present.

But our post-traditional twentieth-century present seems to be distinct from previous senses of the present precisely in our perception of being severed from the past. For us tradition is not even an abstract possibility to be actualized by the vital juices of the present, but "done with" and other to us. In this perception of separation from the traditional past lies our difficulty with tradition, as well as the danger of reactionary and neoconservative movements in our century: they seek to impose aspects of the past that are no longer connected with what is alive in the present, aspects that are even questionable in terms of whether they ever existed (in a way that is similar to some others in our fanciful time who seek to impose something that is not yet here).

II

It is essential to our time that we do in fact live with the perspective of tradition as something with a beginning and an end that are both past, as something completed, as something other to us. Ours is the ambiguous advantage of having stood on the moon. In this chapter I want to discuss the character of the Western drama from the standpoint of this new world perspective. Even after we come to terms fully with the sense of the end of tradition, its radical separateness from us and how we live today, something remains; something flows into our post-traditional lives to energize us. This "something" also resonates in two somewhat mysterious and often quoted statements. One is from the poet Wallace Stevens: "After the final no, there / comes a yes, and upon that yes / the future world depends."[1] The other is from the theologian Paul Tillich: "The courage to be is rooted in the God who appears when God has disappeared in the anxiety of doubt."[2] To understand these statements is to understand our tradition, its absence—and its endurance.

In our time we have become aware of not only the end but also the beginning of tradition. However, awareness of the end comes first, and dawns in negative terms: whether it is dated 1917 with the First World War, with the Holocaust atrocities and totalitarian phenomena of the Second World War, with Hiroshima on August 6, 1945, or with the upheaval of the late sixties in America, there is the sense of a radical break with all that has gone before. Traditional cultures are no longer able to *contain* human life. People leave them and encounter the validity of other lifeways. Or people invade them and introduce the melting agencies of development, the "acids of modernity." We drift or are driven, we are lured or jolted out of the traditional envelope of human life—into the landscape of world war and relativism, consumerism and secularism, identity crisis, technological determinism and nuclear threat. The whole world comes to be wired together in tenuous interdependence. Much of the characteristic art and literature of our time is about this loss of tradition, as, for example, in this letter from D. H. Lawrence, speaking very close to the immediate experience of loss:

> I can't tell you with what pain I think of that autumn at Cholesbury—the yellow leaves—and the wet nights when you came to us, and Gilbert and the dogs—and I had got pork chops—and our cottage was hot and full of the smell of sage and onions—then the times we came to you, and had your wine—those pretty wine-glasses on your long table. Something inside one weeps and won't be comforted. But it's no good grieving. — But there was *something* in those still days, before the war had gone into us, which was beautiful and generous—a sense of flowers rich in the garden, and sunny tea-times when one was at peace—when we were happy with one another, really—even if we said spiteful things afterwards. I was happy, anyway. There was a kindness in us, even a certain fragrance in our meeting—something very good, and poignant to remember, now the whole world of it is lost.[3]

The discovery of the *beginning* of tradition comes after discovery of the end, and this discovery is among the very first positive expressions of our new world perspective. Awareness of beginning centers on a realization about human beings as such, about something fundamental that is shared by all cultures and is prior to the divisions and conflict that mark world history throughout the traditional period, something profoundly common in the midst of—or underneath—our various disputes.

In our earlier discussion of the work of Hannah Arendt, Robert N. Bellah, and Karl Jaspers we have seen that in the "axial period" at about 600 B.C., across the earth, in places having no physical contact with one another, there occured a radical shift in human consciousness. Self-consciousness emerged. Humankind departed from an original structure of consciousness imaged forth as the Garden of Eden in the Hebrew story. Aware of themselves, able to look at themselves, to reflect, think, choose, worry, humans now had both a new freedom and a new anxiety.

Emergence of self-consciousness occurred simultaneously with the discovery and objectification of the One, the unitary character of reality. With this existence itself becomes an issue, something humans must come to terms with. Here there is profound irony. Prior to the discovery of the One, of God rather than gods, humans lived *in* the One. Life itself was sacred, and divine energy was palpably present on the earth: at first it was everywhere and in every moment; and later, approaching the moment of critical transition, the sacred became more specialized, located in particular persons, places, and times. But with the decisive discovery of the One, the sacred was displaced, located in a realm "out there," separated from life in the ordinary. The irony is that discovery or consciousness *of* the One was coincident with alienation *from* the One, with the necessity to distinguish between the sacred and the profane. And at this moment there arose the variety of traditions, each accounting for why it is that humans came to be alienated from the One and what it is that we must do in order to achieve reunion, to overcome "original sin" or "karma." Religion as we know it (*re-ligio*, perhaps from *re-legare*, to "bind back" or "reconnect") was born at this moment—as was the world-rejection of the traditional period.

With their commonly shared beginning, the traditions began to take their distinctive shapes as alternative responses to the complex question about the meaning of self-consciousness and its relationship to the One. To be more specific, the traditions, and human life during the historic period—from its beginning in the axial period between 800 and 200 B.C. until its ending in the twentieth century—can be understood as variations on the answers to three primary questions that are integral to traditional culture. The first is the question of the earth and the world: What is this place and how did it come to be, and what are its central operating principles? The second is about the human condition: In this place, what is the basic human problem, and how is it to be addressed and redeemed? Finally, there is the inclusive question of the ultimate conditions of existence or the nature of the One itself: How are both the earth and the human situation therein related to God—or the good, or Brahman, or Nothingness, or *Logos*—the ultimate?

The early history of each tradition reveals the struggle to establish answers, and in succeeding generations we see codification and elaboration of what was resolved in the formative stage. As the historic period progresses we see conflict, the meetings of the traditions as disagreement at the very basic level of differing answers to these fundamental questions. The disagreements provide reasons for war, exploitation, judgment, and the generally unfriendly terms upon which the traditions have related historically. From the perspective that becomes available to us now in the post-traditional twentieth century, we are able to see the unity that underlies the raucous diversity of the traditional era. And from this perspective we have the opportunity to evaluate both our own traditional past and that of others in light of the shared moment of origin—and in light of the equally shared question of the survival of humans of *any* tradition in the present and future.

III

It is from this perspective that we now focus on the unfolding of the Western drama to develop the overall understanding that is needed at this point in our inquiry. Because the intention of this effort is broad, it is bound to appear as simplistic from the standpoint of any of the subtraditions to be discussed. But here, in a very real way, is the central point: the Western tradition consists of argument about the details within and among the views we are about to explore.

With the intermingling of the Hebrew culture of Jerusalem and the Greek culture of Athens, the Western drama begins. In the West's formative ancient period the relative simplicity of the three questions basic to the formation of tradition gives rise to not one but three complete responses. These alternative Western responses become the basic subsets of the Western worldview. There is one Hebrew response, the theistic orientation, and there are two on the Greek side, the idealistic and the naturalistic. Together these three constitute the strands out of which the Western drama is woven.

In the theistic view the world is the creation *ex nihilo* of Yahweh, God who is completely separate from the world. Humankind is a part, the highest part, of what is created in the original act. Humans are created "in God's image." But humans are not satisfied with their original creation in the Garden of Eden, a place of perfection, innocence, and safety. They disobey God's commandment not to eat the fruit of the tree of knowledge, the tree of the knowledge of good and evil. Not only do they break God's commandment, but, having eaten of that tree, they then present to their Creator the threat that they will eat from a second tree in the garden, the tree of life. This would allow them to become "like us," Yahweh muses in evident alarm, like gods (here is one of the places in the Old Testament where the god-voice switches from the singular to the plural)—they would become immortal. Therefore Adam and Eve, the original humans, are given various punishments for breaking Yahweh's commandment, and they are ejected from the garden. The essence of the state of punishment in which they live forever after is "original sin," the taint of guilt for having rejected the original circumstances of creation and God's commandment. At the moment of ejection God places one of his cherubim with a flaming sword at the gate of the garden, signaling that there will be no way in the future for Adam and Eve or their progeny to return.

The ultimate in this worldview is personified as a being apart from the world and the earth, and he is known to humans through his own commandments and self-revelation. God's actions have the effect of establishing covenants and with them the terms of right relationship among humans and between the covenant community and the divine. Obedience is the mode of relationship, and acceptance of God's actions, independent of reason or any other human standard, is the proper attitude. God acts and chooses in ways that remain mysterious to humankind.

On the Greek side, the idealistic view arises from the writings of Plato, especially his "allegory of the cave" in the *Republic*. Here we find scripture, parallel in its cultural significance to the Pentateuch on the Hebrew side. In this allegory, life on earth is imaged as life in a cave underground: the light in the cave is dim, but there is an opening to the outside world and the direct light of the sun. Yet this opening is not known to most people, and the ascent from the cave to the opening is extremely steep and difficult. Most people are chained in chairs in the cave with their backs to the opening, facing a cave wall on which flickering shadow images appear, cast by a fire behind the people and by objects between their backs and the flames. And by these flickering images the chained watchers are mesmerized.

The flickering shadows represent the everyday awareness of what is apprehended through the senses and the opinions that are fashionable in society. Sense-experience and the opinions of society lie in just the opposite direction from reality itself, as symbolized by the sun, the source and generator of all light and activity in the cave. The human problem is quite literally that we are facing in the wrong direction, orienting ourselves by the shadows of sense-perception and society rather than by reality itself. The beginning of redeeming the human problem is turning around, realizing that reality is 180 degrees from what we have originally assumed. With this realization we can begin the ascent from the cave of ignorance. Plato goes on to say that through mathematical studies it is possible to move to higher and higher levels of abstraction and thus open up and activate human capacities for perceiving the real. Finally, through dialectic, we are able to directly apprehend and participate in the life of the sun itself—the good, the ultimate. Only after this direct apprehension is it possible to return to the cave and operate on the basis of wisdom.

The ultimate here is "outside" the world as the world is normally perceived, but not separate from it as in the theistic view. And neither, for Plato, is it mysterious in its ways or even active in the Hebrew sense. That which is shadowy is just that: dim, relatively devoid of light. But the light is there even so, and ignorance can be overcome through the turning around and realization of the pure light and source of all that exists. Humans in this view, in contrast to the Hebrew perspective, begin in an imperfect state but are capable of achieving perfection, and normal human faculties, properly activated and developed, make this possible. This is clearly distinct from the Hebrew vision in which redemption is possible only through special revelation and unconditioned election by and from an action of God alone.

The other Greek view is the naturalistic, and it finds its definitive formulation in the thought of one of Plato's students, Aristotle. Sometimes also referred to as realism, this set of answers to the fundamental human questions does not provide us with one neat picture or story, as do the other two. This is perhaps consistent with the essence of naturalism, since here the locus of the real is not somewhere else, either in God's commandments and revelations or in an ideal realm removed from the realm of appearances. Rather, the real is to be found right here, in the depth of the actual. This being the case, naturalism can be articulated in terms of two basic notions, which Aristotle uses to explain the character of the actual: *telos* and "the Unmoved Mover."

Telos is the destiny or inner urge that is present in each thing to become what it is meant to be. Aristotle uses the example of the acorn, which contains within it the destiny to become the magnificent oak tree. So it is with humans and everything else in the natural world: each has its own inbuilt program to develop to its fullness. Problems or failures of development are a matter of constraint or obstruction—the acorn is acquired by a squirrel, for instance, or lands under a rock or in my garden. The failure of any particular acorn to become an oak is not a problem with the acorn itself but rather with the circumstances in which it happens to exist, with disruptions or interruptions, or with its being taken into some other telic actualization, such as that of the squirrel or the design of my garden.

Now this becomes somewhat complex with humans, since our telos, in part at least, is to decide who we shall be, and many of our constraints are ones that we ourselves generate in the form of bad or inhibiting habits. But the dynamic is basically the same as it is for the acorn, namely self-actualization or self-determination, and the removing of constraints.

Regarded from this perspective the world is seen as a web of telic actualization and constraint, where at least some of those constraints arise from the inclusion of the lower forms of actualization within the larger—the *teloi* of some acorns are given over to the higher telos of the squirrel. The second of Aristotle's notions, that of the Unmoved Mover, accounts for the inability of some teloi to be actualized, and distinguishes between the lower and the higher forms. Potentialities and actualities, each level giving rise to the next, ascend (for example, from the acorn to the squirrel to humans, who might eat the little beast or use the pelt to keep warm in winter) from lesser causes to greater, and finally to one cause of all causes that is itself uncaused or unmoved. This Unmoved Mover, then, is the ultimate. It resides not outside of nature, as in the theistic view, and not behind, as the light source is behind shadows in the idealist, but rather at the base and as the pinnacle of nature, as the final cause of all causes and telos of all teloi.

In the ancient period, then, these three views, the theist, idealist, and naturalist, were established and set into interaction with one another. But the ancient period does not find its fulfillment with this establishment. There also appear two mysterious characters, two persons, whose lives and deaths exercise tremendous influence on Western culture, and who do not fit very well with any of the three dominant perspectives. These two figures are Socrates and Jesus.

Their stories are remarkable in their similarity. Considered as naively as possible, both were extremely modest, humble, and even marginal by the standards of the societies in which they lived. Each had a career that consisted almost entirely of encounters with other persons, encounters having to do with a transformation or fulfillment that had not been envisioned in the human drama prior to their appearance. Each is associated with wisdom and divinity; each makes paradoxical claims about knowing nothing and being unimportant in himself, while claiming also that somehow "the One" is in them or manifest through them. Neither wrote, and both threatened the existing social order to such a degree that they were executed. And each lives on.

If the three perspectives are the strands out of which Western culture is woven, could it be that the figures of Socrates and Jesus represent the pure energy that courses through those strands, vivifying the culture? Their faces, their enigmatic words, and the conversation between them keep reappearing, energizing and haunting the drama of Western civilization as it unfolds.

IV

After the establishment of the three perspectives and the appearance of Socrates and Jesus, the ancient period gave way to the medieval, as the entire culture became Christian. The Christian energy came to occupy, much in the manner of a hermit crab inhabiting an empty shell, the physically massive but spiritually empty structure of the Roman Empire. After a relatively short time canonization of scripture and dogma occurred, as the culture decided at the Church's Councils of Nicaea (A.D. 325) and Chalcedon (A.D. 451) which of the various accounts of the life and death of Jesus were sacred and which were heresy; likewise, certain standard interpretations of Socrates were established, though in the medieval period Greek philosophy was regarded mostly as only preparation for Christian revelation. Finally, medieval civilization came into full bloom with the emergence of its distinctive organizational style and cultural consensus: medieval civilization became hierarchical, monolithic, and doctrinaire.

Within medieval civilization, the three strands of the Western worldview were melded together, with emphasis on the theistic. But the idealistic and naturalistic strands were visible also. With Augustine, for example, at least in his *City of God,* we see a medieval Christian who articulates the Christ event through the lenses of the idealistic perspective; and later, with Aquinas, we see medieval interpretation in a naturalistic frame. But theism dominated, and the mystery of Jesus was assimilated—many would say lost—in a vast sacramental structure of mediation and commandment. Dostoyevsky's famous "Grand Inquisitor" scene from *The Brothers Karamazov* presents the dynamics of this assimilation with real poignance: the returning Jesus is rejected and condemned by the Church's Inquisitor, who claims to love the people more by giving them miracle, mystery, and authority (and bread) than Jesus does with his ambitious freedom.[4]

In terms of the three primary cultural questions, attention in the medieval period was clearly on the third, on God as the transcendent designer of the grand hierarchy, with heaven above and hell below, a "great chain of being,"[5] with the pope and the Roman Catholic Church at the head of this realm. Perhaps the great cathedrals of the Gothic period can be understood as the most complete symbolic expressions of medieval civilization. With the establishment of medieval catholicity culture entered a phase of stabilization, such that one could argue that prior to this time Western culture did not fully exist as one coherent enterprise. With the Catholic synthesis Western culture was organized, regularized, and integrated into one substance.

As the medieval period developed, there occurred a shift, in Dostoyevsky's terms, from emphasis on miracle and mystery to emphasis on authority. The massive consensus of medieval civilization came to be contained more and more in doctrine, correctness of belief, accord with dogma; *sacrificium intellectús* became the chief mode of obedience—believing what one was told to believe by the Church. There were, of course, exceptions to this orientation, most notably in the monasticism of the period which stood in some tension with the papacy. Some of the fruits of medieval monasticism become available to us today through the mysticism of such figures as St. John of the Cross, Meister Eckhart, and the unknown fourteenth-century author of *The Cloud of Unknowing.*[6] The dominant medieval orientation, however, came to favor strongly, even militantly, intellectual assent and obedience to God through Church rather than mystical prayer and obedience through individual development.

Once stabilization of Western culture was achieved in the medieval period and the rigidity of its structure became manifest in later phases, there began to occur rebellion in the name of the very entity that was most vigorously denied by medieval civilization—the individual. Attention shifted to the second question, the question of self, and "freedom" became the watchword of the modern period.

It is as though sufficient confidence had been established in the existence of one transcendent principle in the medieval period that now individuals could be trusted to act autonomously on the basis of that transcendent principle. The modern emphasis on freedom, then, arose against a backdrop of commonly shared belief that all individuals were relating to and being disciplined by the same transcendent One. Whether in the scientific revolution, the democratic social movements, the Renaissance, or the Protestant Reformation, the same structure of assumption pertained in the modern project: since each individual, through his own powers of belief and reason, was in touch with the same universal, he could be trusted to act on his own, and the result of this autonomous action would be "automatic harmony." The common good would emerge, in the words of the economist Adam Smith, "as though through the presence of an invisible hand."[7]

For some this new affirmation of the dignity and rights of each person meant simply doing what they wanted; for some, freedom was merely the antithesis of what had gone before. But for others there was a positive content to freedom, something more than simply freedom *from* the medieval authoritarianism. In the modern period the positive orientation or subtradition that I have previously referred to as genuine liberalism was most clearly visible in the Radical Reformation and the sectarian free-church tradition that flows out of seventeenth-century England and America.[8] Here there was not just affirmation of the self in isolation, but an understanding of the relation between self and God and self and others, and of relationship as the locus of freedom. It was clear to the eyes of religious liberalism that the voice of God is more subtle than ecclesiastical doctrine, and that God speaks directly and continuously through the person, particularly in those moments when the person is in right relationship with other persons. The paradox of self-development and other-development was rediscovered: that the person can only be engaged in one while at the same time engaged in the other. God was understood not as static and "out there," but rather as dynamic, immanent, and fully relational, present in our midst when we stand in the posture of compassion toward one another. This view made possible the ideas of genuine democracy, of government through discussion, and the importance of transcending private interest for the sake of the common good.

But this relational possibility within the Western inheritance was not sustained when it appeared in the early modern period. Like the visions of Socrates and Jesus, this view entailed responses to the three basic questions that were not contained within the culture's three strands of thought. There was an ambitiousness to the modern relational possibility; it required that persons be "in the maturity of their faculties" (John Stuart Mill), with "a deep insight into the nature of reality" (John B. Cobb, Jr.). Largely as a consequence of limited understandings of self and reality, the early modern liberal view of the relationship between self, other, and the ultimate failed to find support culturally, in ways of articulation and discipline. Since ways of being do not endure long unless people find ways of talking about them and passing them along to the next generation, the relational subset of the Western worldview became less and less accessible as the modern period progressed.

Associated with the failure to sustain the positive vision of modern freedom was the development of an entirely new subset of the Western worldview, a new set of answers to the three primary questions of culture. The new view emerged along with the elevation of reason over faith and the development of modern science. Descartes is remembered as the philosopher who first articulated the influence of the scientific perspective on culture generally, and especially on understandings of personhood, freedom, and relationship. Thus the new subset is widely referred to as Cartesianism.

Human beings came to be conceived of both superficially, in terms of calculating reason and material interests, and atomistically, as radically separate from one another. The deeper but more difficult view of the person as directly in touch with God, and of relationship as the place of God's ongoing revelation and creativity in the world, seems to have been too demanding. Awareness of the mature sense of personhood and the intrinsic need of relationship was overrun by the much more simplistic Cartesian view, in which relationship is construed as extrinsically good insofar as it satisfies the private interest of individuals. In the latter view the image of mechanism prevailed, the push/pull world of hydraulics and the associated ethic of laissez-faire individualism.

Under modern Cartesianism the intellectualist approach, which was already visible in Aristotle, and which in the later medieval period was expressed as a sort of blind faith in doctrine, was now internalized by individuals. In the rise of the modern "Age of Reason," intellectualism came to be applied by free individuals to themselves, others, and the natural world. Hence "mind" and calculating reason replaced "spirit" as the term of opposition to body in the basic world-rejecting dichotomy of the traditional period in the West.

In the modern period the self was largely freed from external authority, and there were initial visions of freedom that recalled Jesus or Socrates, but another view came to prevail. Instead of becoming, in Martin Luther's phrase, a "priest and king before God," there is a real sense in which the modern individual became a microcosm of the world of medieval Catholicism: emotions, the physical body, and all other aspects of the self became the blind followers of the papal dictates of Cartesian reason. And God was lost; not so much argued against, but rendered irrelevant—replaced by the objective knowledge that was worshiped by the Cartesian self. As the modern period worked out its inner logic, even the sense of the ultimate as an order of objective knowledge ceased to be necessary. Instrumentalism and technique took over.

Meanwhile, great confusion was introduced into the culture by the labeling of Cartesian instrumentalism and the related laissez-faire individualism as "liberalism," further eclipsing the relational possibility associated with Socrates and Jesus. Cartesian intellectualism (or its flip side of revolt through materialism, body without spirit) became the only option available, the only model of personhood and relationship. Spirit was lost, the dimension of value, meaning, and enchantment that transcends and stabilizes the tension between the mental and physical poles of human existence that are posited by a dichotomizing culture. Hence the common reference to "Cartesian dualism": in the absence of spirit, human beings, like fish out of water, flip-flop back and forth between disembodied and dispirited intellectualism on the one hand, and unthinking and equally dispirited materialism on the other.

The Cartesian worldview, though shallow and remarkably devoid of metaphysical concerns when compared with virtually all traditional worldviews, was extremely persuasive. By the beginning of the contemporary period—D. H. Lawrence's time of "something lost"—it had been deeply institutionalized in Western society, in workplace and in civic life, as well as in the most intimate elements of the socialization and acculturation process. And this thin but efficient view had spread across the earth, but not as an explicit dogma to be argued or even articulated as in earlier periods characterized by the attempt to convert foreign populations. With Cartesianism there was no "philosophy" argued, no explicit dogma; rather, the appeal of this worldview was directly to the physical and psychological nature of humans in terms of material comfort, higher standards of living and health, and images of well-being associated with consumption. The lure of "development" and "modernization" proved to be enormously persuasive; appealing to a worldwide "revolution of rising expectations," the industrial, technological, and now cybernetic revolutions until quite recently met with very little resistance.

The effect of the Cartesian view was to unify the world around tenets of producing and consuming. What appeared as the physical benefits of this process masked the cultural costs. In the rush of the Cartesian enthusiasm deeper spiritual values were forgotten, and traditional lifeways were neglected, even mocked. And with the meeting of cultures that occurred as a result of the Cartesian activity, a certain cultural cancellation effect set in, giving rise to the relativism of our time and to an increasingly homogenized post-traditional world of producing, consuming, and entertaining.

The modern period has come to an end in the twentieth century with the psychic numbing, inner death, or nihilism that we have been discussing throughout this inquiry. The historical considerations of this chapter enable us to augment and deepen our understanding of this uncomfortable condition. We see how it is that the depressed condition of Western culture in the postmodern period is associated with intellectualism, the progressive elevating and narrowing of one aspect of the human to the exclusion of all others, especially the spiritual dimension, and with the appearance of the question that the intellect cannot answer: What's the use of use?

As early as the turn of the century William James identified the late modern condition in terms of "vicious intellectualism," the purely conceptual approach to life and the refusal to entertain any further evidence or insight once intellectual conclusions have been formulated.[9] Alfred North Whitehead points to much the same orientation with his phrase "the fallacy of misplaced concreteness,"[10] the violation of the actuality of life in the name of conceptual definiteness and closure.

But the intellectualism exists right alongside a materialism that is equally problematic, one that exhibits what we might call the fallacy of misplaced abstraction: for it is an uneasy materialism that is really an endless, abstracted quest for real life that, in its alienation from spirit, is unable to find rest in the body of lived life. Viciousness is present too, always lurking in this materialism: the desperation for real life and immediate experience is capable of consuming anything that might appear to offer this possibility.

Martin Luther King, Jr. speaks of the resultant circumstance in terms of the "culture lag" originally propounded by C. P. Snow: because we have allowed "the internal to become lost in the external," "we suffer from a poverty of the spirit which stands in glaring contrast to our scientific and technological abundance."[11] The effects of the Cartesian worldview have been to project upon the world what Lewis Mumford calls a "megamachine," "a totally organized and homogenized social system,"[12] one that is, in the words of Robert Heilbroner, "dazzlingly rich in every aspect except that of the cultivation of the human person."[13]

As reason was narrowed and lowered in its function, and closed, so that it no longer opened to the divine, and as other aspects of the human were excluded from the hegemony of modern reason, humanity itself began to undergo a change. Human beings underwent a gradual inner death.

This death is difficult to see, since it occurs frequently in the midst of great luxury and stimulation in the physical and psychological dimensions. Indeed, the dualism between intellectualism and materialism makes it hard to see either, since the moment one focuses on one side of the dualism the other side appears as the opposing reality. However, the agreement among the more profound diagnosticians of late modern and postmodern technological society is nearly universal: there is occurring a negative transformation, a forgetting and loss of what is distinctly human, a quiet, persistent erosion of authentic experience, sensibility and perspective. So serious and so advanced is this process that death is the theme.

V

And yet, as I have suggested at the beginning of this chapter with the curiously profound statements from Wallace Stevens and Paul Tillich, something remains: after the final no, a yes; after God disappears, God appears. Out of death there occurs a rebirth. The "survivor" becomes the paradigmatic figure of our time. Speaking on the theme of "survivor as creator," Robert Jay Lifton raises the following question:

> They all tell us that civilization—human life itself—is threatened, dying or dead; that we must recognize this death or near-death, pursue it, record it, and enter into it if we are to learn the truth about ourselves, if we are to live. This capacity for intimacy with (and knowledge of) death in the cause of renewed life is the survivor's special quality of imagination, his special wisdom. But how can that wisdom be shared? Can survivors be mentors to the world?[14]

In terms of the historical perspective of this chapter, I propose that what remains after the end of tradition—alongside the actuality and potentiality of massive death that this end entails—is that possibility within the Western tradition that had been visible from time to time but that had not been sustainable in the past: visible in Socrates and Jesus, in the genuine liberalism of the early modern period, and in the feminist "practice of mutual realization" today. Alfred North Whitehead speaks of this possibility, this slim hope as against the deathfulness of our era, in relation to "the Galilean origin of Christianity":

> There is, however, in the Galilean origin of Christianity yet another suggestion that does not fit very well with any of the three main stands of thought. It does not emphasize the ruling Caesar, or the ruthless moralist, or the unmoved mover. It dwells upon the tender elements of the world, which slowly and in quietness operate by love; and it finds purpose in the present immediacy of a kingdom not of this world. Love neither rules, nor is it unmoved; also it is a little oblivious as to morals.[15]

It is this "another suggestion" that remains after the exhaustion of the "main strands of thought"; and this remaining is intimately associated with the lives of Socrates and Jesus.

In answer to Lifton's question, Jesus and Socrates remain as the ultimate survivors and hence mentors. By this I mean these beings not as they are represented in thoughts or interpretations about them, which exist displaced in intellectual construction, but rather as presences, as tangible possibilities within our own experience—of potential greatness, death, and rebirth. Further, I propose that Socrates and Jesus can come to be present in our experience through dialogue, dialectic, conversation: through the fullness of our relatedness with other human beings.

This statement may seem peculiar, given inherited assumptions that predispose us to conceive of Socrates and Jesus not as ways of being, ways of our own being, but as objects of belief or doctrinal assent. What is being proposed here as the conclusion to our investigation of Western history may also seem strange given our modern habits of seeking vitality and identity in isolation rather than relation. Yet the conclusion we are left with is that the Western tradition is alive and available—as a "new ontology" and beyond "the logic of dichotomy"—through that ambitious possibility that is represented by the surviving of Socrates and Jesus.

But this conclusion is so frail. It is undeveloped, and undefended against massive evidence of a "final no" and a God who "has disappeared." Perhaps it would be more appropriate to call it a hypothesis—or a hope. At the least the conclusion of this chapter provides direction; it serves to set the agenda for what must follow in the inquiry. What *is* the "survivor's wisdom" of Socrates and Jesus? How is it that they can be mentors to us today? What would it mean to say that they in fact do survive and are accessible to us within the immediacy of our experience and our relationships?

ELEVEN

Testimony of Survivors

I

CLEARLY WE WILL need somehow to have direct encounter with Jesus and Socrates to learn the deeper meaning of dialogue, dialectic, and relatedness as locus of the ultimate. But perhaps not just yet. Before these encounters, let us consult some twentieth-century survivors who can be said to have had such an encounter with the reality of Jesus and Socrates, persons in whose experience and articulation we find the voice of the "survivor as mentor": the voice of "the other suggestion" in the Western tradition, the experience of the yes that follows the "final no," of "the God who appears when God has disappeared."

In this chapter I wish to look at the testimony of two of the more lucid and paradigmatic survivors of this century: William James and Etty Hillesum. Then I want to examine the ambiguities of how the "survivor's wisdom" becomes available to us today: through the popular "New Age" movement, through the contemporary genre of personal narrative, and through liberalism in the post-traditional twentieth century. Finally, I will say something about how we might overcome the ambiguities of these sources of wisdom, about what is required to enable us to actualize the positive potential of the survivors' discoveries and avoid the dangers. This, then, will prepare the way for our direct encounter with Jesus and Socrates.

II

William James's mature and full orientation crystallized late in his lively career, with the 1909 Hibbert Lectures, later published under the title *A Pluralistic Universe*.[1] In these lectures he speaks of "a new era of religion as well as of philosophy."[2] For James this new era arises directly out of his own experience, an experience so intense and meaningful that it caused him to break with the prevailing intellectualism and rationalism, which James came to see as the reason "philosophy had been on a false scent ever since the days of Socrates and Plato."[3]

In 1870 James, at the age of twenty-eight and with a recent M.D. degree, suffered what we might call a nervous breakdown, his own death or near-death experience. The resolution of this crisis is indicated in a journal entry, a statement from which the rest of his career would unfold:

> Today I about touched bottom, and perceive plainly that I must face the choice with open eyes: . . . suicide seemed the most manly form to put my daring into; now I will go a step further with my will, not only act with it, but believe as well; believe in my individual reality and creative power. My belief, to be sure, *can't* be optimistic—but I will posit life.[4]

This fundamental experience of "touching bottom" and choice set the themes of James's later work: his "will to believe," and even the sense that the reality of God somehow depends in part on our willingness to believe; his "radical empiricism," the orientation to the "thick" of experience itself rather than to abstraction; and his insistence that we are responsible for the philosophies we choose, as expressions of our most intimate natures.

By 1909 James's root experience was articulated as follows:

> Briefly, the facts I have in mind may all be described as experiences of an unexpected life succeeding upon death. By this I don't mean immortality or the death of the body. I mean the deathlike termination of certain mental processes within the individual's experience, processes that run to failure, and in some individuals, at least, eventuate in despair. . . . Sincerely to give up one's conceit or hope of being good in one's own right is the only door to the universe's deeper reaches. . . . The phenomenon is that of new ranges of life succeeding on our most despairing moments. There are resources in us that naturalism with its literal and legal virtues never recks of, possibilities that take our breath away, of another kind of happiness and power, based on giving up our own will and letting something higher work for us, and these seem to show a world wider than either physics or philistine ethics can imagine.[5]

This realization enabled James to see the way he had thought in the past in a different light: "I had literally come to the end of my conceptual stock-in-trade, I was bankrupt intellectually, and had to change my base."[6] He came to the realization that "an *intellectual* answer to the intellectualist's difficulties will never come"; that "the concepts we talk with are made for purposes of *practice* and not for purposes of insight"; and that he needed to learn "to think in nonconceptualized terms."[7] It was at this point that James broke company with the prevailing modes of thought and articulation.

As against the dominant intellectualism or absolutistic rationalism, which postulated a "static, timeless perfect absolute,"[8] James proposed what he termed the "pluralistic" conception of God as "the only way of escape"[9] from the "foreignness" of the absolutistic conception, the only escape from its inability to make sense of either divine or human action, its inability to affirm any real connection between the human and the divine. In James's pluralistic conception God is thought of as having an "external" environment, and thus as finite and able to act in a finite setting, able to engage in a dramatic struggle of ongoing creation that we can either join or hinder. In this way of thinking, in which reality is "more like a federal republic than like an empire or kingdom,"[10] "we are indeed internal parts of God and not external creations":[11] "because God is not the absolute, but is himself a part when the system is conceived pluralistically, his functions can be taken not as wholly dissimilar to those of the other smaller parts,—as similar to our functions consequently."[12] This enables us to avoid "abandoning the real altogether and taking to the conceptual system":[13]

> The believer finds that the tenderer parts of his personal life are continuous with a *more* of the same quality which is operative in the universe outside of him and which he can keep in working touch with, and in a fashion get on board of and save himself, when all his lower being has gone to pieces in the wreck. In a word, the believer is continuous, to his own consciousness, at any rate, with a wider self from which saving experiences flow in.[14]

The pluralistic conception, then, enables us to be faithful to our most intimate experiences, and to find a way of thinking that serves these experiences and not just our need for intellectual order. It gives us a way to understand both our limitations and our possibilities, and, in the latter, to affirm God acting with us and through us in our better moments. This understanding, James hoped, would open up a "new era," both in his own life and in the larger life of the culture as well.

III

The very same themes of death and survival emerge in perhaps even greater intensity through the experience of a young Jewish woman who was martyred by the Nazis. Etty Hillesum's recently published journals, spanning her life from 1941 to the time of her death in 1943, tell the story of a young person's struggle to find meaning and vitality in the midst of a world of disruption and atrocity.

In Hillesum we see a very compact presentation of coming to spiritual maturity, and the sense in which this development is induced by the horror of twentieth-century circumstances. First, as with James, there is the moment of conscious decision that life is in fact worth living, despite heavy evidence to the contrary, evidence having to do with death in ways up to now unimagined. This is followed by the turning from conceiving of God as "out there" to experiencing God "in here," in the depth of her being: "I imagine that there are people who pray with their eyes turned heavenwards. They seek God outside themselves. And there are those who bow their head and bury it in their hands. I think that these seek God inside."[15] She takes up the latter approach, which she practices in her meditation: "So let this be the aim of the meditation: to turn one's innermost being into a vast empty plain, with none of that treacherous undergrowth to impede the view. So that something of 'God' can enter you, and something of 'Love' too."[16]

This understanding and experience of God moving from within both necessitates and orients work on the self. In fact, this work is seen as the only real solution to the enormous hatred which infects the social situation of the Third Reich: "Each of us must turn inwards and destroy in himself all that he thinks he ought to destroy in others."[17] Her initial metaphor for this work is that of a well: "There is a really deep well inside me. And in it dwells God. Sometimes I am there too. But more often stones and grit block the well, and God is buried beneath. Then He must be dug out again."[18] Later the metaphor shifts to that of unblocking a path: "If only you make certain that your path to God is unblocked—which you can do by 'working on yourself'—then you can keep renewing yourself."[19] It becomes possible to live out of "a vast and fruitful loneliness"[20] that is somehow identical with God and Love.

In living this way we must "forgo all personal desires and surrender completely,"[21] dare to open ourselves to "cosmic sadness" and to "bear your sorrow,"[22] and learn to "eliminate every conventional bulwark. Only then will life become infinitely rich and overflowing, even in the suffering it deals out to us."[23] In this practice "thought doesn't help; what you need is not causal explanations but will and a great deal of mental energy":[24]

> You can't think your way out of emotional difficulties. That takes something altogether different. You have to make yourself passive then, and just listen. Re-establish contact with a slice of eternity.[25]

Finally, what helps most is helping others: "You have to forget your own worries for the sake of others."[26] The ability to "repose in oneself," which is the same as reposing in God, comes with *hineinhörchen* (hearkening unto):

Truly, my life is one long hearkening unto my self and unto others, unto God. And if I say that I hearken, it is really God that hearkens inside me. The most essential and the deepest in me hearkening unto the most essential and deepest in the other. God to God.[27]

The repose of this hearkening is achieved as we "clear the path towards You in them,"[28] in others, so that all people will be "turned into a dwelling dedicated to You, oh God."[29]

In the end this kind of relationship of helping others is extended to helping God himself: "And if God does not help me to go on, then I shall have to help God."[30] Near the time of her death, while she is voluntarily working in the hospital of the transit camp at Westerbork in eastern Holland, Hillesum becomes eloquent on this theme, in what is perhaps the most striking statement to be found in her journals. It is found in the form of a prayer:

But one thing is becoming increasingly clear to me: that You cannot help us, that we must help You to help ourselves. And that is all we can manage these days and also all that really matters: that we safeguard that little piece of You, God, in ourselves. And perhaps in others as well. Alas, there doesn't seem to be much You Yourself can do about our circumstances, about our lives. Neither do I hold You responsible. You cannot help us but we must help You and defend Your dwelling place inside us to the last.[31]

On September 7, 1943, Etty Hillesum was transported to Auschwitz, where she continued to serve others until she was killed on November 30.

IV

In both James and Hillesum, then, we see emerging through intense experience—as though the full weight of the twentieth century were upon them—the direct and personal manifestation of that possible way of being that had not been sustainable by the culture of the traditional period of the West, though it has appeared from time to time as that magnificent "other suggestion" to which Whitehead refers. But how are we to understand and draw guidance from the surviving of James and Hillesum? How are we to lay hold of their experience of "the God who appears when God has disappeared" or of the yes that follows the "final no" in a way that can be effective in our own struggles? How, indeed, are we to interpret and nurture our own experiences of a similar sort?

In historical terms the emergence of this possibility in the twentieth century can be understood as a return to the orientation of immanence in religion and life—the orientation to God "in here" rather than "out there," as dynamic rather than static, as present rather than displaced. Throughout the ancient and medieval periods both transcendentalist and immanentist orientations were present in Western culture, but in the modern period emphasis was placed heavily on the side of transcendence, and there was an active suppressing and repressing of the immanence dimension.[32] As the religious attitude, the religious *a priori* or generalized presupposition of religiosity, faded with the unfolding of the modern era, the secular temper of Cartesianism and preference for technological reason gradually displaced God with "transcendent" scientific objectivity and the atomistic "self" of what has come to be known as Western individualism, and with a faith in consumerism as sufficient to a human life. But now, as the modern period begins to shade into something new, some postmodern way that has not yet been named, we see a surprising return of the spiritual dimension.

Return in our time occurs in the aspect of immanence, which then begins to flow into a culture that had not only fallen into religious slumber but had also avoided aggressively the immanent in its previous religious history. Given this lack of recent experience with the immanent, it is understandable that one of the chief responses to the return of immanence spirituality in the present is denial, and the fundamentalist reassertion of "traditional" transcendentalist forms of religion and culture.

Another chief response to the new return of immanence religiosity is an enthusiastic and frequently naive embracing of it. We see this embracing occurring throughout the twentieth century, in the movements of "progressivism," "new culture," or "human potential" that come and go—alternating as the prevailing mood with fundamentalist "traditionalism" (with both moods reflecting and reacting against a background of numbed secular consumerism). In our time, though the immanence orientation is not presently at the forefront of cultural preference, we see its renewal in the New Age movement. Erich Fromm states the essence of this kind of movement:

> I have said that man is asked a question by the very fact of his existence, and that this is a question raised by the contradiction within himself—that of being in nature and at the same time transcending of nature by the fact that he is life aware of itself. . . . No matter how often he *thinks* of God or goes to church, or how much he believes in religious ideas, if he, the whole man, is deaf to the question of existence, if he does not have an answer to it, he is marking time, and he lives and dies like one of the million things he produces. He *thinks* of God, instead of experiencing *being* God.[33]

But the potential costs of inherent ambiguities in the experience of God from within in post-traditional culture run very high—as Western religious fundamentalists point out time and time again. Robert N. Bellah points this out clearly in relation to the modern situation generally: "No doubt the possibilities for pathological distortion in the modern situation are enormous. . . . Yet the very situation that has been characterized as one of the collapse of meaning and the failure of moral standards can also, and I would argue more fruitfully, be viewed as one offering unprecedented opportunities, for creative innovation in every sphere of human action."[34] At its best the New Age movement both reappropriates what was lost in the rush of the modern period and steps forward, advances the capacity of the human spirit to respond to life—and to God. It presents the same positive aspect that is demonstrated in the life and work of James and Hillesum, and to which Tillich and Stevens point.

On the negative side, however, the New Age movement and the post-traditional mood it presents can become license for anything, a legitimation and reinforcement of the narcissistic tendencies that now infect Western culture, and even a naive opening up to irrationalism and demonic realities. Too frequently the New Age movement emphasizes immanence to the point of denying transcendence, and not only the transcendent dimension of God, but the corresponding human necessity of transcending the immediately given as well. Hence there is an absence of order, authority, reason, and discipline; in effect, the "work" which Hillesum emphasizes is lost. When the message of popular movements of this sort about recovering immanence is broadcast across the land, it is received by some who are ready, who find in these movements the encouragement they need to sustain the revival of religion in their lives, which they intuitively recognize as necessary and already occurring. But the same message falls on other ears also, the ears of those who are inclined to self-absorption and dangerous experimentalism, as well as those who are limited in their resources of interpretation and discipline and therefore vulnerable to all sorts of confusion about "peak experience" and "experiential transcendence." Whitehead reminds us: "Great ideas enter into history with disgusting alliances. But the greatness remains, nerving the race in its slow ascent."[35]

V

We must ask, then, what is required to save and actualize what is positive in the post-traditional rediscovery of immanence, the sense in which it contains authentic stirrings of the religious or the presence of God. Clearly part of both saving what is good in this discovery and guarding against its destructive side is that we need to maintain or rediscover the transcendent dimension and the "work," the attention to proper practice, where one aspect of the work is that of interpretation—relating immanent and transcendent in both understanding and action, theory and practice. But where do we find this interpretation on the contemporary landscape?

In relation to the critical problem of healthy appropriation of the immanent, and integration of it with the transcendent, I would identify two
sources of help that offer themselves to us, though each is limited in a crucial
respect.

The first source of help is the personal testimony of the sort we have
from James and Hillesum. What they present us with is not just intellectual
formulation but autobiography, *story*, the full concreteness of personal
struggle, including process and practice, as well as interpretation.[36] Of course
the problem with these narrative sources is that their usefulness presupposes
some principle of knowing the great stories from what Whitehead calls the
disgusting: some way of distinguishing which of the many narratives of this
individualistic century are actually significant, and which are merely sensa-
tional, frivolous, or even dangerous. Without such a principle of distinction
we are at the mercy of the subjectivism and relativism of our era.

A second source of help to the attempt to articulate and be faithful to
the "survivor's wisdom" of the post-traditional present lies at the heart of
that frequently confused cultural subtradition called "liberalism." Genuine
liberalism, as opposed to the many distorted statements and criticisms of it,
arises from the experience of the simultaneity of immanence and transcendence that occurs quite naturally in the midst of vivid relatedness. Human
beings are capable of having this crucial experience in all kinds of relationship—with God or the ultimate conditions of existence, with nature or the
earth, even with the self, and perhaps most profoundly in our relationships
with other human beings.

I would suggest, then, as sources and mentors for our contemporary
efforts, the great liberals of the twentieth century with whom we have been
in dialogue throughout this inquiry—Arendt, Buber, James, Whitehead, and
Hillesum.

At this point I would also add John Dewey, who is particularly helpful
in the attempt to remain faithful to relational experience, the attempt to
avoid (or accept the death of) the Western temptation to refuse and seek
escape from the relational quality of existence by displacing the crucial experience of relatedness into static systems of thought and belief. Dewey repeatedly reminds us that our culture has been weak in its understanding of
experience, and thus also has had difficulty identifying and affirming the
presence of the divine—as well as the real and full presence of other human
beings.[37] On the constructive side, he helps us move beyond intellectualism
without falling into the irrationalism that characterizes so many of the twentieth-century attempts to deal with the problem. Dewey and the other great
liberals of this century are distinct precisely in that they help us identify our
problem of displacement from relational experience through intellectualism
so that we might, in the words of James, "return to life."

Liberalism, understood in this way, is very much alive and even enjoying a revival in current work in philosophy and theology. In philosophy, for example, Richard J. Bernstein identifies the theme of "community and cooperation" as one that is commonly shared by many thinkers who are prominent today, including Alisdair MacIntyre, Richard Rorty, Jürgen Habermas, Hannah Arendt, and Hans-Georg Gadamer.[38] In theology and religious studies we see emphasis on truth as aletheia, as an uncovering, revealing, or manifestating of reality rather than as a construct of human reason, and on conversation or relatedness as the critical space in which manifestation occurs. The recent work of David Tracy, for example, provides an understanding of human solidarity based on relatedness, and defines the "hermeneutical task" of theology as clarification of the terms of genuine conversation—so that participants "are there not to play their own game, but to lose their usual self-consciousness in the movement of the play itself."[39]

From the standpoint of this inquiry, however, the question arises as to how these hopeful developments of liberalism become actualized in transformative practice, how they enable us to remain faithful to the experience of being fully human. Here we come upon the limitations of twentieth-century liberalism. For liberalism, despite its insistence on experience and immanence, has been remote from practice. It has thus, quite ironically, failed to escape the very intellectualism it deplores, rendering it ineffective for the immediacy of transformation, both personal and political. Twentieth-century liberalism has spoken from the "outside," concerning itself with demarcation of the crucial nexus of relatedness, but it has failed to enter in and engage the actual work of transformative practice within that nexus.[40]

William James provides a good example of the problem. James had great insight into the inner lives of other people, and his influence on Western intellectuals and such social programs as Alcoholics Anonymous has been profound. Yet there is no evidence that he himself was engaged in any consistent discipline of the inner life beyond his essential experience of death and rebirth, his central realization that "sincerely to give up one's conceit or hope of being good in one's own right is the only door to the universe's deeper reaches." In fact, he seems to have maintained himself as an outsider to the "religious experience" he took as his subject matter, exhibiting "the irony of availability" we have discussed earlier. Indeed, his genius itself seems to have involved a withholding or excluding of himself from what he studied, a sort of post-traditional asceticism. Like Franz Kafka's character in the story entitled "The Hunger Artist," James refuses nourishment, speaking about transformation, not from transformation, and about the "varieties" of it rather than recommending any particular practical method, except that of sheer will and his decision to believe in "a *more*" and a "wider self from which saving experiences flow in." There is an absence of connection between what James reports as a scholar and what he endured as a person, exhibiting his own form of the mind/body dichotomy; for all that is interesting and charming about his work, it is as though that which was most significant remained hidden, unspoken—perhaps even to himself.

We can catch a glimpse of what is needed in the writings and life of Etty Hillesum. She speaks both of and from the work of meditation through which "your path to God is unblocked," the work beyond thought through which we can simultaneously repose in ourselves and repose in God. And she specifies the necessity in this work of helping others, of "forget[ting] your own worries for the sake of others." But Hillesum's writing is fragmentary and undeveloped. For she, like Socrates and Jesus, was executed. (James, on the other hand, died of a heart ailment and in some anguish arising from a sense of the incompleteness of his work.)

The struggle of liberalism to move beyond its own intellectualism and achieve a genre of practice is perhaps most visible today in the debate about Richard Rorty. Rorty was once an analytical philosopher, a participant in that recently dominant school of philosophy that exhibits the Western intellectualism at its extreme. Arising out of the Western desire to achieve a universal logic and method of linguistic analysis, this school, I think it is fair to say, became more and more technical, turned in on itself, "professionalized," and thereby isolated from actual human experience. Rorty's career is interesting because it represents a process of defecting from this school, and hence also the unraveling of Western intellectualist philosophy.

In his more recent work, Rorty disavows foundationalism and "philosophy" as attempts to achieve security through conceptualization, embracing the full contingency of our human situation and the impossibility of metaphysics. He recommends that we replace "argument" and "theory" with narratives of self-creation: "We need a redescription of liberalism as the hope that culture as a whole can be 'poeticized' rather than as the Enlightenment hope that it can be 'rationalized' or 'scientized.'"[41] But there are enormous questions in this poeticizing project.[42] For our purposes, the chief question is the same as that which arises from the personal-chronicle approach—that of subjectivism and relativism. For Rorty's liberalism rests on nothing other than the contingent preference of some people to "avoid cruelty," and to protect the private spaces in which "self-creation" could mean almost anything. Hence Rorty's work turns out to be not very helpful in practical terms, except to declare that we need to move beyond our obsession with foundationalist thought. But he himself remains intellectualist in his anti-intellectualism, arrested like Nietzsche in the negativity of revolt against intellectualism without going further, into a positive vision of meaning and relationship and the constructive value of the intellect. Rorty's work, then, can be seen as a flamboyant sort of manifesto, a decisive identification of the problem.

So the problem remains. It might now be described in terms of two halves of a circle. On one side there is the sheer immediacy of our experience of "surviving," of immanence, of being fully human. On the other side there

is the inevitable abstraction of this experience that is contained in any interpretation, any "theory." Each side is fully dependent on the other, since
human experience, in order even to be recalled or remembered, requires
interpretation, and interpretation inevitably predisposes us to certain kinds
of future experience. The problem is to find a way of interpretation that is
adequate to our fully human experience.

A partial solution to our search for transformative practice is addressed
by twentieth-century liberalism. For liberalism has discovered that within
traditional intellectualism "practice" was usually understood as secondary
to and derivative from the interpretive "theoretical." Hence practice came to
be seen as merely a matter of implementation or application of a foundationalist metaphysic which is acquired in a realm of pure thought. Against this
orientation, liberalism has discovered that in actual life—as opposed to
merely intellectual formulation—practice is really the prior term, that theo-
rizing itself is a form or aspect of practice, and that therefore a proper understanding of the practical needs to include the theoretical as one of its
dimensions. This is required in order to remain faithful to the kind of our
full human experience that centers on what we might call radiant paradox—
the paradox of simultaneous immanence and transcendence; in traditional
Christian terms, of particularity and universality; in Tracy's terms, gaining
genuine self through "los[ing] our usual self-consciousness in the movement
of the play itself." This essential paradox of real life and relatedness, that
toward which our practice aims, is not susceptible to any easy intellectual
formulation, or general political policy or program. Twentieth-century liberalism has discovered that the nature of the intellect is such that it can only
point to radiant paradox; it cannot contain or resolve. The intellect is able to
provide resources of identification, discipline, and interpretation, but it cannot by its nature yield a formula or technique for the life of full presence; in
its proper function it may serve what is vital and sustaining in life, but it may
never usurp or grasp that position. But while liberalism has discovered this
fact, in both personal development and political policy, it has not been able
to venture the further step into the zone of full practice, which is necessarily
concrete, local, specific.[43]

Returning to the mind/body dichotomy, we can say that liberalism has
understood the problem of mind as it came to be defined in modern Cartesianism, and even the problem of dichotomizing, but it has failed to move
beyond identification of the problem to living affirmation. The irony is that
while liberalism has been concerned with practice right along, and has
insisted that practice must include theory, it has not been able to acknowledge that its own practice has been for the most part restricted to theory.
Here, it seems, lies the deeper crisis or death of liberalism that has caused it
to devolve into laissez-faire individualism and amorphous poeticizing and to
call forth from others cynicism, suspicion, and claims of hypocrisy.

So we end in dilemma. Both sources of help for appropriation of the orientation of immanence now available in our era are flawed. The personal-chronicle or narrative approach is liable to the peculiarities of individual experience or subjectivism and is too much at the mercy of relativism. Liberalism on the other hand is too distant, too objectivist, abstracted from the concreteness of practice—or else, in the case of Rorty and others, it capitulates to subjectivism. What we need is something that is both subjective and objective, practical and theoretical, and something beyond the opposition between the two, beyond the tendency of each to exclude the other. We need a unifying genre through which the mimetic and the didactic become identical. Madeleine L'Engle, one who perhaps comes closest to speaking directly from the nexus of transformative practice, says that what we need is a form of writing that is also a form of prayer.[44]

We are, then, lacking a solution to our problem of finding resources that enable us to remain faithful to our experience of surviving, immanence, and full human presence. But perhaps this lacking—this emptiness—can be, to paraphrase the Kyoto school, the occasion of fullness. Perhaps we are now prepared for direct encounter with Jesus and Socrates.

TWELVE

The Mystical Christ

I

*E*AST AFRICAN CHRISTIANS call Jesus "the first ancestor"; Lakota
Sioux call him "the buffalo calf of God"; and in Ghana he is referred to
as "the great snake."[1] In a way that is analogous to our possession of pho-
tographs of Planet Earth from outer space, today we have spread out before
us representations of the face of Jesus from many different times and places.
This multiplicity raises the question: What is the one Jesus behind the many,
the one in the midst of the many, or the one as the many? As in cultural relativism generally, do not the many cancel each other out, leaving us with
shades of gray and indifference?

Seeking encounter with Jesus today, we first confront the fact of the
"manyness" of his appearance. From the standpoint of our life in the post-
traditional present, there is no avoiding this fact; there is no simple going
back to the "historic" Jesus or the "fundamental" Jesus. (Escapism and
denial of this fact are basic to the fundamentalist movements of our era; they
deny our own incarnation in the present, including our historicism and relativity.) When we ask about Jesus in the post-traditional situation, we are
confronted with no single image but with a kaleidoscope of many faces. In
order for us to find the genuine and singular presence of Jesus, the one in the
midst of the many, we must first confront the plurality of his manifestations
in history, and the question: How could or can Jesus be one if he appears as
many?

Jesus as the Christ has presented the most difficult and most central
problem in Christian theology. Most Christians have acknowledged that in
his essence he is both human and divine at the same time. But Christologies
in the West usually have dealt with the challenge of this simultaneity by set-
tling on one side or the other, and on one side at the expense of the other.

In some periods the predominant Christologies or images of Christ have
elevated the human or historical aspect, presenting Jesus as the exemplar of

human potential fully realized, as the highest standard of what humans can become. But something is missing in this view, as is revealed by the fact that Christologies of this type have had a remarkable tendency to degenerate into shallow moralisms, reflective of the particular social-cultural-historical context in which they arose. The divine aspect is missing in this view, and hence also theologically there is neglect of the very palpable experience of human depravity and our consequent need of grace and atonement.

In other periods the predominant Christologies have emphasized the divine aspect, but have usually neglected the human side. In this view Christ is understood as revelation of God, and the human figure of Jesus becomes a mere vehicle, thus denying the reality of Incarnation and Cross, as well as any sense that we can make contact with the Christ event within the contours of ordinary human experience.

Much of Christian history is characterized by the oscillation between these two approaches, reflecting the two prevailing stances of Western culture sometimes referred to as free will and determinism. But these are not the only stances. Other orientations that emerge at times, including Whitehead's "other suggestion," can be indicated by reintroducing the terms "transcendent" and "immanent." The human- or historic-Jesus orientation has been associated almost exclusively with the immanence dimension, and its difficulties can be seen as absence of transcendent reference: Jesus is so much "in here" that he dissolves into the culture of the time (in much the same way that the critical insights of the New Age movement are in danger of melting into the culture of Southern California). Likewise the divine-Christ orientation has been associated equally exclusively with the transcendence dimension, and has suffered from absence of immanent reference: Christ is so much "out there" that he never really touches down on earth. But there have been other possibilities as well, correlating with the fact that the historic Jesus has sometimes been linked to the transcendent, and the divine Christ to the immanent; and both historic Jesus and divine Christ have been understood sometimes in relation to the simultaneity of transcendence and immanence.[2]

The point of these distinctions is not to open a full investigation of the relationship between conceptions of Jesus Christ and periods of Western history, but rather simply to underline the fact that Jesus appears in different ways in the Western history of culture, not to mention his many appearances in non-Western cultures. But our awareness of this fact—of the many "faces" of Jesus—does not mean that Jesus appears in all ways today, or that our awareness of so many appearances is necessarily the "highest" or most mature viewpoint. There is no way for us as humans to avoid the particularity and limitations of culture and history, to "transcend" in the sense of moving outside of our human limitations. In fact, our very awareness of the many appearances of Jesus in different periods and cultures can result in distancing, a false sense of transcendence, and an absence of any concrete engagement—the relativistic grayness and indifference. The irony of "availability," as we have seen in the ambiguities of the "many ways" approach to the plurality of religion so common today, is that we are unable to find the singularity of Jesus in the midst of the many. We float in the outer-space perspective of our time, able to admire the marvelous diversity of life on this earth, but unable to be engaged in real relationship and practice.

However, there is one particular way of encountering Jesus that is characteristic of the immanence spirituality and the experience of "surviving" in our time. He is encountered, within the manyness, in the relatively unusual mode that brings divine and immanent together—the mystical or, as William Johnston calls it, the cosmic mode.[3] This orientation has been available only rarely in Western history, and not in any sustained way since the period of the medieval mystics who become so attractive today.[4] And one very powerful locus of the mystical today is right in the midst of East-West dialogue.

II

In order to pursue the encounter we seek, then, I propose that we turn to the work of someone who stands very near that locus: the work of William Johnston, especially his *Christian Zen: A Way of Meditation. Christian Zen* opens with Toynbee's statement about the meeting of Christianity and Buddhism as what is most deeply significant in our era. In light of this, Johnston proposes to speak about how Christianity and Zen have met in his own experience during the twenty years he has lived in Japan as a Roman Catholic priest, and he offers some conclusions that are distinctly practical in nature.

Beyond this modest beginning, though, he is proposing nothing less then the renewal of Christianity through meditation and reappropriation of its contemplative aspect. This can be accomplished through contact with Buddhism, because this offers one the possibility of "practic[ing] Zen as a way of deepening and broadening his Christian faith."[5] This is crucial for Johnston because it is necessary for Christianity to be "renewed at its very heart, that is to say, at the mystical level."[6] What Zen offers, then, is a *method* that Johnston sees as basically compatible with Christianity—hence "Christian Zen." Before turning to Johnston's practical suggestions as to how Christians can achieve renewal at the mystical level through Zen, I think it is helpful to look at some of his other works as a way of grasping the full dimensions of his approach.

Johnston cites Whitehead on the dwindling influence of both Christianity and Buddhism—due, he says, to their refusal of dialogue. In its self-imposed isolation Christianity, locked up in the limitations of its own forms of thought, became rigid and forgot the contemplative or mystical dimension.

It became tied up with "words, words, words," with rationalism and discursive prayer, with an inability to go "beyond the emotional and intellectual consciousness to the deeper, more unified, intuitive or mystical consciousness."[7] In fact, Johnston characterizes the whole of Western civilization as having become "horribly one-sided and unbalanced, so much so that serious people cannot see the distinction between a computer and a man."[8]

In the 1970s many in the West and in the Church became aware of this condition, and there developed a longing for mysticism: "People are now looking for silence, for depth, for interiority, for what has traditionally been called contemplation. They want something that opens up deeper layers of consciousness, bringing into play the more subtle and mystical facilities of the mind."[9] This awareness and longing broke down the barriers to East-West dialogue, and there opened up the possibility for Christianity to be nourished and developed through its meeting with Buddhism, as it had been nourished and developed through its contact with Greco-Roman thought in its formative period.[10]

However, as important as Buddhism and Zen are to Johnston, they are not important as traditions in themselves. What is of greatest importance to him is meditation and the development of an "authentic Christian meditation [that] is a key factor in healing the wounds of a divided society."[11] Johnston's position is that "whatever develops human potential should also develop Christian faith."[12] Therefore Zen stands as one among several possibilities in developing meditation, including, for example, Transcendental Meditation (TM) and biofeedback. In fact, in Johnston's other books he seeks to develop meditation through dialogue with traditional Christian mysticism (in *The Cloud of Unknowing*) and contemporary science (in *Silent Music*). In the latter work meditation is defined very broadly: "For me meditation, in the last analysis, is the search for wisdom or the relishing of wisdom when it has been found. As such it is a word and a practice that unites us all."[13]

What is crucial to any effort to develop meditation for Johnston is that it be "religious." By this he means that the potential that is released through meditation is a "two-edged sword" that can be used for good or for evil. The "new, more mystical man" who becomes necessary in our time must direct meditation in the search "for ultimate truth, for values, for wisdom."[14] This is what makes it religious, and saves people from "the quagmire of illusion and insecurity and mystical evil."[15] While he speaks of the eventual convergence of the historic religions and of the "remarkable harmony" among those who are mystics or meditators, Johnston says that we must find religion in our own particular tradition. This is so because our traditional past is still part of who we are, at least at this stage in evolution, and thus cannot be denied without certain very real dangers.

With this understanding of his basic approach, we return now to Johnston's practical suggestions in *Christian Zen*, and what he says about the experience of Christ. The book ends with a "postscript" entitled "A Way of Meditation" (which is also the subtitle of the book) that begins with Johnston's saying that people have asked him to write a "how-to-do-it book about Christian meditation." He says, "I recoil from this task because I know that meditation is different from cookery and can only be taught by that great teacher whom Augustine calls the *Magister Internus*, the Master Within. Listen to his voice and you will learn to meditate."[16] Having said this, he goes on to set down some "principles or directives" patterned on the Sermon on the Mount.

This is not really a postscript in the sense of an afterthought or something tacked on, but a concluding statement which flows directly from everything he has said before in the book. And the book, while not anything like cookery, certainly is focused on how to do it—"a way of meditation." Taken as a whole, *Christian Zen* explains "meditation," moving from the theological/intellectual to the practical/experiential, and from Christianity to Zen and back to Christianity; and it finally ends with his statement of the centrality of love in the Christian tradition and his criticism of Zen in this light.

Early on in the book he says that every religion teaches people to pray: "Some religions are poor in theology and organization; but if they have prayer or meditation we can respect them and recognize that they are trying to do their job."[17] He then gives a generic definition of prayer or meditation as involving two key elements: (1) detachment—letting go, renunciation, an art that is very highly developed in Zen; and (2) faith, pointing out that, contrary to what is often said, there is great faith present in the practice of Zen, faith that the deepest recesses of the human personality contain the Buddha nature.

From here he moves to a discussion of "monism and dualism" (chapter 3) in the history of Christianity. He explains that the West has been predominantly, even militantly, dualistic (i.e., God is "out there," transcendent), but that monism (i.e., God is in the depth of "in here," immanent) has been present also, though usually repressed—or worse, persecuted. He says that the West now needs "a touch of this so-called monism,"[18] and that the choice needn't be either/or, that we can affirm the monistic or mystical aspect of reality without denying the dualistic aspect.[19] He concludes by implying that the mystical or monistic orientation, which does not deny the dualistic aspect, or define itself merely in opposition, is the more mature religious form:

> Dialogue in Christian prayer reaches its perfection when it is no longer "my dialogue with God" but "Christ's dialogue with the Father in me." That is to say, the real Christian prayer is not *my* prayer but Christ's prayer. It is the voice of Christ within my soul crying out, "Abba, Father!"[20]

In the next two chapters of *Christian Zen* Johnston tells the story of his own life as a method of meditation or of developing the monistic/mystical awareness of reality. Here he is very careful to emphasize that one must not convert to Zen or disappear into the monistic/mystical, denying the dualistic aspect (echoing what I have observed earlier in this inquiry about the danger of disappearing into "the other"). Rather, one must "stand in the stream of one's own tradition and humbly take what is good and valuable from another."[21] He goes on to say that "things like Zen can help us update and demythologize much of the theology that underlies Christian mysticism."[22]

The movement in his book next is fully back to the center of Christianity with "Christ" (chapter 6). Earlier in his text Johnston has acknowledged the problem of reconciling Christ with the imageless void of Zen,[23] and here he speaks to this question of how it is that "Christian Zen" can be Christ-centered. He begins by saying that in different historical periods Christians have approached Christ through various modes of thought, initially those of Judaism and Greece, and that "if we go to Christ through Zen we find him in a different way from the person who goes to him through Aristotle."[24] For the Zen approach Johnston chooses the traditional Buddhist simile likening words and symbols to "a finger pointing to the moon." This he applies to the New Testament writings of Paul:

> Don't let anyone tell me that Paul is here speaking about some simple reality that can be expressed in concepts and images! Nor is he speaking about Jesus just as he was in his earthly, preresurrection form. For Paul, Christ is a "secret" or a "mystery" or whatever you want to call it, and he keeps pointing one finger after another at the moon that no human eye can descry. The poor scholars get all tied up in Paul's fingers; the mystics turn toward the moon.[25]

For Paul, Christ is at the core of his being, such that in the mystical depths there is no separation between his deepest self and Christ. Johnston proclaims: "Here Jesus and Zen are together. No reasoning. No reflection."[26]

The "Christocentric path of Zen meditation" should be pervaded with scripture and liturgy, and may begin with discursive or dualistic prayer—speaking to God in what Johnston calls the "I-thou approach." But as the practice develops, "the thinking process must simplify, the words must decrease, the dualism must give way to the void of emptiness which is the *silentium mysticum*."[27] Finally one comes to the point where "one's life is hidden with Christ in God": "You will be there, very much alive; Christ is there, very much alive; but you are not conscious of yourself or Christ—because your life is hidden with Christ in God."[28]

Following this central statement, the next five chapters of *Christian Zen* are increasingly practical. They read much like the fourteenth-century classic, *The Cloud of Unknowing*, which Johnston recently edited and introduced, except that in *Christian Zen* he is speaking in the now "demythologized" language of Zen. He discusses breathing and posture and other techniques which aid in the maintenance of inner silence without distraction.

Finally comes the "postscript," and his giving of principles and directives with which to continue to learn from the magister internus. Here he concludes by identifying that internal master with the "blind stirring of love."[29] Though Johnston has previously identified his own Zen as *gedo* Zen, unorthodox or heretical Zen, at this late moment in the text he decisively parts company with Zen. The issue is love: "Zen never speaks of love. . . . For [Zen], sentiments or love for God, even for a God who is my deepest being and my truest self, are a species of illusion or *mayko*."[30] This is "the crux of the matter," where Johnston found it "impossible to practice 'pure Zen' or 'Buddhist Zen'."[31]

III

In response to Johnston, I observe that he comes very close to saying that meditation is meditation—the same in any of the world's traditions, or even in biofeedback or what he refers to as "non-religious" Transcendental Meditation (TM). Stopping short of saying that all meditation is the same, he says that we need to be oriented to our own tradition, because that tradition is an undeniable part of who we are, and because mysticism needs the discipline and guidance of "the religious."

But what remains in Johnston's orientation that is distinctively Christian? His answer is love of God—his point at the very end of *Christian Zen*, and underlined in his other writings by his repeated quotation of the First Letter of John (4:16) from the New Testament: "God is love."

But then what does love of God mean, and who is Jesus? Johnston says at the beginning of *Christian Zen* that we must not lose the historical Jesus in the cosmic Christ;[32] but then he goes on to discuss the cosmic aspect, stating that this can be equated with Buddhist realization, without ever returning to the historical Jesus or anything like relatedness as locus of the ultimate.

In the terms of our larger inquiry, it seems fair to conclude that Johnston indeed does rediscover the mystical, contemplative, or immanent aspect of human experience. In so doing he reconverts modern "mind" back to "spirit," but without addressing the dichotomous relation of spirit to body. The effect is that Johnston returns to a premodern form of world-rejection. This raises the question as to whether we have really had an encounter with Jesus as incarnation of the divine, and how the mysticism Johnston describes is related to the body of our own existence.

Evidence of mysticism in our era signals the Western movement toward a deeper view of reality, a rediscovery of the contemplative dimension that has been neglected and nearly forgotten since the medieval period, a reappropriation of our capacity for "another kind of happiness and power" (James) that comes through "repose in God" (Hillesum). The significance of this rediscovery and reappropriation cannot be overemphasized. Surveying the history of human cultures in the way that becomes possible in our time, it appears that Western humanity in the modern period all but completely forgot a fundamental human capacity. Stated most modestly, modern Western people forgot a form of restfulness or centeredness, a way of immanence or repose that has been essential to virtually all previous cultures and visions of being human. The consequences of this lapse, in terms of what Western people did to themselves, to other peoples, and to the earth during the period of forgetfulness, are beyond estimation. And from this standpoint the recovery of the contemplative or mystical dimension that Johnston articulates can be seen as among the most promising developments of our time.

But with Johnston and others who facilitate the reappropriation of mysticism in general, there are serious questions. In terms of our inquiry, the question arises as to what Johnston's orientation says about our previous focus on the fullness of incarnation as relatedness, dialogue, and conversation. The mysticism in general that I get from my reading of Johnston feels unconnected for me to the body of either Jesus or ourselves. It seems "cosmic" to me in the sense of being extraordinary, supernatural, displaced from the ordinariness of everyday life—disembodied. It seems to correspond with "peak" experience or special experiences that are not connected with incarnated life on earth, with a vantage point that can easily regard the life that is actual as entirely arbitrary or forlorn. In terms of political and ethical considerations this outlook can result in callousness and disdain—or even the wish for annihilation of the troubling body of self and world. The mysticism that Johnston seems to identify, the mysticism in general of our era, seems very similar to the problematic "positionlessness" that troubles Cobb, and Rorty's "poeticizing" that we have come upon earlier in the inquiry.

Returning to the question of how we meet Jesus today, the manyness of Jesus' presentations in history certainly has very significant implications for relatedness and dialogue: it can make us aware of the limitations of any understanding of Jesus, and hence also of the possibility of increasing our understanding through appreciation of the understandings of others. And Johnston's suggestion that above the manyness Jesus is a mystic clearly does enable us to move toward spiritual maturity, though it also takes us full circle back to the troubling manyness with which this chapter began (a manyness that, in fact, is now much expanded, to include the mystics of all traditions). We now see that mysticism in general raises very difficult and dangerous issues, as Jesus becomes a doorkeeper who leads us into a hall full of mystics, including our own authentic self, but also perhaps such cult figures as Charles Manson and David Koresh, who claim to be or know Jesus Christ. It appears that there are "bad" mystics as well as "good," failed mystics as well as successful ones.

But perhaps we have not yet had full encounter with Jesus; maybe we need to meet him again within the hall of the mystical. Could it be that we have not yet penetrated the Western tradition fully or arrived at its deep center, but only penetrated as far as the location of the encounter we seek? Perhaps we have so far been dealing with the "aboveness" or transcendental emphasis of the mysticism in general of our era, such that we have not yet met the full immanence of Jesus as Christ.

For now let us simply accept this question, and the frustration or death of our original expectation about where and how we would meet Jesus. It may be that encounter with Socrates will enable us to move beyond the sense of incompleteness and vexation.

THIRTEEN

The Radiance of Socrates

CULTURES IN THE traditional period of human history can be understood as energized by radiant events, events that overflow any interpretation, events that yield not just ideas but an actual energy or inspiration, a breathing of spirit into the life of the culture. These events or founding visions stand at the beginning, as the beginning, as fundamental responses to the mystery out of which traditional cultures arise. Later these events are encapsulated in a partial way in the scripture or classics of a culture, and institutionalized even more partially in its customs and social structure. Periods of greatness or progress can then be understood as a function of faithfulness to or fuller realization of the energizing event, the movement to greater purity of embodiment. The reverse, of course, is true in the case of cultural decline.

In Western culture there are two radiant events, corresponding to the Greek and Hebrew traditions which join in the founding of the Western drama. These events occur in the form of two persons—Socrates and Jesus. These persons stand at the gateway to Western culture, on either side of its opening out of the mystery of what went before. Ever after, at least for the duration of the traditional period, the West is haunted and driven by these two figures and the attempt to understand them and let them live—to actualize their immortality. In a very real way the substance of Western culture is a conversation about who Socrates and Jesus were and are.

In this conversation about what Socrates and Jesus stand for or mean, and what is the appropriate posture of faithfulness to them, I think it is fair to say that there has been a typical misunderstanding of each. Socrates has been misunderstood frequently as being overly harsh and even as setting people up and mocking them, as simply tearing down what people think they know in order to show them that they do not know what they think they know. I recall vividly a moment in my teaching years ago when, in the midst of a heated discussion of what Socrates was up to in the *Euthyphro*, a zip gun was drawn in the back of the classroom—one student had become so frustrated and convinced that Socrates was an SOB that he drew the gun on his fellow student, who had an equally strong sense that Socrates was about something important. Jesus, on the other hand, has been misunderstood frequently in the opposite direction, as being overly mild or passively accepting. Response to the saving grace of his life has often taken the form of simple acceptance of unconditioned election or predestination, merely intellectual assent to doctrine, or crass notions of "works" and shallow moralisms. My point is that energy has been infused into our culture as much by the conversation about these figures, one that admittedly gets out of hand from time to time with zip guns and Inquisitions, as by any of the various resolutions that have issued from the struggle to find right relationship with them.

Turning now to Socrates in particular, his life and work are presented most fully in the famous dialogues of his student Plato. In the *Apology*, the dialogue that contains Socrates' defense of himself at the trial in which he was condemned to death, we have something close to autobiography, a personal chronicle or narrative that is remarkably similar to those we have discussed earlier—except that this one is in dialogue form (a fact that is perhaps suggestive in relation to our current struggles with genre).

In the *Apology* we see that the distinctiveness of Socrates' career began when he received a message from the oracle at Delphi to the effect that there was no man wiser than Socrates. The ambiguity of this statement, which Socrates understood as a riddle (similar to a Japanese koan), drove him to search out and engage in dialogue people who were reputed to be wise. This lifelong investigation he undertook not for his own purposes, but "at the god's bidding" and as "Herculean labors" in "service to the god."[1] What he found out, again and again, was that those who were thought to be wise actually were not, and that Socrates did indeed possess wisdom, a "certain wisdom": "I have gained this reputation, Athenians, simply by reason of a certain wisdom. But what kind of wisdom? It is by just that wisdom which is perhaps human wisdom. In that, it may be, I am really wise."[2]

Socrates' career consisted of pointing out on the god's behalf that people who thought themselves wise really were not, and of employing among young people his dialectical method of moving to "human wisdom." In the course of this activity Socrates roused such indignation that he was convicted of corrupting youth with unorthodox theories and arguments, and he was executed.

But what is this human wisdom? In my own efforts to enter into the conversation with and about Socrates, I have come to see that there are three essential and necessarily interdependent components to his wisdom: knowing nothing, knowing oneself (the "thyself" of the Delphic injunction), and practicing dialectic. These components are so related that the third is inclusive of the first two: knowing nothing and knowing oneself occur in and through dialectic. It is not at all incidental, then, that the Platonic report on the components of Socratic wisdom is presented in the form of dialogues. The dialogues engage us as readers in the very same process of transformation that they discuss, enabling us to solve the riddle of Socrates' wisdom alongside him. They thereby allow us to participate directly in his solution, rather than just thinking about it or "feeling" it (in fact, both thinking and feeling are specifically frustrated and relativized in the movement to Socratic wisdom). The dialogues evoke this participatory quality by their interweaving of all three components into what is said and done within certain human interactions. The interweaving is how the dialogues achieve their greatness—and their difficulty as well; like the parables of Jesus, they can be grasped at different levels. For the components are not only interdependent, but they must be actualized at the same time as part of a single practice leading toward wisdom; they are not to be regarded as separate steps. Again, the third component is inclusive: knowing nothing and knowing oneself become possible and are developed in the context of a particular way of human relatedness. Dialectic, as the inclusive practice, is then synonymous with philosophy, the love of or friendship with wisdom.

The first component is "knowing nothing": "I do not think that I know what I do not know."[3] This not-knowing of Socrates is clearly not the confession of simple stupidity or ignorance, nor is it merely a ploy to disarm or confuse those with whom he is in dialogue. Neither is it only a statement of modesty, knowing that what ordinarily passes for wisdom is worth little or nothing in light of what is really important. There is something deeper than knowing in the usual sense of that term: human wisdom or this deeper kind of knowing consists not in the mastery of doctrine or formulation, not in the knowing of particular things, but rather in the actualization of a power or capacity. We might say that wisdom entails coming into contact with the very source of knowing, rather than only with particular things that are known. In the midst of a certain kind of relationship Socrates is able to know nothing in the sense of suspending his lower forms of knowing, in such a way as to become transparent to Truth.

However, there is an undeniably private and hence mysterious quality to this first component of knowing nothing. It is the "mystical" and "strangeness" aspect of Socrates that has been discussed—and not discussed—over the centuries. Though we have no complete testimony as to the content of his method or practice, there are some powerful clues as to the meaning of this private aspect of knowing nothing. First, in the *Phaedo*, he says that "those who practice philosophy in the right way are in training for dying and they fear death least of all men."[4] By this and related statements he means that the practice of philosophy leads to a transcendence of the physical and ego-self, and a calm acceptance of the limitations and mortality of the lower senses of self. Second, there are reports from several of the dialogues of Socrates' "rapts" or periods of complete absorbtion in contemplation. In the *Symposium*, for example, he is late for the party because he is standing on a neighbor's porch. Someone suggests that he be interrupted. The narrator says, "You'd much better leave him to himself. It's quite a habit of his, you know; off he goes and there he stands, no matter where it is."[5] Later in the same dialogue it is reported that once Socrates stood like this for twenty-four hours straight.

Though we have no report as to exactly what Socrates was doing in these moments, except perhaps through what Plato later says about contemplation in the *Republic*, we do know that this "standing" was an important part of Socrates' life. We are given another clue in the *Apology* as to the content of this mystical experience: "I am subject to a divine or supernatural experience. . . . It began in my early childhood—a sort of voice which comes to me. . . . In the past the prophetic voice to which I have become accustomed has always been my constant companion, opposing me even in trivial things if I was going to take the wrong course."[6] I think it is fair to assume that his "knowing nothing" is similar to other statements of mystical experience or meditation, as the immersion in a "nothing" that is not negative or merely empty but rather is beyond description and the source somehow of everything (perhaps parallel to the Hebrew sense of God creating the world *ex nihilo*). In this regard it is hard not to see a connection between Socrates' wisdom and the "perspective-less perspective" and sunyata of the Buddhists—what Kapleau, for example, refers to as Socrates' "doing zazen." Clearly Socrates is no stranger to the hall of mysticism himself. And yet perhaps part of the essential riddle of Socrates for us today is that he refuses to describe this hall or to provide advice as to how we should move within it, except in the form of occasional comments "in the language of the mysteries."[7]

The second component appears initially to be the opposite of knowing nothing. This component is stated succinctly in the inscription over the entrance to the oracle at Delphi: "Know thyself." It is not possible to unlock the Socratic power of knowing nothing or to hear the inner voice to which he refers unless one has known one's ego or self in the lower or limited sense. Here the Eastern understanding of ego as being comprised of both emotion and intellect applies. In the *Phaedo*, the dialogue which concludes with Socrates' drinking the fatal dose of hemlock, he speaks of the ego's fear that is likened to a child within us: "You seem to have this childish fear that the wind would really dissolve and scatter the soul, as it leaves the body, especially if one happens to die in a high wind and not in calm weather." The remedy for the limitations of this aspect of the self is to know the fears of this child within, and to "sing a charm over him every day until you have charmed away his fears."[8]

On the side of intellect as opposed to emotion, knowing oneself means knowing what one stands for, what position one takes, one's vocation and commitment in life. With Socrates we see this clearly in his keen awareness of vocation, serving the god of the oracle come what may, even to the point of becoming, as he explains in the *Apology*, "in great poverty as a result of my service to the god"[9]—not to mention his commitment to his community, which he held until death. Knowing oneself in the sense of knowing the intellectual aspect of one's being is visible throughout the dialogues in Socrates' insistence on the ability to give an articulate account as an essential mark of any genuine knowing—he will not tolerate instinctual or intuitive claims to knowledge. Neither will he tolerate disbelief, or confusing the "knowing nothing" with skepticism or the mere suspension of belief. Finally, at the level of intellectual knowing it is necessary, as he says in the *Phaedo*, to "risk the belief" in such things as the immortality of the soul and an afterlife, and to repeat the belief to oneself "as if it were an incantation"—even though "no sensible man would insist that these things are as I have described them."[10] The maintenance of certain intellectual beliefs is necessary in order to sustain the life of encounter that is vital.

Without knowing "the self," the knowing nothing is easily perverted or misplaced; it is mistaken, in both the self and others, for vacant silence, for mere idiosyncrasy or animal spontaneity, or untamed parts of the self surreptitiously claiming supremacy, or for mystical exemption from the human condition. Knowing oneself, in both the emotional and the intellectual aspects, is a necessary though not yet sufficient condition for actualizing the fully human wisdom that Socrates exemplifies and leads us to throughout his life.

The third, and inclusive, component to the Socratic wisdom is that activity and capacity known as "dialectic." By this he means not the rehearsing or memorizing of what others have said, or the ability to track complex arguments for their own sake, but inquiry, discussion, fully mutual encounter with others in pursuit of the truth. Dialectic, as is made clear in the *Republic*, is the highest human capacity; it is the art of asking and answering questions with others in the active and continuing quest for truth, and at the same time it is characterized as the direct perception of absolute good—"at the end of the intellectual world."[11] Dialectic, as both continuing quest and direct perception, is at the heart of the famous "examined life" of Socrates' dictum: "I tell you that to let no day pass without discussing goodness and all the other subjects about which you hear me talking and examining both myself and others is really the very best thing that a man can do, and that life without this sort of examination is not worth living."[12] It is as though the examining is a sort of hygiene, a way of cleaning out the false knowing that is continually generated by our ego-self, so that we can "know nothing" and hence know our self in the sense of being receptive to our own "inner voice." So important is dialectic that Socrates warns: "We should not become misologues, as people become misanthropes. There is no greater evil one can suffer than to hate reasonable discourse."[13]

Socrates, the "gadfly to the city" of Athens, practiced his knowing nothing and knowing himself by enabling others to do the same. And this enabling comes not through delivering secondhand answers in the form of intellectual formulation, but rather in a kind of relatedness that guides people to discover truth firsthand and for themselves. The mark of having attained Truth, therefore, is not the possession of intellectual objects but the activation of a capacity and a way of being, a transformation of the whole person. It is in this regard that Socrates is spoken of as a midwife: he engages us in the kind of interaction that gives birth to our own deep self, within the paradoxical simultaneity of knowing and not-knowing, openness and definiteness. The full Socratic method involves both answering and asking questions within a context of transformative movement toward realization of that which is fully human.[14] The highest ideal for Socrates is neither isolated contemplation nor the holding of correct beliefs, as most readers of Plato's dialogues in the traditional period have assumed, but rather a way of relationship in the world.[15]

Socratic wisdom and philosophy, then, entails the practice of knowing nothing, along with knowing that something which constitutes the self, within the activity of making it possible for others to do the same. The "human wisdom"—the practice of it, the *existence* of it—requires others; it is pluralistic (not relativistic), conversational, and ongoing. Philosophy is the love of wisdom, not the holding of it; it arises at that moment in which it is being sought and practiced. And, in our time especially, it must be remembered that though reason is both the path and the vehicle for Socrates, it is not the destination. Intellect is a means rather than an end, a very powerful tool, but a tool nonetheless—a means of arriving "at the end of the intellectual world."

When it became clear to his companions and students that Socrates would in fact be executed, his friend Crito came to him with a plan of escape: Socrates could easily leave the community that would convict him and live out his days in peace somewhere else. He refused. To do so would have been to violate his commitment to the community by qualifying and confusing his vocation. And so the original act of civil disobedience, the act of publicly and articulately questioning the letter of the law in the name of the spirit of the law with a willingness to accept the consequences, was concluded with an execution.

I think that Jon Moline is right that the meaning of Socrates has been eclipsed by an "intellectualist bias" that has held sway in Western culture since Aristotle (I wonder in fact if it began with Plato's own limitations in his attempt to faithfully present the teachings of his master, with the Platonic resolution of Socratic wisdom into a system of thought in the *Republic* and the later Dialogues). Socrates has been understood, for the most part, not as a person, as a living actualization of the highest human capacity, but rather as a mere literary device for the delivery of what came to be taken as Platonic doctrine. The Socratic energy, the energy that arises from the Socratic practice, has been blocked by intellectualism—yet not cut off entirely; we keep coming back to Socrates himself, receiving what energy we can, attracted, despite our cultural blockage, by his radiance. One of the most telling indications of this intellectualist blockage is the virtual absence of attention among traditional Western philosophers, even among those who claim faithfulness to Socrates, to the place and conduct of "contemplation," of Socrates' rapt "standing," or of any other inner discipline. It is peculiar indeed that traditional Western culture elevated "contemplation" to the status of the highest human activity without attending to the context or method of this activity; it is no wonder, then, that contemplation came to mean merely intellectual remove, the priority of thought over action—intellectualism. Likewise, it is astonishing how little attention is given in Western philosophy to the actual dialectical practice of Socrates and the dynamics of the transformative human relationship (perhaps here we have the creative contribution of feminist philosophy in our era).

Fortunately, however, there is strong evidence that the intellectualist orientation is breaking up in our "post-metaphysical" era, and that Socrates is once again becoming available to us. Underneath the noisy clamor of the post-analytic, post-foundationalist postmodernism, a noise that is so obviously the disappointed protest of those who have just discovered the limitations of the intellect but not yet the positive meaning of this discovery, there is also occurring a quiet revival—a rebirth—of Socrates. I want to underscore this revival by citing two works that seem to me particularly vivid examples of this rebirth.

Jacob Needleman's *The Heart of Philosophy* begins with the problem of our present "metaphysical repression," meaning that the essential part of the human psyche is not "known or honored in our culture."[16] This problem arises because of "the repeated failure of great ideas to penetrate the human heart";[17] the ideas have been present but they have made very little actual difference in the way in which we conduct our lives. He cites St. Paul on this: "The good that I would do, that I do not; that which I hate, that I do."[18] Ineffectuality of the great ideas leads to the danger of "inner death"—"man becomes a thing."[19]

Needleman proposes "philosophy" as a remedy for this condition, and philosophy for him is synonomous with Socrates: "Socrates is a metaphor of an activity of mind that defines what it means to be human. Socrates exists as a metaphor of the structure of man, of myself now and here and my possible development."[20] The crucial "activity of mind" is one of questioning through dialectical encounter with one's self and others. This serves to break down false identities and to open a "channel of virtue" within the person, enabling him or her to overcome the division that exists within by establishing contact with the deeper self that had been repressed. When this happens, development and wholeness become possible, as the wisdom of that deeper self (which is identical or confluent with the ultimate, with God or the good) gradually penetrates and transforms the ego. This critical experience of transformation is found in a certain kind of lucid attentiveness, one which is akin to silence, pure listening, or the "knowing nothing" of Socrates.

Needleman takes great pains to point out that Socrates or philosophy is not a system of thought but rather an activity of transformation, a way of being. The middle part of his book is a detailed account of Needleman's own attempts to engage this activity, and much of the value of his work for readers lies in Needleman's sharing of his actual process and practice. He not only argues that philosophy can be effective today, but he shows us how, in the lives of his students and himself. We are able to see how it is that Socrates "lives" in the dialectic encounter in which we experience healing of our inner dividedness and liberation to become our own true selves.

Needleman is decidedly for the general audience; Robert E. Cushman's *Therapeia: Plato's Conception of Philosophy* is more scholarly in its orientation. But Cushman is even more insistent on the basic point about Socrates. Cushman begins by saying that "Plato's *philosophia*, as a method of education, represents the supreme and most influential attainment of classical Greek thought respecting the way of human salvation."[21] This way of salvation is dialectic, which is a therapy, not a doctrine or a set of propositional truths that exist alongside or apart from encounter:

> Philosophy is a way and a life, a way to a moment of existence in which there is direct confrontation with reality. . . . Truth relating to ultimate reality resists propositional status and cannot be corralled and contained. . . . Truth *as* reality is not something admissible of transference by some men to others. Accordingly, the function of philosophy is that of rightly disposing men toward truth.[22]

For Socrates, knowledge is an *event* that is interdependent with virtue; apprehension of the ultimate structure of Being is impossible apart from *ethos* or balance within the soul.

Plato, according to Cushman, was not familiar with reason as a pure, theoretical, or disinterested function. This orientation came to predominate later in Western culture under the influence of Aristotle, "who was subtly lured by definitive answers of supposedly enforceable demonstrations and who, consequently, was impatient with dialogue and preferred the declarative treatise."[23] In contrast to this way of understanding truth, Socrates' "art of midwifery" centered on "decisional truth."[24]

What Plato discovered in the historical figure of Socrates was wisdom as the combination of knowledge and virtue, as expressed in Socrates' dictum:

"It cannot be that the impure attain the pure."[25] The view of reality that corresponds with this understanding is that "the Eternal comes to be truly mirrored in the human soul by being recapitulated there. The man of wisdom is the true microcosm of essential reality."[26] Dialectic, then, is an instrument or a method for bringing this mirroring into actuality. It operates through the destruction of false opinion, which develops through the domination of the self-deceiving sensuous or ego-powers of the soul. The questioning works a conversion or reorientation of *nous*, the organ of cognition, redirecting it from false opinion toward reality. Dialectic ultimately brings the soul to the point of decision: whether to live in a state of accord with both reality and one's true self or in perpetual internal disagreement and strife.

The breakup of intellectualism in our time provides us with the opportunity to have access to and actualize the immortality of Socrates. But this opportunity is demanding. We are called to live beyond our ego's pretenses to knowing, to develop a stance of modesty from which to learn, in both solitude and solidarity, to know nothing. Yet Socrates tells us that we cannot do this by becoming anti-intellectualists, throwing out our formulations altogether, but only by holding the work of the intellect in a different light, as the examined commitments that constitute our own finite beings—knowing ourselves. And it is perhaps the saving grace of Socrates that he shows us that this way of being, which seems impossible when it is merely spoken of or undertaken in privatistic isolation, is precisely what occurs when we enter into the fully human relationship.

Returning to our earlier theme of death and rebirth, in Socrates we do see the survivor: the way to being fully human opens only with the death of our initial inclinations and egoic senses of certainty, and is sustained by an openness to that ultimate source, guidance, and fulfillment which cannot be named or contained within any formulation. Rebirth into this new way of being is described, in a later Socratic dialogue, in what sounds very much like the language of enlightenment: "Acquaintance with [this way] must come rather after a long period of attendance on instruction in the subject itself and of close companionship, when, suddenly, like a blaze kindled by a leaping spark, it is generated in the soul and at once becomes self-sustaining."[27]

Although what appears to us as the "mystical" element in Socrates remains mostly hidden, as a private or preliminary activity, that which it is preparation for is precisely what the dialogues of Socrates bring to light. Perhaps what Socrates is saying in speaking so little about the mystical is that finally there is no difference between the mystical *per se* and that which occurs in dialectic, or that "the mystical" occurs in its genuine and complete form in relationship, not in isolation. The transformative power of the fully and distinctively human encounter is what those dialogues are about; this human encounter is what happens in them and through them, even for us as readers at the remove of many centuries. In terms of our inquiry, the implication is clear: the mark of true and mature spirituality is not detached, otherworldly purity, but rather full immersion in the world. In Socrates we encounter the radiance of full human presence that occurs only in the presence of others, and that is associated with divine presence.

FOURTEEN

Jesus as Christ

*I*N THIS CHAPTER we seek encounter with Jesus as radiant event, in a way that parallels our meeting with Socrates. Given what has already been said about the mystic Christ in a previous chapter, we need to focus here on the relationship between the mystical and the historical Jesus, the figure of an actual person who appeared at one time and also throughout time in the Western drama.

The time immediately preceding the historical appearance of Jesus was characterized by what Bible scholars call "messianic expectation." The Hebrew people knew their time as an unstable one, as a time of interim. There developed the hope and expectation that God would intervene to resolve the confusion and ambiguity, and for the most part they expected grandeur: a powerful Messiah, riding golden chariots from the sky, coming to right injustices and revitalize an unsteady society. Instead they got a child who was born in a barn and grew up to be a carpenter. He began interacting with people and teaching them a new way of life and spirituality, one that cut across all established social designations. The message he brought can be stated simply: We are saved despite our unworthiness by grace alone; those who would seek to save themselves will be lost, but those who give themselves over to the act of grace will be saved; grace and love are the same; and this teaching comes not from Jesus as a person, at least not in the usual way of thinking of personhood, but from "him who sent me" (John 6:39).

This is the teaching. And yet Jesus is the focus, the locus; somehow everything important is located in the person, in what he did, who he was, who he is—in his actual and ongoing life.

The historical record tells us that there gathered about Jesus some disciples and a following, and, like Socrates, he so threatened the existing powers of society that in the end they executed him. Then there followed various reports of his resurrection and reappearance, and there developed a wide range of interpretation about the meaning of all this.

Because of the association of Jesus with divinity, the new religion of Christianity burgeoned. It moved into the cultural structures of the Roman Empire, which had come to a state of material strength but spiritual evisceration. At the great Church Councils of Nicaea and Chalcedon, three and four centuries after the crucifixion of Jesus, the range of acceptable interpretation about the meaning of Jesus as the Christ was determined, with establishment of the canon and the Roman Catholic Church. This orthodoxy prevailed and was elaborated throughout the medieval period. The Protestant Reformation challenged this elaboration, though not the orthodoxy itself, and sought a return to the original message and meaning of Jesus, and especially to the direct rather than mediated prayer of the individual believer. In the modern period, Protestantism progressively lost its footing as orthodoxy broke down and faded into the background, as both individuals and society more and more came to believe in the presuppositions of science. The Christianity that remained spread out in missionary movements across the earth, and there ensued a vast and confusing plurality of interpretations, amidst a twentieth-century cultural situation that increasingly resembled the first centuries of Christianity.

Without the supervision of orthodoxy, and in the midst of the variety of frequently conflicting interpretations, we are left with the question: Who was and who is Jesus? A great mystic? The Son of God? God wearing a human mask? An exemplary human being? A fanatic? Many have held hope of a definitive and objective answer to this question emerging from the development of sophisticated archaeological and literary methods, and in the discovery of new sources like the Dead Sea Scrolls and the Nag Hammadi Library. But the mystery persists and even seems to increase with the gathering of new information. Jesus remains as a salvic mystery, and a somewhat preposterous story; and some of the faithful still confess, as Tertullian did in the third century: "I believe because it is absurd." In a contemporary reflection of the mystery of Jesus, William Johnston reports that a Zen master working with Christians proposes the following as koan: "What do you mean when you make the sign of the cross?"[1]

It is tempting indeed to give up altogether on the historical Jesus and to focus instead on the cosmic Christ and the approach of individual mysticism. But something fundamental is left out if we do this. Jesus is not an invention and not a discarnate archetype. It is clear enough that such a person lived, and it is of enormous significance that he appears as an historical figure throughout Western history, not as a disembodied message. His face and his cross appear and reappear in the deep textures of the historical drama, energizing.[2] Paul, in the New Testament, describes the essential nature of that presence, that "surviving" of Jesus: "I have been crucified with Christ; it is no longer I who live, but Christ who lives in me; and the life I now live in the flesh I live by faith in the Son of God" (Galatians 2:20). Jesus abides historically in the mystery of his actual life and the variety of his appearances in history. And he abides in the experience of Christians who confess their fallenness and ego-centered refusal of atonement alongside Paul's proclamation of Christ within them.[3] For, as Paul says also, Christians are "always carrying in the body the death of Jesus, so that the life of Jesus may also be manifested in our bodies" (2 Corinthians 4:10).

Where is the meaning? In the teaching or in the life, in the "theory" or in the "practice"—or in both, each informing and validating the other? Jesus has been present in Western history in both senses. To submit to the temptation to emphasize the teaching and forget the life is to miss both Incarnation and Cross, as events in the past that we can never quite get to in the "objective" sense (the way we finally got to, for example, the *Titanic*), and as continuing realities throughout Western history and experience. The plainest fact is that the life of Jesus has been important to our ancestors, and it would seem a typical piece of modern foolishness to decide that he did not exist, or that his existence in what we might call the body of historical time is unimportant, only because we are unable to grasp the historical figure to the satisfaction of contemporary standards of science and journalism. To try to take the teaching and forget the radiance of the life as well as the questions it poses is to run the risk of Docetism, the heresy in which the humanity of Jesus is denied, in which Jesus of Nazareth serves only as a costume for God. Resurrection does not occur without Incarnation and Cross.

The cosmic Christ teaches mysticism, in the sense of an inward-focused union with the divine, as Johnston has shown. The incarnation of the historical Jesus reveals that loving presence with others is the highest or most complete form of spiritual actuality and practice. The two—the mysticism and the presence—are inseparable; here is the fullness of incarnation.

The meaning of incarnation, full immersion of the divine as person in the human condition, fusion of the teaching and the life, is most difficult to comprehend. One might say impossible, or respond best by simply pointing to the images of Jesus' face in the art history of the West, rather than to intellectualized church doctrine and theology. The fusion is even more difficult to accomplish in one's own life—to let Christ "live in me." Difficult though this is, Jesus says it is not foreign to the realm of our deepest experience, if only we would resist the temptation to escape and deny the place within us that corresponds with Jesus' proclamation: "The kingdom of God is within you" (Luke 17:21).

And yet this very New Testament passage is sometimes translated as "The kingdom of God is in your midst" or "among you."[4] In this marvelous ambiguity of translation we have an opening onto the identity of the historic with the cosmic aspect, the life and the teaching. We can point to the significance of this identity between "within you" and "among you" in the form of a story:

In the period of the Old Testament, God created the world and acted upon it from above or outside. As transcendent creator and director, God fashioned human beings "in his own image" (Genesis 1:27), and gave them a single commandment, which was then broken in the original human act of self-assertive disobedience. Because of this disobedience God ejected humans from their home in the garden of original innocence into a world of knowledge of good and evil, toil, and exile from "the tree of life." With this world situation established and the human condition in place, God continued to act from outside the situation, giving commandments, punishing disobedience, and forming covenants with his people through his own act of unconditioned election. History unfolded as the drama of this relationship between God and his chosen people.

Then God changed the human condition. Because "God so loved the world" (John 3:16), he became incarnate himself in Jesus Christ. This act constituted a fundamental change in the structure of reality itself, a new creation. God, in an incredible act of self-negation, became fully immersed in the world as an embodied being (even as he at the same time remained also "out there," as the Father of the Christian Trinity, and immanent but unbodied as the "feminine" aspect of divinity as Holy Spirit or Wisdom).

Jesus as the Christ acted not as himself, but "as the Father has bidden me" (John 12:50). Jesus was a human being who was perfectly open to the divine: he was the perfectly transparent opening through which God entered into and found presence in the world. In the very same ontological event God signified to human beings his fundamental decision, his change in the structure of reality. With Christ as "the new Adam," the conditions of existence were altered: from that moment of incarnation the divine would find its way into the world not through God's sole solitary action from outside and beyond the human realm, but through human action and relation, through ordinary people and their associations. With Jesus as the Christ, God "saved" the world by making it possible for humans to come of age, now able to act not only in response to the commandments of an external parent, but through the internal "law of the Spirit" (Romans 8:2). With that event, human action—particularly the action of "the poor in spirit" (Matthew 5:3)—became the channel or doorway through which God would henceforth continue to enter the world and "dwell among us."

With Christ as Jesus we are shown what we need to do; we need to let God be present through Jesus and thereby through us: "Where two or more are gathered in my name, there am I in the midst of them" (Matthew 18:20). This becomes possible through the Atonement: Jesus, as the sacrificial lamb, offers himself to expiate our sins, and promises that we will be saved if we act neither from external commandment nor from egoic concern with saving ourselves, but entirely through faith—which, miraculously, is the same as our simply being who we really are, accepting the incredible fact that we are loved and saved by God.

In Jesus as the Christ there is full incarnation, no distance between the divine and the human, complete transparency to the ultimate. No displacement of the divine into some "out there," either spatially or in intellectual formulation, is possible. No "religion" is possible; no otherworldliness is possible. The message will not be abstracted from the event—or from our own most profound experience of being fully ourselves. The Cross stands as reminder both of the collapse of our efforts to save ourselves and of the radical intersection of the universal with the particular; as reminder that the universal only exists in the immediacy of actual particularity, and the particular in its full realization is none other than the universal. (Perhaps the Buddhist equation of nirvana [salvation] with samsara [the wheel of life and death] helps us to see this anew.) The most we can say is that the Cross is followed by Resurrection, that "God is love" (I John 4:16); all else that is said, no matter how eloquent, is merely a distraction—or else a preparation for this.

Dietrich Bonhoeffer, the Christian pastor martyred by the Nazis and writer on "religionless Christianity," gives magnificent articulation to the simultaneity of God "in you" and "among you," to the meeting of cosmic and historic, to the identity of mysticism and "being there for others":

> Who is God? Not in the first place an abstract belief in God, in his omnipotence, etc. That is not a genuine experience of God, but a partial extension of the world. Encounter with Jesus Christ. The experience that a transformation of all human life is given in the fact that 'Jesus is there only for others.' His 'being there for others' is the experience of transcendence. It is only this 'being there for others,' maintained till death, that is the ground of his omnipotence, omniscience, and omnipresence. Faith is participation in this being of Jesus (incarnation, cross, and resurrection). Our relation to God is not a 'religious' relationship to the highest, most powerful, and best Being imaginable—that is not authentic transcendence—but our relation to God is a new life in 'existence for others,' through participation in the being of Jesus. The transcendental is not infinite and unattainable tasks, but the neighbor who is within reach in any given situation.[5]

Human relatedness is the locus of the ultimate, the temple, the holy place; we meet God in the eyes of our neighbor. Here alone do we answer the koan proposed by Johnston's Zen master about what is meant by the sign of the cross: the answer is compassionate presence for the other. The Jewish writer, Martin Buber, has given one of the fullest statements of this way of being in our century:

> The You encounters me by grace—it cannot be found by seeking. But that I speak the basic word to it is a deed of my whole being, is my essential deed.

The You encounters me. But I enter into a direct relationship to it. Thus the relationship is election and electing, passive and active at once. An action of the whole being must approach passivity, for it does away with all partial action and thus with any sense of action, which always depends on limited exertions.

The basic word I-You can be spoken only with one's whole being. The concentration and fusion into a whole being can never be accomplished by me, can never be accomplished without me. I require a You to become; becoming I, I say You.

All actual life is encounter.[6]

Jesus' life reveals what that essential deed is; his life is more than just "setting an example" for our imitation. The deed is none other than our own presence. Jesus teaches us to pray or to meditate and to be who we are with others, and that these are finally inseparable, one and the same.

How very peculiar, from a world perspective, that the most enduring Christian sacrament involves ingestion of the god. For a moment, let us look at this crudely: Christians eat their god. The bread and the wine, Jesus' body and blood, are among the most perishable of the world's icons, far more so than, for example, granite or gold or wood. The bread and the wine, unlike other icons, do not remain on the altar; within the wonder of incarnation, they are distributed among us, taken into us, digested, and quickly diffused throughout our whole body and spirit.

FIFTEEN

Death and Rebirth

OUR EFFORT TO penetrate the Western tradition in Part II of this inquiry has been a journey. Looking back at the land we have covered, and across as well at the reports from others who have traveled this same landscape, it seems safe to conclude: There is in our time a definite developmental process through which we as humans come to a greatness that can be an effective force in our lives, one that is intimately associated with Socrates and Jesus.

This developmental process can be summarized as follows: people move from waking up to the actualities of the world situation, including encounter with those who have been "other" in the past, to the idea of integration or inclusion as the solution to our post-traditional confusion. We move from the discovery of "dialogue" (or perhaps "participation") as a way of integration that is distinctively Western to the experience of the failure or death of the dialogical way of being in the Western historical drama and in the world of today. We move from our own occasional experiences of immanence and survivorship to frustration with the inability to speak or live these experiences in any sustained way. We move from a curious rebirth associated with Socrates and Jesus or other survivors in our past, through the discovery that our initial meeting with them had been such as to make them "mystical," detached from life in the present, to the discovery of their presence in our own experience and even as one with us in our own fully human presence in relationship with others.

Access to the wisdom of the West, it turns out, is not access to a particular doctrine or way of thinking, as had been assumed throughout much of the traditional period. While ways of thinking are of great significance for how they position us in life, there is something greater still. The wisdom we seek lies beyond thought, in a way of being that honors thinking but does not worship the objects of thought.

But this is not to say access is easy. For access to the Western greatness is possible only through a movement of spiritual development, one that arises from the fundamental human experience of death and rebirth. Access, then, to the wisdom of the West is more like access to a developmental process—a practice of maturation, a pedagogy or way of nurture—than it is to any particular ideas that may be significant to orientation and stabilization along the way. Unconscious awareness of the exertion this movement will demand of us causes many to avoid it, some through continual philosophical arguments about "the end of philosophy" and ever more bizarre and doctrinaire assertions of relativism. It seems that in our time the prevailing relativism, and its expressions as consumerism, psychic numbing, and opportunistic individualism, are the chief impediments to spiritual development.

Beyond these impediments, however, our post-traditional circumstance also enables us to participate directly in the essential act of human transformation. We are able to see the senses in which that essential act of transformation had been hidden by intellectualism or foundationalism throughout much of the traditional period, just as it is blocked from view by relativism now. What has been hidden or blocked from view by an idolatrous devotion to intellectual formulation is the fact that the Western tradition arises out of and is based on the death and immortality of Socrates and Jesus. When we allow ourselves to really experience the end of tradition rather than simply numb ourselves, the hiddenness is dissolved, and we have the possibility of living unencumbered by the blockage. This possibility arises, strange though it may sound at first, as we come to experience *being* the Western tradition, the sense in which the whole of it—its beginning, subsequent unfolding, and present state of unsteady teetering between lethargy and fanaticism—is identical with our own deep experience. As survivors, an identification of microcosm and macrocosm is realized within us, and through this awareness rebirth can occur. Our post-traditional position is the fertile—and therefore also dangerous—ground of possibility in our era.

Turning to the movement in microcosm, the crucial identification of self and Western tradition begins to be possible with the death or despair of our old ways, including our ways of seeking to capture reality in a settled, intellectualized metaphysic. In the early stages of rebirth there is release, a sometimes euphoric rediscovery of the miraculous sheer fact of existence, of the gift-quality of life itself. We experience direct contact with our own deep vitality and its unity with the larger force of reality expressing itself through us. This experience of immanence leads to the rediscovery of mysticism *per se* as a root human capacity, one that most of our ancestors have been alienated from for a very long time—since intellectualism's eclipse of the immortality of Socrates and Jesus.

In our present inquiry this rediscovery of the mystical was manifest in our first contact with Jesus Christ not as the historical Jesus, but rather as the mystical Christ. It is quite instructive that in William Johnston and others who speak from this stage of development there is very little difference between descriptions of the cosmic Christ and of mysticism in general. (Something similar happens quite often today with postmodern readings of Socrates; he is apprehended not in his full particularity but rather as, for example in the writings of Philip Kapleau, one who "does zazen.") The mystical in general, as a universal human capacity in which we participate in extraordinary or "peak" moments of our lives, becomes available to us first.

But this stage can be quite short, and there unfolds another stage in which people today frequently become arrested. This stage, one that is always latent in the relativism of our era, is nihilism. Its full meaning is indicated in a chilling passage from Nietzsche: "Mankind will will the void, rather than be void of will."[1] Nihilism is testimony to the insufficiency of mysticism in general—a mysticism without the support of understanding and discipline—in the context of frustration over the disappearance of traditional structures of meaning and value. It is the most dangerous form of lostness or homelessness in our time. Understood in this way, it is not surprising that Western intellectuals who become the "postmetaphysicians" and "antifoundationalists" of this century are most susceptible to arrest in this phase. They express their confusion, resentment, and desperation over the loss of metaphysics or the spiritual dimension by "willing the void." And this willing of the void persists in its unhappy logic against logic until, as the Kyoto school points out again and again, there is a radicalization of the experience of Nothingness. This occurs in one of two ways: either in self-destruction or in realization, either in the oblivion of will's act of annihilation or in the enlightenment of the void's transformation of will, either in fascism or in awakening.

If one is able to pass through the storm of nihilism, by whatever grace of fortunate insight or mentoring, the next phase of movement is that of the full encounter with Socrates and Jesus, and experience of the deeper meaning of their "mysticism" as presence for others in the midst of the ordinary. This particular Western mysticism unfolds as we relate to Socrates and Jesus fully, no longer as givers of lessons or rules from outside us or above us, or as exemplars of mysticism in general. In the fullness of relation with Socrates and Jesus we encounter them within ourselves and in our relationships with others, and in messages that are no longer about the "extraordinary" but about the ordinary. It is at this stage of return that the universal and the particular come to coincide in the radiance of human presence. That which is distinctly "Western" comes to coincide with "the human" also, as we learn to hear Socrates' "prophetic voice" in dialogue, and to participate in "the life of Jesus" through being there for others.

Turning to the macrocosmic, to the consideration of dynamics of the culture as a whole, we have seen that this very movement to human maturity through full encounter with Socrates and Jesus has been accessible from time to time throughout Western history, and that it can be understood as the underlying vitality of the Western drama. Awareness of the movement toward and celebration of human maturity has been termed "liberalism" in those times and places where this accessibility has achieved cultural recognition. But this vitality has frequently been lost, or distorted, or misplaced in Western history—even as the fundamental experience of death and rebirth is frequently lost in the urgency and complexity of our own lives as well.

The chief reason for the loss of the liberal possibility has been the strenuous nature of the effort required for coming to maturity, the fact that the way of being we have been describing is possible, as John Stuart Mill said, only among persons who are "in the maturity of their faculties."

While the main mode of avoidance or displacement of maturity in our post-traditional era is that of relativism or nihilism (with its threat of fascism), for Western people during the traditional period it was intellectualism. In intellectualism's attempt to capture in formulations of thought those occasional moments of lucidity or full human presence that come upon us quite naturally from time to time, the desire for certainty and control has overshadowed the urge to be fully human. Throughout the traditional period the intellect, which acts like a hand to grasp experience and place it near or far from us, placed the experience of death and rebirth far from us, all the while constructing schemes of absolute knowledge in the foreground. Hence eclipse; no wonder the vehemence of some post-traditionalists today—there is a sense of having been tricked and betrayed. "Philosophy," instead of questioning us as Socrates does, and engaging us in transformative dialogue, turned in on itself, taking reason as an end in itself instead of as a vehicle and a path to transformation. And "theology," rather than providing practical guidance, was seduced by a vision of correctness of interpretation that caused it to turn away from that which is to be interpreted. Philosophy and theology together turned away from our common humanity, preferring to dwell not among us but in abstraction.

In those rare periods in which the experience of being fully human has been accessible, this fundamental experience has not been well supported in, by, and for the culture as a whole. It has not found the interpretation or ways of thinking and talking that are adequate to it, or the ritual and the discipline by which the experience of surviving can move gradually from being an extraordinary and anomalous occurrence to becoming our ordinary way of being. Largely through the displacement action of intellectualization, Socrates and Jesus have remained "out there," in the realm of the unreachably unusual, the supernatural, and the future. We have seen three variations on the theme of accessibility and failure of support in our inquiry: the appearance of Socrates and Jesus, followed by the establishment of the main modes of Western thought; the seventeenth-century experience and vision of the religious significance of democracy, followed by laissez-faire individual-

ism and scientific objectivity; and the twentieth-century experience of surviving, followed by Nietzschean nihilism and fascism.

But in each time when the experience of being fully human has illumi-
nated an era, or even a small community, some light comes into the world
and something like progress occurs. In order to remain faithful to the experience of surviving in our time, we must learn to draw on the past, in order to
not repeat mistakes of displacement. In positive terms the "availability" of
the past and of the wisdom of other cultures in our era makes it possible for
us to place our own experience of death and rebirth in dialogue with this
fundamental human experience as it has occurred in other periods and
places. And we need to remind ourselves constantly to stay practical, "pragmatic" in the best sense of that term, focused on the full body of human
presence instead of the intellectual aspect exclusively. This requires that we
attend in our dialogues to the conditions under which full presence occurs,
the interpretations by which it is remembered, the disciplines by which it is
nurtured—and the acts with which we step beyond thought and self-consciousness, into the radiant simultaneity of the particular and the universal.

With each breath we take we include in our being some number of the
very same atoms that were breathed by Socrates and Jesus. Within the shared
body of earth we take in the atmosphere, draw from it what is needed for
our continued existence, and let go of what is inessential. Socrates and Jesus
are no more distant from us than the breath we are taking now.

And yet, given the sort of creatures we are, we cannot have access to the
way of being in intimate contact with Socrates and Jesus apart from the very
difficult and delicate movement toward full human maturity. In this movement attention to our actual experience and our practice are essential. But
our thought and interpretation are essential also. For we cannot move into
full human actualization if our thinking refuses the incarnational reality of
Socrates and Jesus, if our interpretation is closed to it, if we deny incarnation
in our effort to achieve the control and discipline we need in life. We need
adequate interpretation as a support for being and doing.

In our post-traditional time, even as the ecological, technological, and
political consequences of the modern urge to control threaten the obliteration
that comes from "willing the void," we have great opportunity, the opportunity of becoming fully human. The very dangers that threaten us also provide
the perspective and the opportunity by which we are able to mature. This
occurs as we discover the full weight of what has been done to life on the earth
by our ancestors, and become aware of the dignity of what had been maintained as "other" in the traditional period. Hence we come upon the ambitious suggestion of our inquiry overall, that revitalization of the West becomes
more rather than less possible through encounter with the other generally and
the Eastern tradition in particular. But, again, this is not possible without
interpretation and discipline that are faithful to the reality of incarnation.

What remains in this inquiry is to give as much real body to the relational way of being as we can: to make the relational vision more deeply rooted, and more near to us in terms of how we are and what we do in each moment. This requires that we return very directly to our concern with practice.

After all, nihilism followed by the personal and cultural oblivion that comes out of fascism is not the only possibility, as is obvious from the richness and complexity of the lives that are all around us—if only we would dare consult them. The oblivion that arises out of logic alone or the disembodied reason of fascism is a subtle threat, one that feeds on our impatience with the contingencies, ambiguities, and incompleteness of incarnation and practice. Life in our down-to-earth ordinary existence remains the greatest challenge to us all. Perhaps at this point Socrates and Jesus help us in a surprising way: by their meeting in a confrontation of their differences. For they are not the same. Despite striking similarities, they disagree. Within the vitality of our pluralistic inheritance they converse, the one emphasizing reason and human effort, the other faith and our need to let go. Maybe the tension and dialogue between Socrates and Jesus can save us from the urge to either will the void or void the will—encouraging us to go beyond this fatal opposition, to find revitalization in the ordinary, in the struggle of relating with others in our actual lives.

PART THREE

RELATEDNESS AS PRACTICE

We can be no more satisfied with mere paternalistic Christianity as an occidental form of world religion, than with mere maternalistic Buddhism as an oriental form of world religion. Both father and mother are needed to provide a real 'home' for us. Yet this should not be seen as only a mixture of Christianity and Buddhism. Christianity, we can see from its mystical tradition, is not totally lacking the maternal, receptive aspect, nor is Buddhism, judging from Nichiren, entirely alien to the paternal and justice-oriented aspect. However, neither in Christianity nor in Buddhism have these two essential aspects been thoroughly and harmoniously realized. But, to cope with the radically changing meaning of the 'world' and the resultant human predicament, Christianity and Buddhism must break through their respective occidental-paternal, oriental-maternal structures. Each must develop and deepen itself to achieve a universal form of world religion.

Masao Abe

Do not suppose that what you realize becomes your knowledge and is grasped by your consciousness. Although actualized immediately, the inconceivable may not be distinctly apparent. Its appearance is beyond your knowledge.

Dogen

From time immemorial men have lived by the principle that "self-preservation is the first law of life." But this is a false assumption. I would say that other-preservation is the first law of life precisely because we cannot preserve self without being concerned about preserving other selves. The universe is so structured that things go awry if men are not diligent in their cultivation of the other-regarding dimension. . . . We are in the fortunate position of having our deepest sense of morality coalesce with our self-interest.

Martin Luther King, Jr.

SIXTEEN

Dialogue and Development

I

WE RETURN TO the original problem. There is a lifelessness to the West at this time in history, a lack of zest and coherent direction, an absence at such an utterly basic level that the culture drifts dangerously, alternating between self-deprecation and shrillness. Within the drift many people's attention is lowered to self-interest and individual survival, a lowering that is overlooked in the midst of the orientation to task in which so many of us become caught—the never-ending list of arrangements and details that overgrows our lives. In this unhappy practice it is rarely noticed that our underlying problem is one of the eclipse or inaccessibility of the deeper source of energy, a cultural entropy, what some have called "the sleep of empire."[1]

I have identified this situation in terms of worldview: the fact that the modern Western lifeway is passing and a new one has not yet fully emerged, and, in a larger frame, that the traditional period is giving way to the post-traditional global period in human history. Clearly a major factor in the frustrating condition of the West is the unsteady transitional quality of our time. Circumstances have changed greatly. We now live in what Martin Luther King called "a world house," a world community of peoples from all over the earth who live together in a single interdependent system.[2] It is here that we meet the Japanese with their claim to have a synthesis that provides "the foundations in thought for a world in the making, for a new world united beyond differences of East and West." As those who are among the first generations of world citizens, we meet our Eastern neighbors as people who certainly are not afflicted with paralysis or malaise. They are vigorous, as though the energy of history were with them.

II

In this inquiry what the Kyoto school has offered is not, as their initial claims may have implied, either synthesis as a static formula or position, or a foreign cultural orientation to which we should convert. Rather, what they have provided is the ground of encounter upon which Westerners can reappropriate and revitalize our own traditions, at the same time drawing on Eastern insights, meeting the Japanese and others as citizens of a world now global. There are three elements to this revitalization.

First, meeting with the East provides us, perhaps after an initial phase of infatuation with their otherness, with the opportunity by which to know the greatness of our own tradition. There is an excitement to this knowing, as we are provoked by the meeting to identify and come into possession of the Western vision, to revitalize and awake from the inner lethargy of the present. Here is an opportunity to resolve the ambiguity of availability discussed in Part II, the problem of the world's cultural resources, including our own, being curiously both near and far from us in the post-traditional moment.

This way of Western revitalization through affirming our own tradition while at the same time moving forward to meet with what has been other is to be distinguished from the way of withdrawing into assertion. It seems clear that it is not possible to understand and appreciate fully the genius of the West—much less actually practice or embody it—through the reactionary exhortations and pronouncements of the neoconservatives and fundamentalists of our era. They too recognize worldview as the problem, but want to solve it by going "back"; and, like the cult leaders from whom they are different only superficially, they want solution by assertion rather than by persuasion. (Here, by the way, is a very basic Western distinction, and the source of our best senses of authority and community: the ideal of persuasive rather than coercive relation.)

Later I will want to come back to the *content* of our reappropriation, but for now the point is simply that meeting with the East provides us with the opportunity of becoming aware of our own tradition in a fresh way.

The meeting of cultures in the post-traditional period has functioned in a similar way for the East as well, and is in fact a major source of the Eastern vitality to which I refer. Thich Nhat Hanh, head of the Vietnamese Buddhist Peace Delegation and a teacher and activist who has become quite well known in the American Zen community, gives testimony to this:

> The rebirth of Buddhism in many Asiatic countries in the twentieth century has been indirectly the work of Western scholars who, by their studies and researches, have manifested their admiration for Buddhist art and thought. It is they who have helped the Asiatics to regain confidence in their own cultural heritage. The same thing is now happening with Zen Buddhism. Because Westerners are interested in Zen many Orientals may return to their own spiritual tradition.[3]

It is interesting to note that Thich Nhat Hanh casts this observation in the context of the fact that "the East, like the West, is witness to the spiritual bankruptcy of man."

The second element of revitalization that arises out of our meeting with the East is that we are enabled to see and actually change aspects of our inheritance that are weak or underdeveloped, or that came to be excluded in the traditional period. In particular, we have seen the claim that the East has a deeper apprehension of reality and of the dynamics of personhood. This deficiency of the West has been associated with the development of an "intellectualist bias," with the Aristotelian preference for objective proof and doctrinal answers, and the later Cartesian narrowing and closing of mind to any higher influence. Contact with the East encourages us to move beyond this orientation to a more profound view of Socrates and Jesus, and to reappropriate our own mystical resources that attend to depth or "inner development" of the person. This development might enable us to overcome what the Japanese refer to as "the curse of individualism," the shallow and materialistic sense of self in its essential isolation from all around it—even from its own body.

A third element of revitalization is that our meeting with the East provides a living, ongoing context for drawing creatively from what "the other" has to offer. In this regard the present meeting with the Kyoto school presents an ideal constitution for emerging world community; it provides a space in which we are able to identify and stand in the integrity of our own position, while at the same time respecting and drawing on the most useful insights of the other with whom relationship is unfolding. Could it be that the encounter with the Kyoto school is ideal because it is the same meeting that occurs in (or as) L.A.?—Except that here it occurs on a different level, with a higher order of discipline and communication, beyond the mere noise and ego-inflamation of the entertainment orientation.

In Part II have resisted the idea of synthesis "beyond distinctions between East and West," because it is so imperative at this time that Westerners reappropriate and reengage our own tradition. But looking beyond the immediate present, as we meet with the East on the plane of the transcultural awareness of our era and in the context of a new world in the making, we can see great potential for continued growth toward a fullness of being human that has not yet been possible in human history. We are able to see and include "the other," all that has been excluded in our traditional past: in addition to the "Eastern" sensibility, we can cite the "feminine," the right brain, and the prehistoric dimensions of full humanity. And certainly the work of integration or inclusion, excluding neither body nor spirit in the movement of becoming more fully universal, more fully human, applies to the East as well, though their work toward achieving this universality is different from ours.

III

But at this point there arises the issue of how much of the other we are able to include and hold in the integrity of our own life, before that life disintegrates into a relativistic chaos. There is a need to maintain a point of balance between a rigid holding onto one's own position on the one hand, such that defensiveness and refusal of inclusion set in, and on the other, an excessive openness in which integration is lost by the inclusion of too much. A healthy integration is a balance that is alive and growing, and it is in light of this that some speak of a new universality, a future transcending of distinctions between East and West, and of such things as a Buddhist who is becoming a Christian and vice versa.[4]

It has been suggested that "dialogue" is that form of meeting and discipline through which we are able to maintain a balanced integration and nurture creative growth. Dialogue, in this contemporary usage, is taken to entail much more than the simple transfer of information. Leonard Swidler, convener and participant in many efforts at interfaith and interideological dialogue, makes this point with dramatic clarity:

> The future offers two alternatives: death or dialogue.... Today nuclear or ecological, or other, catastrophic devastation lies just a little ways further down the path of Monologue. It is only by struggling out of the self-centered monologic mind-set into dialogue with The Other as s/he really is, and not as we have projected her/him in our monologues, that we can avoid such cataclysmic disasters. In brief: We must move from the Age of Monologue to the Age of Dialogue.[5]

The Age of Dialogue signals a fundamental shift in paradigm to a different and more mature way of understanding the structure of reality; it is a shift from the understanding that has prevailed in the West since the Enlightenment, Swidler says, a period which was absolutistic, exclusive, static, and monological. The emerging post-traditional view needs to be deabsolutized (though not relativized), mutual, dynamic, and relational. This new (and renewed) understanding arises from the acknowledgment of our need to change and grow, and the perception that "reality is like our view of an object in the center of a circle of viewers. My view and description of the object, or reality, will be true, but it will not include what someone on the other side of the circle perceives and describes, which will also be true."[6] Hence, in this more mature way of apprehending the real, we each need the benefit of the other's view in order that our own may become fuller and deeper.

Finally, we can observe that this dialogical understanding is consistent with what we have previously identified as the vitality of the Western tradition. The appearance of dialogue as a model for the future through Swidler and others can be understood as an expression of the same subtradition we have seen flickering in and out of Western experience over the centuries: as the radiance of Socrates and Jesus, as the "other suggestion" to which Whitehead refers in Western history, as genuine liberalism, as the "survivor's wisdom" that becomes available again in the present. But we need to emphasize, as does Swidler, that this way of being requires a maturity of personhood that has been rare in the Western past, and that this is precisely where dialogue with the East is most helpful—providing the challenge that moves us to achieve the maturity necessary to recall and sustain the dialogical way that is vital to the West.

The East, as we have seen, suggests that world civilization is achievable through the spiritual development that emerges from the experience of sunyata, Absolute Nothingness, and "positionless position." The West suggests that the same ideal of world civilization may be reached through dialogue, encounter, and relatedness. From the standpoint of the marvelous complementarity of our era, we are now able to venture the suggestion that each of these views needs to affirm the other in order to be complete.

SEVENTEEN

The Practical Turn

THE CONCLUSIONS OF the previous chapter are formal and abstract, distant from the concrete immediacy of our struggles. And in the condition of personal struggle, the separation of abstraction and concreteness is the very problem.

In the inquiry overall to this point I see that I've actually said very little about particulars of the Kyoto school in presenting what I think is the significance of that school's "positionless position." So I wonder if the Kyoto school has had a full hearing. Perhaps I need to say something more about the concrete textures of my own experience in dealing with the works of the Kyoto school.

Part of the challenge with Eastern sources is that they tend to be written almost exclusively from the perspective of practice, as opposed to what has become the traditional Western preference for theory. This is instructive in itself (and may shed new light on elements of the Western inheritance that predate the theory/practice distinction, in particular the dialogues of Socrates and the life of Jesus). In the Eastern tradition, certain kinds of frustration of the intellect are intentional, seeking to "cut the root" of the intellect in ways that lead to insight. The structure of this frustration is generally tripartite: affirmation, negation, affirmation—first a mountain, then no mountain, then a mountain. As a way of leading the reader into "nonduality," for instance, Zen expression involves a paradoxical logic of enlightenment that is "beyond" normal logic. Repetitions, silence, non sequiturs, enigmatic statement, and tautologies are all quite common in the effort to break the barrier of intellectualism or closed discursive thinking. Here is a way of speaking that is quite distinct from the Western treatise, the presentation of intellectual argument leading to a necessary theoretical conclusion.

With the Kyoto school, however, the challenge is complicated enormously by their attempt to "express Eastern insights in Western philosophical categories." This leads to a mix of the logic of Buddhist enlightenment and Western categories—usually German categories at that—which can be

169

rather cumbersome. I cannot say that this is conscious on their part, as an expression of an Eastern sense of superiority, but there are points at which there is almost a toying with those deadly serious German concepts. This sort of synthesis can lead not to insight but to headaches. And this difficulty reminds us of our problem in the post-traditional period, in cultural and personal life as well as philosophy, of distinguishing those sources that lead to genuine insight from those that lead to trouble.

Perhaps it is more fruitful to pursue dialogue with the East through the increasing number of primary sources that now become available in our era. At present I am reading a new translation of the writings of Zen master Dogen, who brought Zen from China to Japan in the thirteenth century. I can recommend *Moon in a Dewdrop* to the reader, and offer in particular Dogen's suggestion that in practice there is something more important than knowledge: "Do not suppose that what you realize becomes your knowledge and is grasped by your consciousness. Although actualized immediately, the inconceivable may not be distinctly apparent. Its appearance is beyond your knowledge."[1]

The Eastern emphasis on practice reminds us that return to the integration of one's own position after one cycle of dialogue, if it is to be complete and part of an authentic reaching out, must be not only theoretical or ideational but practical as well. Here, as we have noted before, is a subtle problem for us as Westerners. We tend to be intellectuals, despite our popular rhetoric of disdain for "eggheads" and "ivory tower" types. All the while that we (especially Americans) prize ourselves on being a practical people, ours is revealed in the East-West encounter to be an extremely rationalistic culture. We tend to live in and lead with our heads, more as the offspring of Aristotle and Descartes than of Socrates or Jesus. Unless we are aware of this fact there is continued danger.

Historians of religion speak of two functions that are always present in humankind's religious responses to existence: myth and ritual, word and deed, theory and practice. The ancient separation of East and West seems to have involved separation along precisely these lines. Eastern cultures tended to focus on the practical and to be casual or even negligent of the theoretical, while the reverse is the case in the West. Sissela Bok, in her book *Lying*, helps us to see the Western problem. We are deficient in "applied ethics," she says, because of the Western assumption that epistemology should be prior to ethics, "knowing" prior to "doing," that we must always have things figured out before we can act.[2] The problem with this orientation is that, in addition to diminishing the richness of life and reducing it to that which is known and controlled through the intellect, it also reduces action and relation to the mere implementation or application of what is settled elsewhere. No room is left for disclosure or creativity in the encounter between self and self, or self and world. Thus we cut ourselves off from relatedness as the locus of the ultimate; we are separated from the dialectic of Socrates and the being there for others of Jesus.

Following the discovery of this Western disposition, much of the creative work in Western ethics today is going on in the field that Bok has pioneered—"practical ethics." Philip Hallie's *Lest Innocent Blood Be Shed* is an excellent example of this newer orientation of ethics. Given the overwhelming presence of evil in the Holocaust and the twentieth century generally, as well as the obvious failure of theoretical ethics to make much of a difference in the world and in our lives, Hallie goes in the opposite direction: he goes not into the intellect to construct a better theory, but rather into the world to see if he can *find* goodness anywhere. Hence his extremely powerful study of the people of the French village of Le Chambon, a place "where goodness had happened."[3]

What is necessary is that this turn to the practical happen in religion as well as in ethics, and in the necessary nexus of relation between the two. But "the practical" in this turn cannot exclude theory, or be merely its opposite. Rather, the practical or action approach that so many Western movements seek to achieve needs to include theory and the work of the intellect *within* the wider field of our human presence.[4]

Yet attempting to speak from the standpoint of practice clearly has its dangers, as we have observed in relation to Nietzsche's will to power, Rorty's poeticizing, and John Cobb's anxiety about going beyond the intellect in positionlessness. In light of the dangers, the wish to remain within the enclosure of theory, concerning ourselves exclusively with how to think, is certainly understandable. For there is no way around the fact that speaking from the standpoint of practice presumes a standard of authority and discipline that is higher than that of the reader or the student, a standard that may or may not be authentic. Here again we meet one of the fundamental problems of our post-traditional circumstance, that of the absence of authorities that can be accepted without question—a problem that leads people not only to engagement with false authority, but also to pervasive skepticism about any authority and hence any practice. But perhaps there is a crucial distinction to be made between forms of authority that speak to our own deep experience and are validated there, and those that remain external.

EIGHTEEN

Finding Western Practice

*T*HE CENTER OF religious practice is located within the same radiant paradox that has been reappearing throughout this inquiry; the paradox involves learning to do two things that appear to the naked intellect and to the ego as contradictory, but which in actuality are so related that each of them occurs fully only when it is simultaneous with the other. Through religious practice we learn to be open and to concentrate at the same time. To be open is to have a clear mind, to participate in the Socratic "knowing nothing," the Nothingness of sunyata, or Jesus' being transparent to the ultimate. To concentrate, on the other hand, is to focus completely in the moment on the concrete activity in which one is engaged, without any extraneous consideration. In Socrates and Jesus we see extraordinary focus, attentiveness, the definiteness of complete location in the present—complete embodiment or incarnation.

As we continue to learn and to refine our practice in the larger curriculum of life, the openness and the concentration begin to converge, in the simultaneity of full human presence. For we learn that openness without concentration drifts off into sleep, other-directedness, proteanness, or otherworldliness; we need the gravity, the concreteness of concentration and commitment. We also learn that concentration without openness becomes "trying too hard," effort sustained by the insufficient energies of the ego alone, closed off from any higher or deeper influence; we need the sustenance of energies that are beyond our control and self-interest. In either openness or concentration that does not develop toward convergence, the spiritual dimension is lost and the practice atrophies. Presence is lost.

There could be much intelligent discussion of this central paradox of religious practice, the necessary simultaneity of openness and concentration, and some of it could be useful. But here, with the issue of practice itself, we come to a crucial juncture in our discussion, one at which we could turn our attention in either the theoretical or the practical direction. This is the point at which we need to follow Hallie's lead, to choose the practical path. We

173

need to resist the inherited tendency to forsake religious practice in the name of an intellectual practice that may appear to be "about" religious practice but which is actually a subtle avoidance, or is itself a form of religious practice that is unself-conscious and unexamined. We cannot exclude or repudiate the work of the intellect in this turn to the practical path, but only insist that it serve the life which is actual. It seems appropriate to ask that intellectual work become self-conscious and be evaluated as a form of practice.

From this perspective the most useful thing to say is that religious practice is already operative to some degree in almost all human lives, and that we only need to identify where and how, and what can be done to allow it to develop more fully. Most of us have a context of practice that centers on the learning to be open. This can range from meditation, prayer, or the affirmation of "Thy will be done" or a "listening to God" to "stress release," or even the ideal of recreation (re-creation), something like what William James once referred to as "the gospel of relaxation."[1] Most of us also have a context in which we are learning to concentrate, whether it be an artistic or athletic activity or some aspect of our primary vocation or work.

Finally, for most of us there is also present somewhere in our lives a third context in which we are striving simultaneously to be open and to concentrate—to be fully present. The potential contradiction between the learnings we get from the first two contexts of practice, and the sense in which each is insufficient by itself, is resolved by the experience of a third context in which the simultaneity itself between openness and concentration is pursued. Recently some interpreters have discussed this third context as that of "the flow experience,"[2] an experience or way of being that is quite similar to what Bromwich describes as the state of "attentiveness" that arises from the practice of liberal education.

What I am saying is quite simple. When we become conscious of these three contexts as they are already operative in our own lives, then we can begin to examine and develop them. Without this crucial identification there is no way for the insights of Parts I and II of this inquiry or any other to be of use at all; insights become mere intellectual exercises or entertainments, either too objective or too subjective, in either case missing the full body of our existence. It is necessary to identify our own practice, however surprising or modest it may appear to be (for example, I see I am practicing openness while doing the dishes; I am practicing concentration while driving the car). This essential identification is what the Zen tradition means by referring to the first stage of religious process as the connecting of a tether, seeing the "mind-ox" of selfhood as a problem and developing some initial connection by which change can occur. It is simply making contact with one's own actual practice, without which everything of thought and resolve becomes confused, frustrating, or dangerous. This point is so easy to say, yet it seems profoundly foreign to Western experience, at least in recent centuries. The orientation to practice requires a subtle shift of perception, one that is curiously both delicate and vast.

Where does this lead us in our inquiry's concern for a reappropriation of the Western vision? Just here: the Western vision specifies the third context of practice as the encounter between human beings. It is clear throughout the Western tradition—from the Socratic interrogation which delivers the other person of himself to Jesus' "being there for others," from the Greek love of the polis to the Hebrew obsession with obedience, covenant and "right relationship"—that relatedness is the the temple or holy place, the place of full religious practice and presence. One practices openness through prayer or meditation in isolation from the world until one can do it in every moment and in the presence of the other. One practices concentration in various disciplines of respect, study, and "work" until one is able to meet the gaze of the other.

But the tension between openness and concentration is not easily resolved, nor is it easy to find and sustain their convergence in the inclusive relational form of practice. The Western inheritance itself is helpful, perhaps comforting, on this point. For we find the very tension between openness and concentration in the differences between Jesus and Socrates. The Hebrew orientation to the openness of faith and unconditioned election and the Greek orientation to the concentration of reason and human development have maintained all along a vital tension within Western culture, a dialogue in itself out of which Western culture has arisen. On one side there is the Hebrew subtradition, with its orientation to unquestioned obedience and Jesus' acting not on his own "but for the Father through him," the human necessity of atonement and grace that is radically beyond all human effort. On the other side there is the Greek subtradition, with Socrates' meticulous attention to the logic of dialectical argument and the effort of the examined life that leads to full human actualization. Yet in each subtradition, as we have seen in our encounters with Jesus and Socrates, there is powerful recognition of the complementary form of practice that is not emphasized there (in Jesus' advice that "by their fruits ye shall know them," for example, and in Socrates' "not-knowing"), as well as the specifying of relatedness as the activity in which the radiant simultaneity of the two forms occurs.

One advantage of dialogue with the East is that it can wake us up to what is humanly possible. Once we awake from our slumber and numbness it becomes possible to see the magnificence of our own tradition and practice, and to reappropriate the fully human act at the center of the Western vision. In a state of wakefulness we come to see that in its fullness Western action is a capacity far deeper than either Aristotelian implementation of doctrine or modern technological manipulation. From the Golden Rule to John Cobb's emphasis on "giving form," and from Greek democracy to Hannah Arendt's insistence that "with the creation of man, the principle of beginning came into the world itself,"[3] human action has been associated with our being created "in God's image," as beings who are capable of creating something out of nothing.

But in order to reclaim this capacity a new kind of effort is required, one which appears from the standpoint of our old ways as either a sort of effortlessness (when viewed in terms of openness) or as an impossible task (when viewed in terms of concentration). Yet in reality it is neither of these, but both together.

NINETEEN

Sitting and Relating

*I*N MASAO ABE'S book he speaks again and again of the necessary movement from national sovereignty to a new sovereignty of humankind. In order for this critical transition to occur, people as individuals must come to self-awakening: "The foundation of this position is for *each of us* to awaken to his or her true Self."[1] This is required, according to Abe, because the survival of the world itself calls for a sovereignty of wisdom and compassion rather than authority and justice, and because "true investigation of the self is always the investigation of the world and of history."[2]

In this inquiry we have seen that there is striking agreement between Eastern and Western views on the human need to overcome the ego-orientation to reality and move to the more mature, more spiritual way of being. While access to this message may be difficult in the West because of the dominance of modern materialistic and mechanistic values, the testimony of our tradition is quite clear on this point: painful and difficult though it is, and potentially dangerous as well, the coming to human maturity entails a necessary death of the ego-self and subsequent birth of a deeper selfhood. What Abe is saying is that now world dynamics and history make this movement imperative, in order to save the world and humanity from the forces of destruction that loom all around us. World dynamics drive us to the movement of individual maturation; coming of age is induced in us by our historical circumstance, whether we have access to reliable messages about how to undertake it or not. And yet, as Abe points out, this movement remains in its essence a voluntary act.

From the standpoint of the Kyoto school, the possibility of this movement to human maturity occurring in the present is provided by the experience of Nothingness. Here, simply put, is the point of contact between Western experience and Eastern wisdom as the Kyoto school sees it: the quality of life in the West (or any modernized society) drives people to Nothingness, to the death of ego; and if this experience can be radicalized or fully embraced, the East provides a way of awakening on the far side of that sunyata experience of *absolute* Nothingness, through "the 360-degree movement of return."

Hence sunyata becomes a sort of koan that is provided for Western people by the Kyoto school. There remain, then, certain questions and ambiguities that we must meet and come to terms with.

Nothingness, the void, nihilism, experience of existential dread and meaninglessness, total futility. Yes, these are familiar experiences, at least according to the mainline interpreters of Western culture in the twentieth century. In the traditional period there were structures of value, authority, and commonly accepted meaning that protected or insulated people from these experiences, as well as providing support, interpretation and discipline for the few who were permitted to journey in and through this territory. But in the post-traditional twentieth century these traditional structures have collapsed or are no longer available, lost in the sea tide of relativity, or eclipsed by the superficial values of producing and consuming. The situation of spiritual deprivation—the loss of protection and guidance, as well as an oppressive superficiality—becomes humanly intolerable. We have been told this repeatedly in our century of spiritual wasteland, and the Kyoto school joins with the Western artists and intellectuals that it has followed in this understanding.

But there is a problem, one that the Kyoto school has perhaps not taken into account. Most of us do not actually *have* this experience of "wasteland." As we drift close to it another reality sets in, psychic numbing or "the sleep of empire." It seems that the primary response to our late-twentieth-century cultural moment is not the grand identity crisis or the crying out of the human spirit that we read about in the literature of existentialism and nihilism, but rather an amputation or anesthetizing of that part of our humanity which is concerned with higher or deeper meaning and value. As we approach the twenty-first century, then, we worry not only about the crisis of meaning but also about a new form of life that is not quite human, a forgetting of what it means to be human, a forgetting of meaning itself—the death T. S. Eliot describes, not with a bang but a whimper. And the worst part is, of course, the numbing's self-enforcing power: it becomes so pervasive that it is taken for granted, for normal. It becomes very difficult to raise questions about this adaptation to the rigors of life in our time: people change the subject, and return to the slumber of consumerism and task.

It is as though we put on the cloak of psychic numbing as we come close to the sunyata experience. We can be stripped of this cloak, jarred out of our false consciousness and into wakefulness, and there arise from time to time groups and figures who attempt to do just this. But then what? We resist because we "know better": Why allow the stripping to occur if it only leaves me naked and vulnerable, if there is no answer as to what to do next, how to develop and actualize the deeper self, how to "return"? There are those who proffer guidance and method in this situation, but many of them have turned out to be charlatans or cult leaders whose teachings were false or evil. People have learned this, so the resistance to the full sunyata experience is quite understandable. It seems better to remain in the apparent safety of psychic numbing than to risk the dangers that lie beyond.

It should be observed that from the traditional perspective, both Eastern and Western, the sunyata type of experience is a natural fact of human development and maturation. And it should also be recalled that there are both negative and positive forms of this experience. In this regard I recall Alfred North Whitehead's statement: "Religion . . . runs through three stages, if it evolves to its final satisfaction. It is the transition from God the void to God the enemy, and from God the enemy to God the companion."[3] Although in the present inquiry and in the works of the Kyoto school the initially negative forms of the sunyata experience have been emphasized, the positive forms remain also, both before and after the critical experience of the death of ego: in the natural senses of wonder and awe, in the appreciative awareness of the miraculousness of everything that exists, in the enchantment of life on this earth which comes over us in unexpected moments. But under conditions of psychic numbing these are all lost, and there arises in their absence the addiction to entertainment and an underlying mood of boredom or tedium, a bland existence with neither highs nor lows. Without reliable sources of interpretation, support, and discipline, much of what we associate with the fullness of human experience simply ceases to be visible, ceases to be identified, confirmed, and nurtured. People close down in their essential humanity, opt for inhuman adaptation, relinquish the innate longing to achieve their potential. In the face of our own fear, oblivion seems preferable to sunyata.

But suppose that one could not resist the *nihil*, could not any longer wear the cloak of psychic numbing? Suppose one caught wind in some compelling way of the imperative of our era to which Abe refers? Here we enter a zone of excruciatingly difficult personal questions: How does one know if one has had the sunyata experience or not? How is it different, for example, from depression or other clinical diagnoses of dysfunction? Does the death-and-rebirth experience happen all in one dramatic occasion, as the Kyoto school and others sometimes imply, or rather in a series of less momentous events? Should one force or drive oneself and others to this experience? Where is the line between being open or not resisting, on one side, and on the other the masochism which Saul Bellow and others find typical of our time? And assuming that the experience has occurred, how does one prevent oneself from slipping back into old ways, or into new ways that are perverse?

How is one to navigate these treacherous waters? Surely the magister internus is essential, as Johnston points out: the understanding that once on a path of development one does or will receive the necessary messages from within one's own experience as to what needs to happen by way of direction, discipline, and making choices between what is creative and what is destructive. (This is basic to "faith" in the Buddhist tradition also: that the Buddha nature is present in the depth of each person and will serve as a guide to development.) Under post-traditional circumstances, with the requirement of maturation or what Karl Jaspers refers to as becoming a "self-existent self,"[4] attentiveness to the self-regulating principle of the master within assumes even greater importance than it had in the traditional period. In fact, it seems to be a most basic component of the elusive "post-traditional wisdom" that we have been pursuing like the rare snow leopard throughout this inquiry.

Two voices come to mind just now. One is William James's with his suggestion that at some point it is necessary for us to simply *decide* to risk stepping beyond the numbing, decide to trust the master within in order to avoid the "morbid introspection" that troubled him so; his famous "will to believe" must be applied to ourselves, to what we can be and do, as well as to the reality outside us.[5] The second is that of Huston Smith: "Humility has nothing to do with low self-esteem. It is the capacity to distance oneself from one's private, separate ego to the point where one can see it objectively and therefore accurately, as counting for one, but not *more than* one, even as charity sees one's neighbor as counting *for* one."[6] This, in my recent reading, echoes Dogen's repeated references to the importance of "giving to the self" and directing one's own development. Although it is not easy to do.

There is no way to avoid or neglect the insistence of Kapleau and others that one needs a teacher, a guide, sources of wisdom that are external and that one can trust and surrender to, at least to some extent; even if the center of their wisdom is the lesson that there *is* no external, one still needs to learn this and progress toward it from somewhere, from where one is. And so post-traditional wisdom might consist in part in a reappropriation of the Judeo-Christian recognition of the teacher's appearing in the form of the stranger or the neighbor—right in the midst of our most mundane moments. If we are attentive, angels appear where and when we least expect them! Yet, again, examples of the disasters that occur when people choose false teachers come to mind.

The question becomes urgent: How, in our period of great and ironic cultural availability, when the resources of all of human history are so near and yet so far, can we choose among sources, teachers, and alternative directions for our own development? How can we know which is reliable and suitable for our own process?

I know of no better way to answer this crucial question than by turning to the traditional Christian "marks of salvation"; criteria which were used by medieval Christians to distinguish spiritual progress from diversion, or a saint from a dangerous pretender. These "marks" have been articulated in twentieth-century language by two theologians, Paul Tillich and Henry Nelson Wieman, and they can be simply listed for the very substantial guidance that they provide.

Tillich, concerned about the loss, with the influence of secular criticism, of traditional criteria for interpreting the process of sanctification, provides "four principles determining the New Being as process": "first, increasing awareness; second, increasing freedom; third, increasing relatedness; fourth, increasing transcendence."[7] His point is that sanctification or religious development entails the increase of all of these terms together, and that any resource or choice that is deficient in any one of these principles should be reexamined.

Like Tillich, Wieman also wants to interpret the Christian tradition in such a way as to provide guidance under contemporary circumstances. His criteria for distinguishing what he calls "the creative event" are as follows: "emerging awareness of qualitative meaning derived from other persons through communication; integrating these new meanings with others previously acquired; expanding the richness of quality in the appreciable world by enlarging its meaning; deepening the community among those who participate in this total creative event of intercommunication."[8] Here also we are talking about mutual and interdependent increase of the four "subevents," and, without going on a long excursion of comparison between his list and Tillich's, we can note their compatibility. Wieman's emphasis on meaning and communication could perhaps be seen as giving context and interconnection to the somewhat austere principles of Tillich.

With the fully practical nature of our present considerations in mind, I want to stress, as does the Kyoto school and Zen itself, that the mature and creative forms of spiritual development always involve "return." (Here is another of the positive benefits of our post-traditional world perspective, that we are enabled to see this.) Return, in this context, means that choices and development must be considered in relation to the ordinary, the wholeness of the actual life we are living; return, in a certain sense, means simply living in the present. This is in contrast to unhealthy forms of choice and development that appeal to some part of our lives that is abstracted from the whole; appeal is to our future or potential life that is either dislocated from or buried beneath the actuality of who we are in the present, disconnected in either case from the "ordinary" of our actual incarnation.

But the ordinary is neither simple nor always easy to identify; the world is constituted of many spaces and many activities, such that the image of a Zen master cleaning toilets or engaged in some other humble or unexpected activity is only a partial and potentially misleading answer to the question as to the location of the ordinary. Many have suggested that "the ordinary" is especially difficult to locate under contemporary circumstances of "homelessness," with the wide variety of entertainments, anesthetics, and ideologies that can carry us away, transport us, deliver us from an ordinary that is too painful, or too demanding, or too elusive. Hence the question: Where do I return to, how do I locate the ordinary? How do I get home?[9]

Throughout this inquiry I have suggested two answers to this question, two responses that may at first appear in contradiction but move toward convergence in practice: return to "sitting" in prayer, meditation, or contemplation, and return to relatedness. I have also stressed that in the Western tradition relatedness is the inclusive or "third" form of practice. Let us look at these two activities and their convergence once again.

It may be that the hardest part of sitting is to carve out the space and time from the task-orientation of our society—and its flip side, entertainment within its broader environment of consumerism—to even begin. Having begun, however, we are assured that this human activity will naturally develop. One only needs to enter what the unknown Christian mystic of the fourteenth century calls "the cloud of unknowing," to "think nothing," to empty one's mind, to be in that Nothingness so basic to the Eastern tradition—to enter into a state of radical openness. In doing this, paradoxically, it is helpful to have something on which to concentrate: one's breathing, or a mantra, or a short phrase like "God is love" (1 John 4:16) to repeat over and over. Through the presence of the magister internus and the selection of resources according to the principles I have described above, the sitting can be trusted to evolve in its depth and effectiveness. We only need to give this activity a place in our lives, to enter that place one or two times each day, and to listen for the messages that would enable us to refine our method. It is ironic, though I think finally positive, that the effectiveness of this essentially human activity of mystical prayer, meditation, or contemplation, which had been largely lost in the rush of the modern period, is now being confirmed and validated according to scientific criteria; without even considering its significance in spiritual progress, researchers tell us, sitting turns out to be a most efficacious form of rest, one that increases our "efficiency" in the world of task.[10]

Moving to the second activity: return to relatedness is return to who we are when we are most faithful to the gift-quality of life, the way that life is given to us as human beings on earth. It is return to what Hannah Arendt calls "the paradoxical plurality" of beings who are "all the same, that is, human, in such a way that nobody is ever the same as anyone else."[11] But we are not in fact both the same and different in all relationships; in many the radiant paradox is dim, such that we become either the same or different in ways that preclude the fully human relationship. Return to relatedness as locus of the ultimate or the holy place is return to those relationships that exhibit the full simultaneity of sameness and difference, closeness and distance, intimacy and independence; it is return to those relationships in which we find ourselves being fully present. Return occurs when we identify those relationships that in fact do have this quality of synergy or "mutual realization"; it occurs when we nurture and remain faithful to those relationships and the people (including ourselves) within them. Return occurs when we do what we can in the worlds of child-rearing, interpersonal relations, vocation and public policy to build a common life in which this kind of relationship can occur more widely and more freely. In addition to contributing to the spiritual maturation process in itself, return to relatedness also provides us with an ethic, a coherent and reliable way of being in the world, and a political principle, the same one that is envisioned in our best senses of democracy.

Certainly the practice of relatedness requires work on the self, developing the capacity to treat the self "as one, but not more than one," and coming into "the maturity of our faculties." And one essential component must be the sitting, the prayer, meditation, or contemplation, the learning to be open and to concentrate in that mode, the coming into right relationship with God or the ultimate conditions of existence. But this component and the work on the self generally must not be thought of in sequential terms, as prior to relatedness with others. Here is a frequent pitfall in our culture: people will accept—almost intuitively, it seems—the notion of relatedness as practice, yet exempt and exclude themselves from the fullness of this practice until they "get it together" privately. They are, in effect, entirely focused on the internal, and thereby alienated from the very space of relationship they have affirmed. This splitting of the internal and the external, the public and the private, and the associated pathology of James's "morbid introspection" or narcissism, is one of the great dangers of our psychologizing era. To enter into the practice of relatedness, as not the "final" component but the most inclusive context of practice, is to begin right away.

How? The first step is realization, something analogous to the Eastern "connecting of a tether": we must be able to see and appropriate those moments of mutual realization or full relatedness we have in our personal and cultural history and in the present geography of our lives. This is very simple in one sense: we only need to look at our lives from the perspective of vivid relatedness. And yet it is difficult in another sense, especially in a society that teaches us to "see" and evaluate relations in other terms, primarily those of exchange and authority (including rebellion against authority). But once the crucial recognition of synergetic relationship has occurred, something very like the refinement of meditation through the voice of the magister internus begins to become possible. Refinement occurs through our ever fuller response to certain basic questions: Where in my life are my relationships of mutual realization, what are their essential qualities, and what changes would be involved in giving them fuller priority? What is it that I or we do in those relationships to nurture and support them, and what does this imply for how I might take action in my less vivid relationships? And what do I do by way of preparation and personal discipline that enables me to stand in and body forth the radiance of full relationship? Responding to these questions and making the choices that response implies, we come to the "new kind of effort" we have discussed before, a discipline of openness that requires and facilitates my full definiteness, and a way of definiteness that is open to further illumination.

Within East-West dialogue, I have observed that traditionally the East has emphasized return as sitting, while the West has focused primarily on relatedness. But there are voices within both of these traditions telling us that each of the essential activities in their completeness involves convergence and simultaneity with the other, demonstrating again the complementarity of East and West. However, from a Western standpoint, it appears that while the East is insistent on *the ordinary* as the point of convergence and hence the most sophisticated context of religious practice (for the goal is to be meditating all the time and right in the midst of everyday life), it is less clear about identifying our relatedness with other human beings as the most profound *location* of the ordinary. But the West is very definite on the point that sitting and relatedness each find their maturity when they converge in the act of full human presence. Here, through our relational vision, the West might contribute to Eastern development, through the practice of that presence with the other in which we finally become ourselves: that practice of giving ourselves to the other in which we find ourselves complete, that practice of encountering the completeness of the other in which we find ourselves truly giving.

TWENTY

Earth as Home

WE MUST REACH for a form of humanity that is as new as our global circumstance, one that is "beyond distinctions between East and West." We must move toward a new universality—not one of thought only, but of human being, one which includes the East in our "effective historical memory."

Masao Abe's recommendation for achieving this universality is remarkably similar to what appeared earlier in this inquiry as the need to integrate the dimension of our humanity that had been "other" in the traditional period. Abe says that both West and East must break through their historical limitations in order for each to achieve "a universal form of world religion." He goes on to describe this in terms of "two essential aspects" that need to be "thoroughly and harmoniously realized": Christianity and the West has emphasized "the father" or the "paternal and justice-oriented aspect," while Buddhism and the East has emphasized "the mother" or the "maternal, receptive aspect." In order for both cultures to break through their respective occidental-paternal, oriental-maternal structures and become truly universal, each must now integrate and include the other aspect: "Both father and mother are needed to provide a real 'home' for us."[1] The achievement of a "universal form of world religion," through integration and inclusion of that which had been "other" to each, is Abe's final goal and ideal, though it is approached from different directions by Westerners and Easterners respectively (and hence is no mere mixture of the two traditions). In this chapter I attempt to point in the direction of universality from a Western location.

Yet we already have a conclusion from a previous chapter that appears to be at odds with this: that the West must reappropriate its own tradition of relatedness as locus of the ultimate, and that dialogue with the East and the Kyoto school provides the context in which this becomes possible. However, I suggest that there is no opposition between the two conclusions of reappropriation and integration, though their co-presence certainly makes for complexity, at least as it is grasped initially by the intellect. But the complexity melts away as we receive and begin to work on these two conclusions in our actual practice.

We must reappropriate our own Western tradition, and we must include the East and "the other" generally, or Abe's "maternal" other aspect, in the larger integration of who we are. We cannot properly do one without also doing the other: reappropriation of the West without integration of the East leads to absolutistic neoconservative rigidity and fundamentalist parochialism, and indiscriminate assimilation of the East without possession of the Western wisdom leads to relativistic deconstructionist dispersion and false universalism.

The common ground of these two conclusions, the ground upon which there is no contradiction between rediscovering the West and integrating the East, is our new world situation, the situation of our earth itself, earth as home. Technological developments, capacities, and dangers have brought us together into a new interdependence. In order to inhabit this interdependence as human beings rather than as mere servants of technology we must become universal citizens of the globe itself. Yet we cannot become global in outer space. We are only authentically global when we are at the same time *from* somewhere. For here is how life is given to us, "located," as John Cobb says. Between the dual dangers of rigid parochialism, exhibited in the new fundamentalism we have seen sweep across the earth in recent decades,[2] and false universalism, as in much of the New Age movement, we are challenged to be particular and universal at the same time, to activate both conclusions of this inquiry.

In real or actual life—as distinct from those moments in our life when we are estranged, either disembodied spirits or merely body without spirit—universal and particular are not opposed. They are certainly not opposed in those forms of practice that are vital. This brings us back to the same essential paradox that has been appearing and reappearing in our inquiry from the very beginning, as the necessary simultaneity of openness and concentration, as sitting and relatedness, and now as the co-presence of reappropriation and integration, universality and particularity. The middle term is real life, presence, the earth.

Paradox, by definition, is an affront to the intellect. But we are at a moment in history when we must go beyond the intellectualist orientation that dominates the West and threatens the whole earth through its expression as technology undisciplined by genuinely human value and purpose. This going beyond is an extraordinarily delicate matter. For to say that we must go beyond the intellect is frequently confused with saying that we must throw it out altogether. So we are afflicted in our post-traditional period with dangerous outbursts of the irrational, as well as with persistence of the mere reverse of intellectualism that is expressed as spiritless and numbed materialism. The challenge is not to eliminate or act against the intellect, but rather to realize its proper function, to use it as a preparation and a stepping-stone for the real life that always lies beyond its grasp.

We must integrate the intellect within a life that honors it in its harmonious relation with other human faculties. Through the intellect we are able to remember and discipline ourselves in order to truly accept the gift-quality of life and be who we really are. The function of the intellect, as Martin Buber and many of the Zen masters say, is to point. It is simply not able to resolve paradox, except by breaking it and drawing back from real life. When it serves the ego, the intellect draws back from paradox through the denial of complexity and possibility, and its preoccupation with closure and control. The certainty the intellect promises when it acts in the service of ego turns out to be a certainty that is removed from real life, and hence illusory. But the intellect can also serve real life, becoming an indispensable tool for reminding us and pointing us to the life of encounter, as well as maintaining the discipline and work that are necessary prerequisites of encounter.

The going forward into the fullness of practice and our own real life is vexingly simple, utterly decisive, and the most difficult thing we will ever do. Part of the difficulty lies in overcoming the world-rejection of the traditional period, learning to affirm body and the immanent aspect of reality, incarnation as the unity of body and spirit. The work or effort in this movement forward is subtle, and different from work as it has been construed in the traditional and modern past. In order to overcome the world-rejection we are called to celebrate the gift-quality of life, rather than seeking to control life through the scheming of the ego in its ownership of the intellect. The work, in essence, is a deep act of affirmation. On the way to this essential act of affirmation we must meet and dare to live beyond what Rollo May calls "the life fear"—the fear of actualization, the fear of real life.[3] Living beyond this basic fear is excruciatingly difficult, because the ego prefers the certainty and apparent comfort of constricted existence and even failure to the expansiveness of real life.

What could persuade us to take the decisive "leap of faith" beyond the egoism of modern individualism and into the life that embodies who we really are? What could induce us to do what is absolutely counterintuitive from the standpoint of the ego (something like learning to do a back flip from a diving board, when the dominant voice inside says *no* and needs to be overridden)? The answer that returns again and again in this inquiry is the earth itself and that which arises upon it, especially the world of our relatedness with other human beings. Once we actually take the leap we discover firsthand the truth of what we have been told: that acting on behalf of world survival is both our most profound duty and finally the best thing we can do for ourselves as well. But this cannot be known, except in a fragmentary way, before the leap—which may actually be just a single step.

I recall Alexander Solzhenitsyn's now-famous address at Harvard University in 1978:

> If the world has not come to its end, it has approached a major turn in history. . . . It will exact from us a spiritual upsurge, we shall have to rise to a new height of vision, to a new level of life where our physical nature will not be cursed as in the Middle Ages, but, even more importantly, our spiritual being will not be trampled upon as in the Modern Era.
>
> This ascension will be similar to climbing onto the next anthropologic stage. No one on earth has any other way left but—upward.[4]

My decision, my act of affirmation, may not be tolerable from the standpoint of my little ego in its isolation. But the incentive I need to take the decisive step beyond ego that Solzhenitsyn speaks of as a surge may be provided by the world itself: the world of my children and their unborn children; the possible survival of certain forests, lakes, and cities I love, institutions I cherish, and riches of the world that have not yet been revealed to me; the thriving of friends, the wonder of their lives; the beauty of the human form in the midst of the great biodiversity of the earth, and the earth itself in the unfathomable vastness of outer space. To not answer that call to affirmation now is to answer on the side of oblivion.

In the end, what more can be said?—Especially since the specifics of your practice and the point from which you take the decisive step may be quite different from mine. I have tried to describe the central components of vital practice and their interrelations: the necessity of making contact with and learning to trust the magister internus, the importance of maintaining both integration and openness, the significance of exercising careful choice of support and resources.

Throughout this inquiry I have spoken from the perspective of liberal education. I have sought to recommend it as a practice that is not only effective in its own right, but also illuminating in relation to other forms of practice, and therefore helpful as we make the choices that are necessary to our growth in this period when the cultural resources of the whole world are ambiguously available. The practice of inquiry can enable us to find and become rooted in our own authentic practice, even if ours turns out to be different from that of liberal education. Beyond this orienting and stabilizing quality, the effectiveness of inquiry in itself arises from the fact that, fully engaged, liberal education is none other than the Western practice of relatedness as locus of the ultimate. Within the "examined life" of liberal education we learn to know ourselves through knowing others, and to know the world through knowing ourselves, as we move beyond knowing in the usual sense to the way of being that becomes possible in synergetic relationship. We are enabled to grow into our own distinctive vocation, as our way of presence in the world that is both accepting and active, open and definite—an ongoing practice of encounter.

What more can be said? Maybe a couple of other things *can* be said by way of bringing the particular inquiry of this work to a close and illuminating the nature of genuine practice. First, we can identify our genuine practice, that activity of transformation or "clarifying consciousness" by which we are able to move from ego-self to deeper self, as an activity that serves as a model and an ideal for all other activities in our lives, and one by which those other activities can be evaluated. Vital practice overflows its particularity, breathes spirit into, inspires the whole body of our life, as that activity through which we receive and more fully incarnate the finer energy that is available to us. Second, our practice, when it is healthy and effective, is expressed as compassion for those other beings we encounter along the path of "mutual transformation," even to the point of deferring what we envision as our own "enlightenment" for the sake of others. Finally, love is everything, the central, saving mystery.

Martin Luther King makes this last and most fundamental point with eloquence, underlining that in our practice we must remain aware of the first law of life:

> From time immemorial men have lived by the principle that "self-preservation is the first law of life." But this is a false assumption. I would say that other-preservation is the first law of life. It is the first law of life precisely because we cannot preserve self without being concerned about preserving other selves. The universe is so structured that things go awry if men are not diligent in their cultivation of the other-regarding dimension. . . . We are in the fortunate position of having our deepest sense of morality coalesce with our self-interest.[5]

It seems appropriate in terms of my own practice to bring this inquiry to its conclusion with King's statement, since the essay in which it appears is one I draw upon again and again in my own practice of teaching. It is appropriate too in the inquiry we have shared: King's statement is a contemporary manifestation of that subtradition of the West I have been celebrating throughout this inquiry, in the service of what might now be called a postliberal liberalism.

The theme of death and rebirth enters once more. For King is no longer with us; he is dead, assassinated. However, the fortunateness of which he speaks is very much in our midst, awaiting rebirth in our own lives. All we need to comprehend, in order for rebirth to begin, is the imperative of spiritual development of which King, Solzhenitsyn, Abe and others speak. Comprehension—as embracing, embodiment, affirmation of incarnation—begins when we realize that this development is necessary not only from the standpoint of the world, but also necessary for the self, though the ego will inevitably protest and resist this movement.

What the ego resists is birth of the true self through surrender to the first law of life: other-preservation, mutual realization, the fullness of our own presence that only occurs when we are present with and for the other. Awareness of this basic resistance of the ego-self is the key to resolving the paradox of contemporary obsession with "self" (we must learn to love and care for our self; at the same time selfishness is our problem). For it is only after achieving the perspective of that first law that we have access to the revitalizing sense in which each self, including our own, is a microcosm of the whole and an opening onto divinity. At this point we become able to experience the act of submitting to our own transformation as the essential human act, as identical with the step forward to deep life affirmation. Here lies the birthing act through which the radiant energy begins its work, transforming our lives and the larger life we share on this fragile and still-enchanted earth.

Notes

Prologue

1. Hans-Georg Gadamer, *Truth and Method* (New York: Crossroad, 1988). For a discussion of the significance of Gadamer's work, see Richard Rorty, *Philosophy and the Mirror of Nature* (Princeton: Princeton University Press, 1979), chapter 8, "Philosophy Without Mirrors" (pp. 357–394).

2. Reflecting uncertainty about our location in history, there is much potential for confusion in terminology. I use the terms "historic" and "traditional" simultaneously to indicate the large period between roughly 600 B.C. and the time in the twentieth century when both the beginning and end of this period were discovered. By "modern" I mean the shorter period roughly from Descartes (d. 1650) to that point in the twentieth century when the dominant mind-set of the West came to be criticized in both the West and other cultures. Hence claims about the "post-traditional" and the "postmodern" arise at the same time, though their reference is quite different: postmodernists can appeal to tradition; post-traditionalists appeal to an aspect of humanity that has been repressed, suppressed, or oppressed throughout the traditional period. These distinctions and their significance are spoken to in the body of the text that follows.

3. Plato, *The Republic*, trans. Francis MacDonald Cornford (New York: Oxford University Press, 1945), p. 261.

4. David Bromwich, "The Future of Tradition: Notes on the Crisis of the Humanities," in *Dissent*, Fall 1989, p. 548.

5. William James, *Essays in Radical Empiricism and a Pluralistic Universe* (New York: Dutton, 1971), p. 150.

6. Alfred North Whitehead, *Process and Reality* (New York: Free Press, 1969), p. 10.

7. Madeleine L'Engle, *A Circle of Quiet* (New York: Seabury Press, 1979), p. 40.

8. Charles S. Peirce, *Selected Writings (Values in a Universe of Chance)*, ed. Philip P. Wiener (New York: Dover, 1958), pp. 383–393. Josiah Royce, *The Problem of Christianity* (Hamden, CT: Archon, 1967), p. 118.

9. Stanley Rosen, *The Ancients and the Moderns: Rethinking Modernity* (New Haven: Yale University Press, 1989), p. 36.

10. Plato, *Phaedo*, trans. G. M. A. Grube (Indianapolis: Hackett Publishing, 1977), p. 40.

11. Plato, "Socrates' Defense," in *Plato: The Collected Dialogues*, eds. Edith Hamilton and Huntington Cairns (Princeton: Princeton University Press, 1985), p. 23. I present an expanded interpretation of liberal education and an anthology of

basic statements about and instances of practice in this tradition in *Claiming a Liberal Education: Resources for Realizing the College Experience* (Needham Heights, MA: Ginn Press, 1990).

12. The issue of genre has been basic in my own work, and I understand the struggle to achieve appropriate "voice" to be central to creative scholarship in our time. In *Leaving and Returning: On America's Contribution to a World Ethic* (Lewisburg, PA: Bucknell University Press, 1989) I attempt to practice "a way of writing that is both more generous and inclusive than the traditional forms of philosophy and theology, and more spirited and committed than the contemporary forms of social science" (p. 20), "through which the didactic and mimetic acquire a persuasively simultaneous character" (p. 23). Another way to indicate the genre challenge is to say that we need a way of communicating that is somewhere between the traditional, intellectualist treatise and the contemporary, subjective chronicle or autobiography. I suggest the following as examples of writing that effectively engages the practice of liberal education, inquiry, or dialogue as genre of revitalization: Madeleine L'Engle, *A Circle of Quiet*; Peter Mattheissen, *The Snow Leopard* (New York: Viking, 1978); Robert M. Pirsig, *Zen and the Art of Motorcycle Maintenance* (New York: William Morrow, 1974); and David Tracy, *Plurality and Ambiguity: Hermeneutics, Religion, Hope* (San Francisco: Harper & Row, 1987).

13. James, *Essays*, p. 260.

14 Karl Jaspers, *Man in the Modern Age* (Garden City, NY: Anchor Books, 1957), p. 193.

15. Rosen, *The Ancients and the Moderns*, p. 188.

16. Robert Pirsig, *Zen and the Art of Motorcycle Maintenance*, p. 242.

17. Andrienne Rich, *On Lies, Secrets, and Silence* (New York: Norton, 1979), p. 64. The essay in which this statement appears, "Women and Honor: Some Notes on Lying," is also included in my anthology, *Living Beyond Crisis: Essays on Discovery and Being in the World* (New York: Pilgrim Press, 1980), p. 71.

18. Robert Jay Lifton, *History and Human Survival* (New York: Vintage Books, 1971), p. 376.

19. Plato, "Socrates' Defense," in Hamilton and Cairns, eds., pp. 8, 24.

Part I. Seeing the World with Zen

Chapter 1. Western Teetering and the Japanese Claim

1. Cited in Tiziano Terzani, "Behind Japanese Superiority," in *World Press Review*, March 1987, p. 27.

2. Keiju Nishitani, cited in Hans Waldenfels, *Absolute Nothingness: Foundations for a Buddhist-Christian Dialogue* (New York: Paulist Press, 1980), p. 61.

3. Keiji Nishitani, ed., *Philosophy in Contemporary Japan* (Kyoto: Yukonsha Press, 1967), p. 4.

Chapter 2. Worldview as the Problem

1. T. S. Eliot, "Choruses from 'The Rock'," *The Complete Poems and Plays: 1909–1950* (New York: Harcourt, Brace and Co., 1952), p. 96.

2. Hannah Arendt, *Men in Dark Times* (New York: Harcourt, Brace and World, 1955), p. 82. The essay in which this statement appears, "Karl Jaspers: Citizen of the World?," is also included in *Living Beyond Crisis*, p. 252.

3. Many of the presentations of this conference are available in an important anthology of postmodern thought: David Ray Griffin, ed., *Spirituality and Society: Postmodern Visions* (Albany, NY: SUNY Press, 1988). For other Western sources on emerging worldviews, see Ruth Nanda Anshen, ed., *Our Emergent Civilization* (New York: Harper & Brothers, 1947), and her subsequent World Perspectives Series, with the same publisher. My *Living Beyond Crisis* is also an attempt to contribute to this same discussion.

Chapter 3. Buddhist Perspective and Zen

1. The Third North American Buddhist-Christian Theological Encounter was held at Purdue University, Oct. 9–12, 1986. To the best of my knowledge there has been no publication of the proceedings. The contact person at Purdue for this event was Professor Donald W. Mitchell of the Philosophy Department, Purdue University, West Lafayette, IN 47907. The major papers to which I refer in this chapter were distributed by mail in advance of the encounter.

2. Francis H. Cook, "Just This: Buddhist Ultimate Reality," p. 4.

3. Ibid., p. 11.

4. Ibid., p. 12.

5. Ibid., p. 22.

6. Thomas Merton, *Zen and the Birds of Appetite* (New York: New Directions, 1968), p. 3.

7. Ibid., p. 4.

8. Ibid., pp. 55–56.

9. Ibid., p. 119.

10. Ibid., p. 10.

11. Ibid., p. 49.

12. Ibid., p. 50.

13. Ibid., p. 62.

14. Keiji Nishitani, *Religion and Nothingness* (Berkeley: University of California Press, 1982), p. 285.

15. Ibid., p. 33.

16. Ibid., p. 71.

17. Ibid., p. 99.

18. Ibid., p. 151.

19. Ibid., p. 151.

20. Ibid., p. 131.

Chapter 4. Eastern Presence in Encounter

1. James W. Fowler, *Stages of Faith: The Psychology of Human Development and the Quest for Meaning* (San Francisco: Harper & Row, 1981).

2. See, for example, "The Six Oxherding Pictures," in Zenkei Shibayama, *A*

Flower Does Not Talk: Zen Essays (Rutland, VT: Charles E. Tuttle, 1970), pp. 152–203.

3. John B. Cobb, Jr., *Beyond Dialogue: Toward a Mutual Transformation of Christianity and Buddhisms* (Philadelphia: Fortress Press, 1982). On the meaning of dialogue from a Western/Christian standpoint, see also Harvey Cox, *Many Mansions: A Christian's Encounter with Other Faiths* (Boston: Beacon Press, 1988), and David Tracy, *Dialogue with the Other: The Inter-Religious Dialogue* (Grand Rapids: Eardmans, 1990). Tracy is especially helpful in relation to postmodern circumstances and contemporary hermeneutics.

4. John B. Cobb, Jr., "Ultimate Reality: A Christian View," p. 6. This paper was presented at the Third North American Buddhist-Christian Encounter, 1986, cited above.

5. Cobb, *Beyond Dialogue*, p. 59.

6. Cobb, "Ultimate Reality: A Christian View," p. 5.

7. Masao Abe, "A Buddhist Response to John Cobb, Jr.'s 'Ultimate Reality: A Christian View,'" p. 20. This paper was presented at the Third North American Buddhist-Christian Encounter, 1986, cited above..

8. Masao Abe, *Zen and Western Thought* (Honolulu: University of Hawaii Press, 1985), p. 4.

9. Ibid., p. 7.

10. Ibid., p. 7.

11. Ibid., p. 15.

12. Ibid., p. 187.

13. Ibid., p. 73.

14. Ibid., p. 22.

15. Ibid., p. 236.

16. Ibid., p. 134.

17. Ibid., pp. 149–150.

18. Ibid., p. 148.

19. Ibid., p. 134

20. Ibid., pp. 192–193.

21. Ibid., p. 193.

22. Ibid., p. 193

Chapter 5. World Perspective

1. Alfred North Whitehead, *Religion in the Making* (Cleveland: Meridian Books, 1960), pp. 140–141.

2. Karl Jaspers, *The Origin and Goal of History* (New Haven: Yale University Press, 1953).

3. Ibid., p. 2.

4. Arendt, "Karl Jaspers: Citizen of the World?," in Rowe, ed., *Living Beyond Crisis*, P. 257.

5. Robert N. Bellah, *Beyond Belief: Essays on Religion in a Post-Traditional World* (New York: Harper and Row, 1970), p. 22. The essay in which this statement appears, "Religious Evolution," also appears in Rowe, ed., *Living Beyond Crisis* (p. 93).

6. Hannah Arendt, *The Human Condition* (Chicago: University of Chicago Press, 1958), pp. 2–3.

7. Note that the following could be taken as a central riddle or koan (Zen teaching statement) of our era: What is the difference between East and West? Abe, as we have seen, speaks directly to this. On the Western side, I would recommend the following as speaking in significant and helpful ways to the question: Joseph Campbell, *Myths to Live By* (New York: Bantam Books, 1973); Denis de Rougemont, *Man's Western Quest* (New York: Harper & Brothers, 1957); William Johnston, *The Still Point* (New York: Fordham University Press, 1982); F. S. C. Northrop, *The Meeting of East and West* (New York: Macmillan, 1946); Arnold Toynbee, *An Historian's Approach to Religion* (New York: Oxford University Press, 1956).

8. Waldenfels, *Absolute Nothingness*, p. 162.

9. John Stuart Mill, "On Liberty," in *Utilitarianism*, Mary Warnock, ed. (New York: New American Library, 1974), p. 135.

10. Carol Gilligan, *In a Different Voice: Psychological Theory and Women's Development* (Cambridge: Harvard University Press, 1982). See also Jean Baker Miller, *Toward a New Psychology of Women* (Boston: Beacon Press, 1976), Mary Field Belenky, et al., *Women's Ways of Knowing: The Development of Self, Voice, and Mind* (New York: Basic Books, 1986), and Nel Noddings, *Caring: A Feminine Approach to Ethics and Moral Education* (Berkeley: University of California Press, 1984).

11. See Robert E. Ornstein, *The Psychology of Consciousness* (New York: Penguin Books, 1972), and Roger Sperry, *Science and Moral Priority: Merging Mind, Brain and Human Values* (New York: Columbia University Press, 1983).

12. See C. G. Jung, *The Undiscovered Self* (New York: New American Library, 1957); Joseph Campbell, *Myths to Live By*; and Bruno Bettelheim, *The Uses of Enchantment* (New York: Alfred A. Knopf, 1976).

13. On the theme of body as inclusive "other," see Margaret R. Miles, *Fullness of Life: Historical Foundations for a New Asceticism* (Philadelphia: Westminster Press, 1981). On earth as body and the global challenge of overcoming the earth-rejection of the modern materialistic worldview, see J. Ronald Engel and Joan Gibb Engel, eds., *Ethics of Environment and Development: Global Challenge, International Response* (Tucson: University of Arizona Press, 1990).

14. William Dean, *American Religious Empiricism* (Albany, NY: SUNY Press, 1987), p. 83. Dean's book, though less than fully persuasive, is richly suggestive in its connections between American radical empiricism, the Chicago school of theology, postmodern literary criticism, and the American literary tradition.

15. Arnold J. Toynbee, in Arnold J. Toynbee and Daisaku Ikeda, *The Toynbee-Ikeda Dialogue* (Tokyo: Kodansha International Ltd., 1976), p. 27.

16. Ibid., pp. 238–239.

17. Ibid., pp. 238, 280.

Chapter 6. Ram Dass, the Roshi, and Liberal Education

1. Toynbee and Ikeda, *The Toynbee-Ikeda Dialogue*, p. 27.

2. Masao Abe, *Zen and Western Thought*, p. 251.

3. Peter Matthiessen, *Nine-Headed Dragon River: Zen Journals 1969–1982* (Boston: Shambhala, 1986), p. 46.

4. See especially Saul Bellow, *Herzog* (Greenwich, CT: Fawcett Publications, 1961).

5. Baba Ram Dass, "Nobody Special." A talk delivered December 6, 1981 at Unity of the Palm Beaches, West Palm Beach, Florida.

6. An interview with Roshi Philip Kapleau, Rochester, NY, November 6, 1986. Used by permission.

7. Philip Kapleau, *The Three Pillars of Zen* (New York: Harper & Row, 1965).

8. Philip Kapleau, *Zen: Dawn in the West* (Garden City, NY: Anchor Books, 1979). On the theme of Zen in America, see also Matthiessen's *Nine-Headed Dragon River*, and Janwillem van de Wetering, *A Glimpse of Nothingness* (New York: Washington Square Press, 1978).

9. Philip Kapleau, *The Wheel of Life and Death: A Practical and Spiritual Guide* (New York: Doubleday, 1989).

10. Eugene Kennedy, "A Dissenting Voice: Catholic Theologian David Tracy," in *The New York Times Magazine*, Nov. 9, 1986, pp. 20–30. See also David Tracy, *Plurality and Ambiguity: Hermeneutics, Religion, Hope*.

11. Paul Tillich, *Systematic Theology* (New York: Harper & Row, 1967), vol. 3, p. 245.

12. I seek to make available this literature and wisdom in *A Tradition Beyond Traditions* (forthcoming). This anthology presents the vertical or historical dimension of the same school of ethics and religion that *Living Beyond Crisis* presents in the horizontal or contemporary dimension.

13. Jaspers, *Man in the Modern Age*, pp. 206–214. On this same theme of the emergence of a new nobility in our era, see Dietrich Bonhoeffer, *Letters and Papers from Prison* (New York: Macmillan, 1976), pp. 12–13, and Rosen, *The Ancients and the Moderns*, pp. 20–21.

14. Bonhoeffer, ibid., p. 282.

15. David Bromwich, "The Future of Tradition," p. 541.

16. Alfred North Whitehead, *The Aims of Education and Other Essays* (New York: Free Press, 1967), p. 14.

17. Michael Oakeshott, *The Voice of Liberal Learning*, cited in David Bromwich, "The Art of Conversation," in *The New Republic*, July 10, 1989, p. 34.

Chapter 7. L.A.: Searching for Post-Traditional Wisdom

1. Abe, *Zen and Western Thought*, p. 251.

2. Matthiessen, *The Snow Leopard*.

3. Ibid., p. 246.

4. An interview with John B. Cobb, Jr., Claremont, California, December 29, 1986. Used by permission.

5. Madeleine L'Engle, *A Circle of Quiet*.

6. Martin Buber, *I and Thou* (New York: Charles Scribner's Sons, 1970).

Part II. Rediscovering the West

Chapter 8. Standing Our Ground

1. Jan Van Bragt's translator's introduction in Nishitani, *Religion and Nothingness*, p. xxxvii.

2. Paul Tillich, *Christianity and the Encounter with the World Religions* (New York: Columbia University Press, 1963), p. 97.

3. John B. Cobb, Jr., *Beyond Dialogue*, p. vii.

4. Ibid., p. 52.

5. Ibid., p. 47.

6. Ibid., p. 51.

7. Ibid., p. 50.

8. Ibid., p. 49.

9. Ibid., p. 52.

10. Lifton, *History and Human Survival*, p. 376. See also Lifton's *The Life of the Self: Toward a New Psychology* (New York: Basic Books, 1983), p. 114. The essay in which this last statement appears, "The Survivor as Creator," is included in Rowe, ed., *Living Beyond Crisis* (p. 179). On the related theme of "proteanness," see Lifton's "Protean Man," in *History and Human Survival*, pp. 316–331. William Perry, in *Forms of Intellectual and Moral Development in the College Years* (New York: Holt, Rinehart and Winston, 1968), pp. 134–135, speaks of much the same phenomenon in terms of "going limp."

11. William H. Whyte, *The Organization Man* (New York: Simon and Schuster, 1956). On numbing as it entails the appearance of a new disturbingly less-than-human personality type, see also David Riesman, *The Lonely Crowd: A Study of the Changing American Character* (New Haven: Yale University Press, 1950), Hannah Arendt, *Eichmann in Jerusalem: A Report on the Banality of Evil* (New York: Viking Press, 1963), and Woody Allen's film *Zelig*.

12. See Philip Rieff, *The Triumph of the Therapeutic: Uses of Faith After Freud* (New York: Harper Torchbooks, 1968), and Christopher Lasch, *The Culture of Narcissism: American Life in an Age of Diminishing Expectations* (New York: Norton, 1979).

13. In this understanding of fascism, I have found most helpful Hannah Arendt's *The Origins of Totalitarianism* (New York: Meridian Books, 1968), especially vol. 3, chapter 13, "Ideology and Terror: A Novel Form of Government." On the cultural and religious dimensions, see Ernst Nolte, *Three Faces of Fascism*, trans. Leila Vennewitz (New York: Mentor Books, 1969). For very helpful interpretation of the relationship between fascism and contemporary styles of personhood, cults, or "soft fascism," see Peter Marin, "The New Narcissism," in *Harper's* (vol. 251, no. 1505), October 1975, pp. 45–46, and "Spiritual Obedience," in *Harper's* (vol. 258, no. 1545), February 1979, pp. 45–58.

14. Aldous Huxley, *The Perennial Philosophy* (New York: Harper Colophon, 1970); Joseph Campbell, *The Power of Myth*, ed. Betty Sue Flowers (New York: Doubleday, 1988); John Hick, *God Has Many Names* (Louisville, KY: John Knox Press, 1982); Paul Knitter, *No Other Name?: A Critical Survey of Christian Attitudes Toward the World Religions* (Maryknoll, NY: Orbis Books, 1985); Huston Smith, *Beyond the Post-Modern Mind* (New York: Crossroad, 1982). For Smith's response to critics of the "many paths" approach, see "Is There a Perennial Philosophy?" in *Journal of the American Academy of Religion* (vol. 55, no. 3), Fall 1987, pp. 553–566.

15. On the ambiguity of availability as it is manifest in the work of Campbell,

see Brendan Gill, "The Faces of Joseph Campbell," in *The New York Review of Books*, Sept. 28, 1989, pp. 16–21.

16. Paul Tillich, *Systematic Theology*, vol. 1, p. 124.

Chapter 9. From Dialectic to Feminism

1. Jon Moline, *Plato's Theory of Understanding* (Madison: University of Wisconsin Press, 1981).

2. Ibid., p. 183.

3. Ibid., p. x.

4. Ibid., p. xi.

5. Ibid., pp. 27–28.

6. Ibid., p. 33.

7. Ibid., p. 43.

8. Ibid., pp. 39–41.

9. Ibid., pp. 6–7.

10. Ibid., p. 78.

11. Rowe, *Leaving and Returning*.

12. Barbara Herrnstein Smith, *Contingencies of Value: Alternative Perspectives for Critical Theory* (Cambridge: Harvard University Press, 1988), p. 112.

13. Ellen Rooney, *Seductive Reasoning: Pluralism as the Problematic of Contemporary Literary Theory* (Ithaca, NY: Cornell University Press, 1988), p. 4.

14. Ibid., pp. 57–58.

15. Ibid., p. 6.

16. Ibid., p. 59.

17. Bromwich, "The Future of Tradition," p. 548. For Bromwich's full presentation of this understanding of tradition, see his *A Choice of Inheritance* (Cambridge: Harvard University Press, 1989).

18. Rooney, *Seductive Reasoning*, p. 8n.

19. Bromwich, "The Future of Tradition," pp. 541–542.

20. Ibid., p. 544.

21. On the loss of genuine liberalism to laissez-faire individualism, see Benjamin Barber, *Strong Democracy: Participatory Politics for a New Age* (Berkeley: University of California Press, 1984); Steven Lukes, *Individualism* (New York: Harper Torchbooks, 1973); Anthony Arblaster, *The Rise and Decline of Western Liberalism* (New York: Basil Blackwell, 1984); and C. B. Macpherson, *The Political Theory of Possessive Individualism: Hobbes to Locke* (Oxford: Oxford University Press, 1962).

22. Whitbeck, "A Different Reality: Feminist Ontology," in Carol C. Gould, ed., *Beyond Domination: New Perspectives on Women and Philosophy* (Totowa, NJ: Rowman & Allanheld, 1983), p. 64.

23. Ibid., p. 68.

24. Ibid., p. 65.

25. Ibid., p. 81.

26. Ibid., pp. 79, 81, 82.

27. Ruth Nanda Anshen, "World Perspectives: What This Series Means," in Werner Heisenberg, *Physics and Beyond: Encounters and Conversations* (New York: Harper & Row, 1971), p. xvi.

Chapter 10. A View on the Western Drama

1. Wallace Stevens, "The Well Dressed Man with a Beard," in *The Palm at the End of the Mind*, ed. Holly Stevens (New York: Vintage Books, 1972), p. 190.

2. Paul Tillich, *The Courage to Be* (New Haven: Yale University Press, 1952), p. 190.

3. D. H. Lawrence, *The Letters of D. H. Lawrence*, eds. James T. Boulton and Andrew Robertson (Cambridge: Cambridge University Press, 1984), vol. III, p. 252.

4. Fyodor Dostoyevsky, *The Brothers Karamazov*, trans. Constance Garnett (New York: Penguin, 1986), pp. 227–244.

5. For a study of the central role of this idea in Western history, its components and ambiguities, see Arthur O. Lovejoy, *The Great Chain of Being* (Cambridge: Harvard University Press, 1936).

6. St. John of the Cross, *The Collected Works*, trans. Kieran Kavanaugh, O.C.D. and Otilio Rodriguez, O.C.D. (Washington, DC: ICS Publications, 1979); Unknown mystic of the fourteenth century, *The Cloud of Unknowing*, ed. William Johnston (Garden City, NY: Image Books, 1973); Meister Eckhart, *The Essential Sermons, Commentaries, Treatises, and Defense*, trans. Edmund Colledge, O.S.A. and Bernard McGinn (New York: Paulist Press, 1981). For a discussion of these works and the issues of their appropriation in the present, see William Johnston, *The Still Point: Reflections on Zen and Christian Mysticism* (New York: Fordham University Press, 1982).

7. Adam Smith, *An Inquiry into the Nature and Causes of the Wealth of Nations*, ed. Edwin Cannan (New York: Modern Library, 1937), p. 423.

8. For a selection of documents from this tradition and discussion of their significance, see A. S. P. Woodhouse, ed., *Puritanism and Liberty* (Chicago: University of Chicago Press, 1951). The works of A. D. Lindsay, especially *The Essentials of Democracy* (Oxford: Clarendon Press, 1967), provide direct interpretation of these documents. For contemporary articulation both from and about this tradition, see the works of James Luther Adams, in James Luther Adams, *Voluntary Associations: Socio-Cultural Analyses and Theological Interpretation*, ed. J. Ronald Engel (Chicago: Exploration Press, 1986).

9. James, *Essays*, P. 150.

10. Whitehead, *Process and Reality*, p. 10.

11. Martin Luther King, Jr., *Where Do We Go from Here: Chaos or Community?* (Boston: Beacon Press, 1968), p. 171. The essay in which this statement appears, "The World House," is also included in Rowe, ed., *Living Beyond Crisis* (p. 77).

12. Erich Fromm, *The Revolution of Hope: Toward a Humanized Technology* (New York: Harper & Row, 1968), p. 30.

13. Robert Heilbroner, *An Inquiry Into the Human Prospect* (New York: Norton, 1974), p. 77.

14. Lifton, "The Survivor as Creator," in Rowe, ed., *Living Beyond Crisis*, p. 189.

15. Alfred North Whitehead, *Process and Reality*, p. 404.

Chapter 11. Testimony of Survivors

1. William James, *Essays*, pp. 121–284.

2. Ibid., p. 270.

3. Ibid., p. 225.

4. William James, "Diary: April 30, 1870," in John J. McDermott, ed., *The Writings of William James* (Chicago: University of Chicago Press, 1977), p. 8.

5. James, *Essays*, pp. 265–266.

6. Ibid., p. 261.

7. Ibid., p. 260.

8. Ibid., p. 272.

9. Ibid., p. 269.

10. Ibid., p. 274.

11. Ibid., p. 272.

12. Ibid.

13. Ibid., p. 257.

14. Ibid., p. 267.

15. Etty Hillesum, *An Interrupted Life: The Diaries of Etty Hillesum 1941–43*, trans. Arno Pomerans (New York: Washington Square Press, 1981), p. 44.

16. Ibid., p. 27.

17. Ibid., p. 222.

18. Ibid., p. 44.

19. Ibid., p. 228.

20. Ibid., p. 96.

21. Ibid., p. 176.

22. Ibid., p. 100.

23. Ibid., p. 178.

24. Ibid., p. 30.

25. Ibid., p. 47.

26. Ibid., p. 175.

27. Ibid., p. 214.

28. Ibid.

29. Ibid., p. 215.

30. Ibid., p. 181.

31. Ibid., pp. 186–187.

32. For a study of the return of immanence in postmodern religiosity, see David Ray Griffin, "Introduction: Postmodern Spirituality and Society," in Griffin, ed., *Spirituality and Society*. For a fuller presentation of Griffin's interpretation, see his *God and Religion in the Postmodern World* (Albany, NY: SUNY Press, 1989), especially "Spiritual Discipline in the Medieval, Modern, and Postmodern Worlds," pp. 109–125.

33. Erich Fromm, in Erich Fromm, D. T. Suzuki, and Richard DeMartino, *Zen Buddhism and Psychoanalysis* (New York: Harper Colophon, 1970), p. 92. This volume provides a good example of the attractiveness of Eastern perspective in relation to the developments of Western culture discussed in this chapter. See also John Welwood, ed., *Awakening the Heart: East/West Approaches to Psychotherapy and the Healing Relationship* (Boston: Shambhala, 1985), especially Jacob Needleman's essay, "Psychiatry and the Sacred," pp. 4–17.

34. Robert N. Bellah, "Religious Evolution," in *Beyond Belief: Essays on Religion in a Post-Traditional World*, p. 44, and in Rowe, ed., *Living Beyond Crisis*,

p. 112). For a work that speaks very clearly of the post-traditional reemergence of immanence in terms of the crucial distinciton between "God-man" and "man-god," see Glenn Tinder, "Can We Be Good Without God?: On the Political Meaning of Christianity," in *The Atlantic Monthly* (vol. 264, no. 6), December 1989, pp. 69–85.

35. Alfred North Whitehead, *Adventures of Ideas* (New York: Free Press, 1933), p. 18.

36. For discussion of autobiography as representative contemporary genre, see James Olney, ed., *Studies in Autobiography* (New York: Oxford University Press, 1989). For a constructive statement that is consistent with my own concerns with genre as indicated in the prologue to the present inquiry, see Janet Varner Gunn, *Autobiography: Toward a Poetics of Experience* (Philadelphia: University of Pennsylvania Press, 1982). For an example of an autobiography that is consistent in both form and content with the intentions of this inquiry, see Natalie Goldberg, *Long Quiet Highway: Waking Up in America* (New York: Bantam Books, 1993).

37. See John Dewey, *A Common Faith* (New Haven: Yale University Press, 1934), and *Experience and Education* (New York: Collier Books, 1963).

38. Richard J. Bernstein, *Philosophical Profiles: Essays in a Pragmatic Mode* (Philadelphia: University of Pennsylvania Press, 1986). For a work that is parallel to the attempt of my inquiry overall, in terms of both genre and the development of a "theory of pragmatic meaning" (see note 1, chapter 17), see Bernstein's *Beyond Objectivism and Relativism: Science, Hermeneutics, and Praxis* (Philadelphia: University of Pennsylvania Press, 1983).

39. David Tracy, *Plurality and Ambiguity: Hermeneutics, Religion, Hope*, p. 17. On the larger conversation out of which Tracy's statement emerges, see Francisca Cho Bantly, ed., *Deconstructing/Reconstructing the Philosophy of Religions* (Chicago: The Divinity School, University of Chicago, 1990).

40. For a study of liberalism that develops this theme, see my essay, "The Transformation of Liberalism: Our Legacy from James Luther Adams and the Need for a Theory of Pragmatic Meaning," presented at a February 1990 consultation on James Luther Adams and the Democratic Prospect at Meadville/Lombard Theological School in Chicago, sponsored by the Lilly Endowment.

41. Richard Rorty, *Contingency, Irony and Solidarity* (Cambridge: Cambridge University Press, 1989), p. 53.

42. For critical discussion of Rorty's work, see Sheldon S. Wolin, "Democracy in the Discourse of Postmodernism" and Richard J. Bernstein, "Rorty's Liberal Utopia," in *Social Research*, vol. 57, no. 1 (Spring 1990), pp. 4–30, 31–72. In chapter 11 I seek to show how the view I am developing is not only similar to Rorty's but also very different. There I suggest that Rorty's work presents the full ambiguity of our situation, philosophically speaking.

43. For two works that are suggestive on the matter of liberalism's failure to address the concrete actualities of practice, see William Barrett, *The Illusion of Technique: A Search for Meaning in a Technological Civilization* (Garden City, NY: Anchor Books, 1979), especially the epilogue, "Nihilism, Faith, Freedom"; and Bruce Wilshire, *The Moral Collapse of the University: Professionalism, Purity, and Alienation* (Albany, NY: SUNY Press, 1990). Wilshire speaks specifically of William James and John Dewey in chapters 5 and 8 respectively.

44. Madeleine L'Engle, *The Irrational Season* (San Francisco: Harper & Row, 1977), p. 122. For a work that well states the agenda for a new genre, though it does not deliver what it promises, see Robert Nozick, *The Examined Life: Philosophical Meditations* (New York: Simon & Schuster, 1989). Nozick's concern is to address "the whole of our being" (p. 17) and hence to overcome "the prodominant current perspective on philosophy [that] has been 'cleansed' to leave a tradition in which the rational mind speaks only to the rational mind" (p. 18). He wishes to present a "portrait" rather than a "snapshot" (p. 12), in service of the following aim: "My thoughts do not aim for your assent—just place them alongside your own reflections for awhile" (p. 15). The mode of writing is proposed as "mulling" or "dwelling," in relation to "life and living," which is "not the kind of topic whose investigation philosophers find especially rewarding" (p. 12). Nozick's ultimate purpose is developmental, because there is a loss "when we are directed through life by the not fully mature picture of the world we formed in adolescence or young adulthood" (11), and because "by becoming our ideal parent ourselves finally the circle is closed and we reach completeness" (p. 303).

Chapter 12. The Mystical Christ

1. Cited in an excellent review essay on the historical Jesus by Cullen Murphy, "'Who Do Men Say That I Am?'," in *The Atlantic Monthly* (vol. 258, no. 6), December 1986, p. 58. For a Japanese perspective on Jesus, see Shusaku Endo, *A Life of Jesus*, trans. Richard A. Schuchert, S.J. (New York: Paulist Press, 1973). For a presentation of the figure of Jesus in the art history of the world, see Joseph Jobe, *Ecce Homo: The Life of Jesus as Artists of Many Cultures Have Seen It Since the Beginning of the Christian Era* (New York: Harper & Row, 1962).

2. For works that address these historical possibilities, see H. Richard Niebuhr, *Christ and Culture* (New York: Harper & Brothers, 1951) and Ernst Troeltsch, *The Social Teachings of the Christian Churches*, 2 vols., trans. Olive Wyon (New York: Harper & Row, 1960).

3. As representative of this orientation I would cite, in addition to the works of William Johnston discussed in this chapter, Joseph Sittler, *Essays on Nature and Grace* (Philadelphia: Fortress Press, 1972) and Matthew Fox, *The Coming of the Cosmic Christ: The Healing of Mother Earth and the Birth of a Global Renaissance* (San Francisco: Harper & Row, 1988).

4. For works of the medieval Christian mystics that are readily available today, see above, chapter 10, note 2.

5. William Johnston, *Christian Zen: A Way of Meditation* (San Francisco: Harper & Row, 1971), p. 2.

6. Ibid., p. 9.

7. William Johnston, *Silent Music: The Science of Meditation* (San Francisco: Harper & Row, 1976), p. 17.

8. Johnston, *Christian Zen*, p. 19.

9. Johnston, *Silent Music*, p. 18.

10. Ibid., p. 169.

11. Johnston, *Christian Zen*, Preface, p. 2.

12. Johnston, *Silent Music*, p. 21.

13. Ibid., p. 10.
14. Ibid., p. 20.
15. Ibid., p. 21.
16. Johnston, *Christian Zen*, p. 110.
17. Ibid., p. 15.
18. Ibid., p. 21.
19. Ibid., p. 26.
20. Ibid., p. 28.
21. Ibid., p. 44.
22. Ibid.
23. Ibid., p. 36.
24. Ibid., p. 49.
25. Ibid., p. 52.
26. Ibid., p. 54.
27. Ibid., p. 55.
28. Ibid., p. 56.
29. Ibid., p. 129.
30. Ibid., p. 130.
31. Ibid., p. 132.
32. Ibid., p. 54.

Chapter 13. The Radiance of Socrates

1. Plato, "Apology," in *Euthyphro, Apology and Crito*, trans. F. J. Church (New York: Liberal Arts Press, 1948), p. 26.
2. Ibid., p. 25.
3. Ibid., p. 26.
4. Plato, *Phaedo*, in Grube, p. 16.
5. Plato, "Symposium," in *Plato: The Collected Dialogues*, eds. Hamilton and Cairns, pp. 529–530.
6. Plato, "Apology," in Church, pp. 37, 46.
7. Plato, *Phaedo*, p. 10.
8. Ibid., p. 28.
9. Plato, "Apology," in Church, p. 28.
10. Plato, *Phaedo*, p. 64.
11. Plato, *The Republic*, trans. F. M. Comford (New York: Oxford University Press, 1945), p. 51.
12. Plato, "Apology," in Church, p. 23.
13. Plato, *Phaedo*, p. 40.
14. Plato, *The Republic*, p. 255.
15. For a study of this crucial question as to whether contemplation or return to dialectical encounter in the world is the highest ideal in Plato, see Mitchell Miller, "Platonic Provocations: Reflections on the Soul and the Good in the *Republic*," in *Platonic Investigations*, ed. Dominic J. O'Meara (Washington: Catholic University of American Press, 1987), pp. 163–193. Insofar as this question is related to the difference in Socrates between the early and the middle dialogues, and the difference

between Socrates and Plato, see Gregory Vlastos, *Socrates: Ironist and Moral Philosopher* (Ithaca, NY: Cornell University Press, 1991), and Jacob Needleman, *The Heart of Philosophy* (New York: Bantam Books, 1984).

16. Jacob Needleman, *The Heart of Philosophy*, p. 3.

17. Ibid., p. 19.

18. Ibid., p. 26.

19. Ibid., p. 3.

20. Ibid., p. 25. On the sense in which the development that is essential to Socrates and philosophy involves "awakening," see Jacob Needleman, *Consciousness and Tradition* (New York: Crossroad, 1982), especially the introduction, pp. 1–11.

21. Robert E. Cushman, *Therapeia: Plato's Conception of Philosophy* (Chapel Hill: University of North Carolina Press, 1958), p. xi.

22. Ibid., p. xviii.

23. Ibid., p. xvii.

24. Ibid., p. xix.

25. Ibid., p. 296.

26. Ibid., p. 295.

27. Plato, "Letters: VII," in *Plato: The Collected Dialogues*, eds. Hamilton and Cairns, p. 1589.

Chapter 14. Jesus as Christ

1. Johnston, *Silent Music*, p. 17.

2. For presentation of the facial appearance of Jesus in Western art history, see Marion Wheeler, ed., *His Face: Images of Christ in Art* (New York: Chameleon Books, 1988). For a study of the impact of the figure of Jesus on artistic, literary, political, and economic history of the West, see Jaroslav Pelikan, *Jesus Through the Centuries* (New York: Harper & Row, 1987).

3. For a discussion of this dual confession—of the exaltedness and fallenness of the individual—and its impact on the modern world and our world today, see Glenn Tinder, "Can We Be Good Without God?: On the Political Meaning of Christianity."

4. For example, in the following translations Luke 17:21 is translated as "The kingdom of God is within you": King James Version, New King James Version, and American Standard Version. In the following the same passage is translated as "The kingdom of God is in your midst": New American Standard Bible and Revised Standard Version. In the New International Version, presenting the full ambiguity, the same passage is "The kingdom of God is within (or 'among') you."

5. Dietrich Bonhoeffer, *Letters and Papers from Prison*, p. 381.

6. Buber, *I and Thou*, p. 62.

Chapter 15. Death and Rebirth

1. This is the last sentence of Nietzsche's *The Genealogy of Morals*, in Friedrich Nietzsche, *The Birth of Tragedy and the Genealogy of Morals*, trans. Francis Golffing (Garden City, NY: Doubleday Author, 1956), p. 299. For examples of the impact of this statement in efforts to interpret our era, see William Barrett, *The Illusion of Technique*, p. 219; and Bruce Wilshire, *The Moral Collapse of the University*, p. 1.

Part III. Relatedness as Practice

Chapter 16. Dialogue and Development

1. Peter Marin, "The Human Harvest," in *Mother Jones*, p. 35, December 1976, and also in Rowe, ed., *Living Beyond Crisis*, p. 223.

2. King, "The World House," in *Living Beyond Crisis*, pp. 74–90.

3. Thich Nhat Hanh, *Zen Keys* (Garden City, NY: Anchor Books, 1974), p. 150. The essay in which this statement appears, "The Regeneration of Man," also appears in my anthology, *Living Beyond Crisis*, pp. 38–49.

4. For a discussion of this possibility, see Waldenfels, *Absolute Nothingness*, p. 63.

5. Leonard Swidler, "Death or Dialogue: From the Age of Monologue to the Age of Dialogue," a lecture delivered at Grand Valley State University May 24, 1990, pp. 1–2. See also John B. Cobb, Jr., Monika K. Hellwig, Paul F. Knitter, and Leonard Swidler, *Death or Dialogue? From the Age of Monologue to the Age of Dialogue* (Philadelphia: Trinity Press International, 1990).

6. Ibid., p. 17.

Chapter 17. The Practical Turn

1. Kazuaki Tanahashi, ed., *Moon in a Dewdrop: Writings of Zen Master Dogen* (San Francisco: North Point Press, 1985), p. 15.

2. Sissela Bok, *Lying: Moral Choice in Public and Private Life* (New York: Vintage Books, 1979), chapter 1, "Is the 'Whole Truth' Attainable?" Note the similarity between what she is saying and the earlier references to James on "vicious intellectualism" and Whitehead on "the fallacy of misplaced concreteness."

3. Philip Hallie, *Lest Innocent Blood Be Shed* (New York: Harper & Row, 1979), p. 7. On the move to "practical ethics," see also Peter Singer, *Practical Ethics* (Cambridge: Cambridge University Press, 1979), especially "About Ethics," pp. 1–13.

4. I seek to develop this point in relation to the American tradition of pragmatism in "The Transformation of Liberalism."

Chapter 18. Finding Western Practice

1. William James, "The Gospel of Relaxation," in *Talks to Teachers on Psychology; And to Students on Some of Life's Ideals* (New York: Norton, 1958), pp. 132–148.

2. See Mihaly Csikszentmihaly, *Flow: The Psychology of Optimal Experience* (New York: Harper & Row, 1990), and also Marvin C. Shaw, *The Paradox of Intention: Reaching the Goal by Giving Up the Attempt to Reach It* (Atlanta: Scholars Press, 1987).

3. Arendt, *The Human Condition*, p. 177.

Chapter 19. Sitting and Relating

1. Abe, *Zen and Western Thought*, p. 251.

2. Ibid.

3. Alfred North Whitehead, *Religion in the Making*, p. 16.

4. Jaspers, *Man in the Modern Age*, p. 194. I recommend the entire last part of this work, "What Mankind Can Become" (pp. 179–228), for its practical value in relation to the Abe point about the necessity of self-awakening, and the theme of a "new nobility."

5. William James, "The Will to Believe," in McDermott, *The Writings of William James*, pp. 717–735.

6. Smith, *Beyond the Post-Modern Mind*, p. 55.

7. Paul Tillich, *Systematic Theology*, vol. 3, p. 231.

8. Henry Nelson Wieman, *The Source of Human Good* (Carbondale: Southern Illinois University Press, 1946), p. 58.

9. For a work that addresses the problems of the ordinary and "the recovery of the human," see Stanley Cavell, *In Quest of the Ordinary: Lines of Skepticism and Romanticism* (Chicago: University of Chicago Press, 1989). For an insightful review of this book that pursues the issues in a way that is consistent with my approach, see Richard Rorty, "The Philosophy of the Oddball," in *The New Republic*, June 19, 1989, pp. 38–41.

10. On the "efficiency" of meditation, see Herbert Benson and Robert Wallace, "The Psychology of Meditation," in *Scientific American*, January 1972, pp. 84–90. For a comprehensive survey of meditation across the globe, see Herbert Benson, *The Relaxation Response* (New York: William Morrow, 1975), and Claudio Naranjo, M.D., *How to Be: Meditation in Spirit and Practice* (Los Angeles: Tarcher, 1971). My best sources of advice on the actual practice of meditation or mystical prayer (perhaps also Socratic contemplation) are Thich Nhat Hanh, *The Miracle of Mindfulness* (Boston: Beacon Press, 1977); Johnston, *Christian Zen*; and Philip Dessauer, *Natural Meditation* (New York: P. J. Kennedy & Sons, 1965). Useful on integrating this practice with one's larger life of encounter, moving toward full presence, is Ira Progoff's *The Practice of Process Meditation* (New York: Dialogue House, 1980). Also of great practical value are the medieval mystics, St. John of the Cross, the unknown mystic of the fourteenth century (author of *The Cloud of Unknowing*), and Eckhart (see chapter 10, note 2 above).

11. Arendt, *The Human Condition*, pp. 176–178. It is important to note that Arendt's systemic work is cast in terms of faithfulness to the gift-quality of life, as opposed to the earth- and life-denying orientation that had come to dominate Western culture in the traditional period (see Prologue). Bellah, in "Religious Evolution," goes even further and says that "world rejection" was characteristic of all cultures in the traditional period (Rowe, ed., *Living Beyond Crisis*, pp. 93–94).

Chapter 20. Earth as Home

1. Abe, *Zen and Western Thought*, p. 274.

2. See Martin E. Marty and R. Scott Appleby, eds., *Fundamentalisms Observed* (Chicago: University of Chicago Press, 1990).

3. Rollo May, *The Courage to Create* (New York: Norton, 1975), pp. 18–19. The essay in which this discussion appears, "The Courage to Create," is also included in Rowe, ed., *Living Beyond Crisis* (p. 54).

4. Alexander Solzhenitsyn, untitled address delivered at Harvard University, June 8, 1978. Available through the News Office, Harvard University, Cambridge, MA.

5. King, "The World House," in Rowe, ed., *Living Beyond Crisis*, pp. 82–83.

Bibliography

Abe Masao. *Zen and Western Thought*. Honolulu: University of Hawaii Press, 1985.

Adams, James Luther. *Voluntary Associations: Socio-Cultural Analysis and Theological Interpretation*. Edited by J. Ronald Engel. Chicago: Exploration Press, 1986.

Anshen, Ruth Nanda. "World Perspectives: What This Series Means." In Werner Heisenberg, *Physics and Beyond: Encounters and Conversations*. Edited by Ruth Nanda Anshen. New York: Harper & Row, 1971.

———, ed. *Our Emergent Civilization*. New York: Harper and Brothers, 1947.

Arblaster, Anthony. *The Rise and Decline of Western Liberalism*. New York: Basil Blackwell, 1984.

Arendt, Hannah. *Eichmann in Jerusalem: A Report on the Banality of Evil*. New York: Viking Press, 1963.

———. *The Human Condition*. Chicago: University of Chicago Press, 1958.

———. *Men in Dark Times*. New York: Harcourt, Brace and World, 1955.

———. *The Origins of Totalitarianism*. New York: Meridian Books, 1968.

Bantly, Francisca Cho, ed. *Deconstructing/Reconstructing the Philosophy of Religions*. Chicago: The Divinity School, University of Chicago, 1990.

Barber, Benjamin. *Strong Democracy: Participatory Politics for a New Age*. Berkeley: University of California Press, 1984.

Barrett, William. *The Illusion of Technique: A Search for Meaning in a Technological Civilization*. Garden City, NY: Anchor Books, 1979.

Belenky, Mary Field, Blythe McVicker Clinchy, Nancy Rule Goldberger, and Jill Mattuck Tarule. *Women's Ways of Knowing: The Development of Self, Voice, and Mind*. New York: Basic Books, 1986.

Bellah, Robert N. *Beyond Belief: Essays on Religion in a Post-Traditional World*. New York: Harper & Row, 1970.

Bellow, Saul. *Herzog*. Greenwich, CT: Fawcett Publications, 1961.

Benson, Herbert. *The Relaxation Response*. New York: William Morrow, 1975.

Benson, Herbert and Robert Wallace. "The Psychology of Meditation." *Scientific American,* Jan. 1972, pp. 84–90.

Bernstein, Richard J. *Beyond Objectivity and Relativism: Science, Hermeneutics, and Praxis.* Philadelphia: University of Pennsylvania Press, 1983.

———. *Philosophical Profiles: Essays in a Pragmatic Mode.* Philadelphia: University of Pennsylvania Press, 1986.

———. "Rorty's Liberal Utopia." *Social Research,* vol 57, no. 1 (Spring 1990), pp. 31–72.

Bettelheim, Bruno. *The Uses of Enchantment.* New York: Alfred A. Knopf, 1976.

Bok, Sissela. *Lying: Moral Choice in Public and Private Life.* New York: Vintage Books, 1979.

Bonhoeffer, Dietrich. *Letters and Papers from Prison.* New York: Macmillan, 1976.

Bromwich, David. *A Choice of Inheritance.* Cambridge: Harvard University Press, 1989.

———. "The Future of Tradition: Notes on the Crisis of the Humanities." *Dissent,* Fall 1989, pp. 541–557.

Buber, Martin. *I and Thou.* New York: Charles Scribner's Sons, 1970.

Campbell, Joseph. *Myths to Live By.* New York: Bantam Books, 1973.

———. *The Power of Myth.* Edited by Betty Sue Flowers. New York: Doubleday, 1988.

Cavell, Stanley. *In Quest of the Ordinary: Lines of Skepticism and Romanticism.* Chicago: University of Chicago Press, 1989.

Cobb, John B., Jr. *Beyond Dialogue: Toward a Mutual Transformation of Christianity and Buddhism.* Philadelphia: Fortress Press, 1982.

Cobb, John B., Jr., Monika K. Hellwig, Paul F. Knitter, and Leonard Swidler. *Death or Dialogue? From the Age of Monologue to the Age of Dialogue.* Philadelphia: Trinity Press International, 1990.

Cobb, John B., Jr., An interview with Stephen C. Rowe, December 29, 1986, Claremont, California. Used by permission.

Csikszentmihaly, Mihaly. *Flow: The Psychology of Optimal Experience.* New York: Harper & Row, 1990.

Cushman, Robert E. *Therapeia: Plato's Conception of Philosophy.* Chapel Hill: University of North Carolina Press, 1958.

Dean, William. *American Religious Empiricism.* Albany, NY: SUNY Press, 1987.

de Rougemont, Denis. *Man's Western Quest.* New York: Harper & Brothers, 1957.

Dessauer, Philip. *Natural Meditation.* New York: P. J. Kennedy & Sons, 1965.

Dewey, John. *A Common Faith.* New Haven: Yale University Press, 1934.

————. *Experience and Education.* New York: Collier Books, 1963.

Dogen. *Moon in a Dewdrop: Writings of Zen Master Dogen.* Edited by Kazuaki Tanahashi. San Francisco: North Point Press, 1985.

Dostoyevsky, Fyodor. *The Brothers Karamazov.* Translated by Constance Garnett. New York: Penguin, 1986.

Eckhart, Meister. *The Essential Sermons, Commentaries, Treatises, and Defense.* Translated by Edmund Colledge, O.S.A. and Bernard McGinn. New York: Paulist Press, 1981.

Eliot, T. S. "Choruses from 'The Rock'." In *The Complete Poems and Plays 1909–1950.* New York: Harcourt, Brace and Co., 1952.

Endo Shusaku. *A Life of Jesus.* Translated by Richard A. Schuchert, S.J. New York: Paulist Press, 1973.

Engel, J. Ronald, and Joan Gibb Engel, eds. *Ethics of Environment and Development: Global Challenge, International Response.* Tucson: University of Arizona, 1990.

Fowler, James. *Stages of Faith: The Psychology of Human Development and the Quest for Meaning.* San Francisco: Harper & Row, 1981.

Fox, Matthew. *The Coming of the Cosmic Christ: The Healing of Mother Earth and the Birth of a Global Renaissance.* San Francisco: Harper & Row, 1988.

Franck, Frederick, ed. *The Buddha Eye: An Anthology of the Kyoto School.* New York: Crossroad, 1982.

Fromm, Erich. *The Revolution of Hope: Toward a Humanized Technology.* New York: Harper & Row, 1970.

————, D. T. Suzuki, and Richard DeMartino. *Zen Buddhism and Psychoanalysis.* New York: Harper Colophon, 1970.

Gadamer, Hans-Georg. *Truth and Method.* New York: Crossroad, 1988.

Gill, Brendan. "The Faces of Joseph Campbell." In *The New York Review of Books,* Sept. 28, 1989, pp. 16–21.

Gilligan, Carol. *In a Different Voice: Psychological Theory and Women's Development.* Cambridge: Harvard University Press, 1982.

Goldberg, Natalie. *Long Quiet Highway: Waking Up in America.* New York: Bantam Books, 1993.

Gould, Carol C., ed. *Beyond Domination: New Perspectives on Women and Philosophy.* Totowa, NJ: Rowman & Allanheld, 1983.

Griffin, David Ray, ed. *God and Religion in the Postmodern World.* Albany, NY: SUNY Press, 1989.

————. *Spirituality and Society: Postmodern Visions.* Albany, NY: SUNY Press, 1988.

Gunn, Janet Varner. *Autobiography: Toward a Poetics of Experience.* Philadelphia: University of Pennsylvania Press, 1982.

Hallie, Philip. *Lest Innocent Blood Be Shed.* New York: Harper and Row, 1979.

Heilbroner, Robert. *An Inquiry Into the Human Prospect.* New York: Norton, 1974.

Hick, John. *God Has Many Names.* Louisville, KY: John Knox Press, 1982.

Hick, John and Brian Hebblethwaite, eds. *Christianity and Other Religions.* Philadelphia: Fortress Press, 1980.

Hillesum, Etty. *An Interrupted Life: The Diaries of Etty Hillesum 1941–43.* Translated by Arno Pomerans. New York: Pantheon, 1984.

Huxley, Aldous. *The Perennial Philosophy.* New York: Harper Colophon, 1970.

James, William. "Diary: April 30, 1870." In John J. McDermott, ed., *The Writings of William James.* Chicago: University of Chicago Press, 1977.

———. *Essays in Radical Empiricism and a Pluralistic Universe.* New York: Dutton, 1971.

———. "The Gospel of Relaxation." In *Talks to Teachers on Psychology; And to Students on Some of Life's Ideals.* New York: Norton, 1958.

Jaspers, Karl. *Man in the Modern Age.* Garden City, NY: Anchor Books, 1957.

———. *The Origin and Goal of History.* New Haven: Yale University Press, 1953.

Jobe, Joseph. *Ecce Homo: The Life of Jesus as Artists of Many Cultures Have Seen It since the Beginning of the Christian Era.* New York: Harper & Row, 1962.

Johnston, William. *Christian Zen: A Way of Meditation.* San Francisco: Harper & Row, 1971.

———. *Silent Music: The Science of Meditation.* San Francisco: Harper & Row, 1976.

———. *The Still Point: Reflections on Zen and Christian Mysticism.* New York: Fordham University Press, 1982.

———, ed. *The Cloud of Unknowing and The Book of Privy Counseling.* Garden City, NY: Image Books, 1973.

Jung, Carl G. *The Undiscovered Self.* New York: New American Library, 1957.

Kapleau, Philip. *The Three Pillars of Zen.* New York: Harper & Row, 1965.

———. *The Wheel of Life and Death: A Practical and Spiritual Guide.* New York: Doubleday, 1989.

———. *Zen: Dawn in the West.* Garden City, NY: Anchor Books, 1979.

Kapleau, Roshi Philip. An interview with Stephen C. Rowe, November 6, 1986, Rochester, New York. Used by permission.

Kennedy, Eugene. "A Dissenting Voice: Catholic Theologian David Tracy." In *The New York Times Magazine* (Nov. 9, 1986), pp. 20–30.

King, Martin Luther, Jr. *Where Do We Go from Here: Chaos or Community?* Boston: Beacon Press, 1968.

Knitter, Paul. *No Other Name?: A Critical Survey of Christian Attitudes Toward the World Religions.* Maryknoll, NY: Orbis Books, 1985.

Lasch, Christopher. *The Culture of Narcissism: American Life in an Age of Diminishing Expectations.* New York: Norton, 1979.

Lawrence, D. H. *The Letters of D. H. Lawrence.* Edited by James T. Boulton and Andrew Robertson. Cambridge: Cambridge University Press, 1984.

L'Engle, Madeleine. *A Circle of Quiet.* New York: Seabury Press, 1979.

————. *The Irrational Season.* San Francisco: Harper & Row, 1977.

Lifton, Robert J. *History and Human Survival.* New York: Vintage Books, 1971.

————. *The Life of the Self: Toward a New Psychology.* New York: Basic Books, 1983.

Lindsay, A. D. *The Essentials of Democracy.* Oxford: Clarendon Press, 1967.

Lovejoy, Arthur O. *The Great Chain of Being.* Cambridge: Harvard University Press, 1936.

Lukes, Steven. *Individualism.* New York: Harper Torchbooks, 1973.

Macpherson, C. B. *The Political Theory of Possessive Individualism: Hobbes to Locke.* Oxford: Oxford University Press, 1962.

Maranhao, Tullio. *Therapeutic Discourse and Socratic Dialogue.* Madison: University of Wisconsin Press, 1986.

Marin, Peter. "The Human Harvest." In *Mother Jones,* December 1976, pp. 30–38, 52–54; and in Rowe, ed., *Living Beyond Crisis,* pp. 217–236.

Marty, Martin E., and R. Scott Appleby, eds. *Fundamentalisms Observed.* Chicago: University of Chicago Press, 1990.

Matthiessen, Peter. *Nine-Headed Dragon River: Zen Journals 1969–1982.* Boston: Shambhala, 1986.

————. *The Snow Leopard.* New York: Viking Press, 1978.

May, Rollo. *The Courage to Create.* New York: Norton, 1975.

Merton, Thomas. *Zen and the Birds of Appetite.* New York: New Directions, 1968.

Miles, Margaret R. *Fullness of Life: Historic Foundations for a New Asceticism.* Philadelphia: Westminster Press, 1981.

Mill, John Stuart. *Utilitarianism.* Edited by Mary Warnock. New York: New American Library, 1974.

Miller, Jean Baker. *Toward a New Psychology of Women.* Boston: Beacon Press, 1976.

Miller, Mitchell. "Platonic Provocations: Reflections on the Soul and the Good in the *Republic.*" In Dominic J. O'Meara, ed., *Platonic Investigations.* Washington, DC: Catholic University Press of America, 1987.

Moline, Jon. *Plato's Theory of Understanding.* Madison: University of Wisconsin Press, 1981.

Murphy, Cullen. "'Who Do Men Say That I Am?'" In *The Atlantic Monthly*, Dec. 1986, pp. 46–59.

Naranjo, Claudio, M.D. *How to Be: Meditation in Spirit and Practice.* Los Angeles: Tarcher, 1971.

Needleman, Jacob. *Consciousness and Tradition.* New York: Crossroad, 1982.

———. *The Heart of Philosophy.* New York: Bantam Books, 1984.

Nhat Hanh, Thich. *Being Peace.* Berkeley: Parallax Press, 1987.

———. *The Miracle of Mindfulness.* Boston: Beacon Press, 1977.

———. *Zen Keys.* Garden City, NY: Anchor Books, 1974.

Niebuhr, H. Richard. *Christ and Culture.* New York: Harper & Brothers, 1951.

Nishida Kitaro. *An Inquiry into the Good.* Translated by Masao Abe and Christopher Ives. New Haven: Yale University Press, 1990.

Nishitani Keiji. *Religion and Nothingness.* Translated by Jan Van Bragt. Berkeley: University of California Press, 1982.

———, ed. *Philosophy in Contemporary Japan.* Kyoto: Yokonsha Press, 1967.

Noddings, Nel. *Caring: A Feminine Approach to Ethics and Moral Education.* Berkeley: University of California Press, 1984.

Nolte, Ernst. *Three Faces of Fascism.* Translated by Leila Vennewitz. New York: Mentor Books, 1969.

Northrop, F. S. C. *The Meeting of East and West.* New York: Macmillan, 1946.

Novak, Michael, ed. *Democracy and Mediating Structures: A Theological Inquiry.* Washington, DC: American Enterprise Institute for Public Policy Research, 1980.

Nozick, Robert. *The Examined Life: Philosophical Investigations.* New York: Simon & Schuster, 1989.

Oakeshott, Michael. *The Voice of Liberal Learning.* New Haven: Yale University Press, 1989.

Olney, James, ed. *Studies in Autobiography.* New York: Oxford University Press, 1989.

Ornstein, Robert E. *The Psychology of Consciousness.* New York: Penguin Books, 1972.

Peirce, Charles Sanders. *Selected Writings (Values in a Universe of Chance).* New York: Dover, 1958.

Pelikan, Jaroslav. *Jesus Through the Centuries.* New York: Harper & Row, 1987.

Perry, William. *Forms of Intellectual and Moral Development in the College Years.* New York: Holt, Rinehart and Winston, 1968.

Phillips, Anne. *Engendering Democracy.* University Park: University of Pennsylvania Press, 1991.

Pirsig, Robert M. *Zen and the Art of Motorcycle Maintenance.* New York: William Morrow, 1974.

Plato. "Apology." In *Euthyphro, Apology, and Crito.* Translated by F. J. Church. New York: Liberal Arts Press, 1948.

———. *Phaedo.* Translated by G. M. A. Grube. Indianapolis: Hackett Publishing, 1977.

———. *The Republic.* Translated by Francis MacDonald Cornford. New York: Oxford University Press, 1945.

———. "Symposium," "Letters: VII." In *Plato: The Collected Dialogues.* Edited by Edith Hamilton and Huntington Cairns. Princeton: Princeton University Press, 1985.

Progoff, Ira. *The Practice of Process Meditation.* New York: Dialogue House, 1980.

Ram Dass, Baba. "Nobody Special." A talk delivered December 6, 1981 at Unity of the Palm Beaches, West Palm Beach, Florida.

Rich, Adrienne. *Lies, Secrets, and Silence.* New York: W. W. Norton, 1979.

Rieff, Philip. *The Triumph of the Therapeutic: Uses of Faith After Freud.* New York: Harper Torchbooks, 1968.

Riesman, David. *The Lonely Crowd: A Study of the Changing American Character.* New Haven: Yale University Press, 1950.

Robertson, D. B., ed. *Voluntary Associations: A Study of Groups in Free Societies.* Richmond, VA: John Knox Press, 1966.

Rooney, Ellen. *Seductive Reasoning: Pluralism as the Problematic of Contemporary Literary Theory.* Ithaca, NY: Cornell University Press, 1988.

Rorty, Richard. *Philosophy and the Mirror of Nature.* Princeton: Princeton University Press, 1979.

———. *Contingency, Irony and Solidarity.* Cambridge: Cambridge University Press, 1989.

———. "The Philosophy of the Oddball." *The New Republic,* June 19, 1989, pp. 38–41.

Rosen, Stanley. *The Ancients and the Moderns: Rethinking Modernity.* New Haven: Yale University Press, 1989.

Rowe, Stephen C. *Leaving and Returning: On America's Contribution to a World Ethic.* Lewisburg, PA: Bucknell University Press, 1989.

———. "The Transformation of Liberalism: Our Legacy from James Luther Adams and the Need for a Theory of Pragmatic Meaning." Unpublished consultation paper presented at February 16–18, 1990 consultation on "James Luther Adams and the Democratic Prospect" at Meadville/Lombard Theological School in Chicago, sponsored by the Lilly Endowment.

———, ed. *Claiming a Liberal Education: Resources for Realizing the College Experience.* Needham Heights, MA: Ginn Press, 1990.

———, ed. *Living Beyond Crisis: Essays on Discovery and Being in the World.* New York: Pilgrim Press, 1980.

Royce, Josiah. *The Problem of Christianity*. Hamden, CT: Archon Books, 1967.

Shaw, Marvin C. *The Paradox of Intention: Reaching the Goal by Giving Up the Attempt to Reach It*. Atlanta: Scholars Press, 1987.

Shibayama Zenkei. *A Flower Does Not Talk*. Translated by Kudo Sumiko. Rutland, VT: Charles E. Tuttle, 1970.

Singer, Peter. *Practical Ethics*. Cambridge: Cambridge University Press, 1979.

Sittler, Joseph. *Essays on Nature and Grace*. Philadelphia: Fortress Press, 1972.

Smith, Adam. *An Inquiry into the Nature and Causes of the Wealth of Nations*. Edited by Edwin Cannan. New York: Modern Library, 1937.

Smith, Barbara Herrnstein. *Contingencies of Value: Alternative Perspectives for Critical Theory*. Cambridge: Harvard University Press, 1988.

Smith, Huston. *Beyond the Post-Modern Mind*. New York: Crossroad, 1982.

———. "Is There a Perennial Philosophy?" In *Journal of the American Academy of Religion*, vol. 55, no. 3 (Fall 1987).

Solzhenitsyn, Alexander. Untitled address delivered at Harvard University June 8, 1978. Available through the News Office, Harvard University, Cambridge, MA.

Sperry, Roger. *Science and Moral Priority: Merging Mind, Brain and Human Values*. New York: Columbia University Press, 1983.

St. John of the Cross. *The Collected Works*. Translated by Kieran Kavanaugh, O.C.D. and Otilio Rodriguez, O.C.D. Washington, DC: ICS Publications, 1979.

Stevens, Wallace. "The Well Dressed Man with a Beard." In *The Palm at the End of the Mind*. Edited by Holly Stevens. New York: Vintage Books, 1972.

Stout, Jeffrey. *Ethics after Babel: The Languages of Morals and Their Discontents*. Boston: Beacon Press, 1988.

Streng, Frederick J. *Emptiness: A Study of Religious Meaning*. Nashville: Abingdon Press, 1967.

Swidler, Leonard. "Death or Dialogue: From the Age of Monologue to the Age of Dialogue." Lecture delivered at Grand Valley State University, Grand Rapids, MI, May 24, 1990.

Takeuchi Yoshinori. *The Heart of Buddhism*. Translated by James W. Heisig. New York: Crossroad, 1991.

Thoreau, Henry David. *A Week on the Concord and Merrimack Rivers*. Boston: Houghton Mifflin, 1929.

Tillich, Paul. *Christianity and the Encounter with the World Religions*. New York: Columbia University Press, 1963.

———. *Systematic Theology*. Harper & Row and University of Chicago Press, 1967.

———. *The Courage to Be.* New Haven: Yale University Press, 1952.

Tinder, Glenn. "Can We Be Good Without God?: On the Political Meaning of Christianity." In *The Atlantic Monthly,* vol. 264, no. 6 (Dec. 1989), pp. 69–85.

Toynbee, Arnold. *An Historian's Approach to Religion.* New York: Oxford University Press, 1956.

Toynbee, Arnold J. and Daisaku Ikeda. *The Toynbee-Ikeda Dialogue.* Tokyo: Kodansha International, 1976.

Tracy, David. *Plurality and Ambiguity: Hermeneutics, Religion, Hope.* San Francisco: Harper & Row, 1987.

———. *Dialogue with the Other: The Inter-Religious Dialogue.* Grand Rapids, MI: Eerdmans, 1990.

Troeltsch, Ernst. *The Social Teachings of the Christian Churches.* 2 vols. Translated by Olive Wyon. New York: Harper & Row, 1960.

Tworkov, Helen. *Zen in America: Profiles of Five Teachers.* San Francisco: North Point Press, 1989.

Unknown mystic of the fourteenth century. *The Cloud of Unknowing.* Edited by William Johnston. Garden City, NY: Image Books, 1973.

van de Wetering, Janwillem. *A Glimpse of Nothingness.* New York: Washington Square Press, 1978.

Vlastos, Gregory. *Socrates: Ironist and Moral Philosopher.* Ithaca, NY: Cornell University Press, 1991.

Waldenfels, Hans. *Absolute Nothingness: Foundations for a Buddhist-Christian Dialogue.* Translated by J. W. Heisig. New York: Paulist Press, 1980.

Welwood, John, ed. *Awakening the Heart: East/West Approaches to Psychotherapy and the Healing Relationship.* Boston: Shambhala, 1985.

West, Cornell. *The American Evasion of Philosophy: A Genealogy of Pragmatism.* Madison: University of Wisconsin Press, 1989.

Wheeler, Marion, ed. *His Face: Images of Christ in Art.* New York: Chameleon Books, 1988.

Whitbeck, Caroline. "A Different Reality: Feminist Ontology." In Carol C. Gould, ed., *Beyond Domination: New Perspectives on Women and Philosophy.* Totowa, NJ: Rowman & Allanheld, 1983.

Whitehead, Alfred North. *Adventures of Ideas.* New York: Free Press, 1933.

———. *The Aims of Education and Other Essays.* New York: Free Press, 1967.

———. *Process and Reality.* New York: Free Press, 1969.

———. *Religion in the Making.* Cleveland: Meridian Books, 1960.

Whyte, William H. *The Organization Man.* New York: Simon and Schuster, 1956.

Wieman, Henry Nelson. *The Source of Human Good.* Carbondale: Southern Illinois University Press, 1946.

Wilshire, Bruce. *The Moral Collapse of the University: Professionalism, Purity, and Alienation.* Albany, NY: SUNY Press, 1990.

Wolin, Sheldon S. "Democracy in the Discourse of Postmodernism." In *Social Research*, vol. 57, no. 1 (Spring 1990), pp. 4–30.

Woodhouse, A. S. P., ed. *Puritanism and Liberty.* Chicago: University of Chicago Press, 1951.

Zweig, Paul. *The Heresy of Self-Love: A Study of Subversive Individualism.* New York: Harper Colophon, 1968.

Index